NOBO

Jordan "Gizmo" Bearss

Copyright © 2018 Jordan Bearss

All rights reserved.

ISBN: 1987553160
ISBN-13: 978-1987553161

CONTENTS

	From The Editor	i
	Preface	iii
1	THE FIRST STEP	Pg # 1
2	PREPARATION, OR SOMETHING LIKE THAT...	Pg # 6
	CONCERNING GEAR	Pg # 14
3	TAKE FLIGHT	Pg # 18
4	THE FLORIDA TRAIL	Pg # 26
5	THE ROAD TO SPRINGER	Pg # 54
	CONCERNING THE AT	Pg # 79
6	THE APPALACHAIN TRAIL	Pg # 82
7	HOME, BUT AWAY FROM HOME	Pg # 105
8	NEW FRIENDS AND NEW COUNTRY	Pg # 127
9	DEVOTION AND ENDURANCE	Pg #144
10	DON'T FORGET TO REMEMBER	Pg # 173
11	NEW SOULS	Pg # 189
12	JOEL	Pg # 210
12.5	THE ROAD TO KATAHDIN	Pg # 235
14	THE FINAL FRONTIER	Pg # 251
15	ON HOME	Pg # 279

BOOK TITLE

FROM THE EDITOR:

I've always been a sucker for the narrator. As I read, I develop this secret relationship with the character, unbeknownst to him, unable to separate fact from fiction. Plotting our life together, I empathise with every struggle, I hurt with every setback, I glow with every victory; I fall in love.

Which is why I was screwed from the beginning.

I met Jordan while he was in the process of writing this book; fresh off the trail, dirty and quasi-homeless, he was just a regular who ordered unlimited coffee from me late at night. He would sit in the back, put on headphones and type viciously on his computer, fueled by--what? Boredom? Angst? Years later I understand the comedown off a trip like that, the inevitable post-adventure funk that sets in when you re-emerge into society a changed man, a wild animal. Jordan wrote every day on the trail, crossing state lines on foot and climbing mountains in his underwear, and now he spent every day recollecting those moments, feverously, mysteriously behind a junk Asus laptop at a coffee shop in Holland, Michigan.

Cut to the chase: six weeks later, we quit our jobs, gave away our stuff and skipped town together, barely more than strangers. Which is when I started editing this book.

Rife with spelling errors and poor grammar, let me just say: You're welcome. It took me six months of finding free WiFi and cheap coffee while living out of a car or in the woods in order to make sense of 300 pages of phonetic spelling and no less than 8,257 "proved-to-bes" (probably). That being said, our budding relationship coincided with this epic narrative of a low-life, a father, an outdoorsman and adventurer, a beautiful human as he so enthusiastically discovered the joy of everything, all his for the taking, unencumbered by anxieties or presumptions or second thoughts, just DOING it, and loving it. Through the eyes of the narrator I saw the beauty and worth of every vista, every sunrise, every stranger, every partner, every struggle, every failure, every danger, every victory. Literary me was in love. But this character, my secret love, my hero, was REAL, was always next to me, my sole companion for six months as we toured around the country, chasing backcountry trails and hunting breweries. My partner in crime. My person. My secret love had become my real love, and I never stood a chance.

A year to the day from when we left, he asked me to marry him. The rest is history.

And so, my friends, while you won't (can't; I won't allow it) have QUITE the same experience as I have had reading this wonderful tale (is it a coming of age if you're already 30?) I certainly expect you will enjoy it for the same reasons that made me fall in love with the wonderful human who lived it. And if you find a misspelling, I'm sorry. There were a lot.

Dani R Bearss

Editor and Wife

Preface

Do you know the difference between a war story and a fairy tale? An old friend of mine explained the difference to me once, though exactly when I can't remember. He said they share a lot of the same characteristics, both usually being larger than life, utilizing many of the same adjectives and mannerisms. Compelling to listen to and a pleasure to tell. In fact, many times it would be impossible to tell one from the other if not for one simple, yet very important fact. A fairy tale starts with 'Once upon a time' while a war story begins 'No shit, there I was'.

So this now brings us to my story, and I must admit I've long struggled with how to start it. In a way it doesn't seem fitting to write my own story, seeing as I have no idea as to how it ends, but why would anyone care to write the ending if they had never read the beginning? Much as history isn't history until it's over. The biggest problem I currently face is that there seems to be too many places to start rather than having nothing worth writing. I've heard it said to 'start at the beginning', but what exactly does that mean? Do I start at the beginning of my life? Perhaps I would if I could remember it, however I'd like to think there's a reason my mind has blocked out the several years of lying useless and shitting myself. Do I start at the moment I set off on my greatest adventure to date? I could, but it'd almost be like running on a treadmill, still good for you but lacking any real reason. Perhaps the best place to start is when the idea first hit my mind, but therein lies the problem--I'm not entirely sure when that was.

They say one is not supposed to judge a book by its cover, but if you're looking at this one I image you're picturing some sort of tale about adventure and self discovery across America. If that's the case, I'm pleased to inform you that you have gambled wisely! However, it would have personally brought me far more joy to tell you that this is in fact a cookbook, novel about a fictional, purple raccoon, or some other completely random, off topic tale absolutely unrelated to what you assumed it to be. I, for one, tend to find the unexpected to make for a far more enjoyable experience then exactly what was planned.

Not to digress, this is in fact a story of my 3000 mile expedition on foot across the eastern coast of North America mainly via nature trails and back roads. While I must admit this was far from the most efficient method of travel the purpose for traveling was not to get somewhere but rather to see everywhere along the way. To quote an old Taoist parable 'the journey is the destination', perhaps more on that later.

And so I decided to walk the Appalachian Trail, a 2000+ mile trek thru the the eastern mountain ranges of America; a good section of the Florida Trail, over 1000 mile of scenic swamp and farmland across the southern most state, and some highways through Georgia to connect the two. The notion first struck me while watching a documentary on the Appalachian Mountains in my younger years and stuck with me throughout my life. In December 2013, life opened an opportunity to go, and I decided to take it.

Upon my return I've decided to write a book about my trip, which has been an adventure all its own. However, after countless hours and enough coffee to fill Lake Michigan, I've managed to succeed, though I feel it should come with a few words of caution.

First of all, I believe it's worth noting that I am in fact a Christian, and therefore vocationally take a line or two to thank the Lord amidst a rather risky or rewarding endeavor. That being said this book is in no way meant to evangelize or alienate those of other religious beliefs, or the lack thereof for that matter, but rather it tells the story the way I have seen it. Just as with a good belt, not all people will wear it the same way, but I do believe everyone can find a notch where it will fit comfortably.

Second, I refuse to refrain from using what some people would call bad language, simply because I do not believe such a thing exists. Language has no notion to whether it is good or bad, words are simply words and it is the meaning that we put behind them that is truly offensive or not. I personally have heard a good Christian, southern-born woman intend to speak far more ill by saying 'bless your heart' than a construction worker offering condolences by saying 'that's fucked up'. In short, if I feel like dropping in a sentence enhancer every now and then, you damn well better believe I will! Perhaps there's more to note here at the beginning, but at the moment nothing comes to mind, and so I shall continue on.

Furthermore, how to format the story of such a bold journey has been a constant pain, for everyone who I talk to about my travels has different questions. It would be impossible to cover everything without having the book read like a dictionary, a title that has never managed to hold my interest for very long, but I also believe that no one would have the slightest idea what I was talking about should I leave out some of the seemingly trivial components. Thus, I have compiled several sections that are meant to be more information than story; I feel they will be valuable to future long distance hikers, but for those who just want a good read such sections can easily be skipped for the sake of continuity. Also, every now and then I have dropped in what I like to call a Hiker-ism, which is meant to describe a word or idea that long distance hikers frequently use. I have placed them along the way to keep things reading smoothy and avoid confusion, plus I found them to be a fun way to answer some of the smaller questions I have been asked more than once.

Currently the question I'm most frequently asked to answer about the whole endeavor is 'How was it?' asked almost out of automation. It's amazing how such a simple question can stir up such deep thought and emotion. In a way, it's like trying to describe air. I can tell you the composition of air, mainly Nitrogen by the way, or the physical properties of air and how it reacts in various situations. I could go on about how it's vital for the life of every single surface-dwelling plant and animal on this planet, or to the origins of the atmosphere. Yet sadly, even if I made the most valiant effort ever recorded to describe the substance it would all fall in vain because until you're breathing one really has no idea just how awesome air is. At times the trip was amazing! There are no words in all the languages of man that can begin to describe it. Other times, I think I would rather repeatedly bash my fingers with a rubber mallet than experience it again. This trip evoked every emotion imaginable, and in every possible degree, from intense, uncontainable joy to sole crushing depression. So when people ask me 'How was it?' the only answer I find appropriate is simply 'Yes.'

So, now that you have an idea of what you're getting into, I suppose it's time to begin, bearing in mind that while the trail has been traveled before, this story is mine. In spirit of such an idea, I can think of no better way to start then taking my friends words and adding my own sort of spin to them.

        And so: No shit, once upon a time, there I was...

1 THE FIRST STEP

It's cliche, but they say the journey of a thousand miles begins with a single step, but the thing of it is, of the insurmountable number of steps a person takes in their life it's impossible to tell exactly which step that may be. Would it be a ground shaking stride into adventure, resonating with grandeur and purpose, or would it slip by quietly, perhaps a wrong turn or even a single pace down a familiar street. Would it be a conscious effort, venturing forth to seek the unknown, or something that came and went without ever being known. A neighborhood walk resulting in an epiphany perhaps. Having to run from something, or running towards something. Or maybe a misstep that sends one tumbling head over heals for a brief moment. At this point in my life however, I wasn't taking many steps at all, and more often then not I could be found sitting behind a pint of cold beer at my favorite pub.

My friend Lector had put quite a bit of work into fixing up the place, and the rest of us worked hard to keep it in good repair. The effort becomes pretty apparent right away actually, as one pulls open the door via a monkey wrench wielded in place to serve as a badass, aesthetically pleasing handle. Just past the door is a pool table and a pinball machine, both of which have occupied countless hours of my time, and are essentially the only things to break up the long, narrow space of the interior apart from a few places to sit. The lights are kept low and the orange and black walls blend well with the stained cedar bar running through the whole space, creating a cool, laid-back atmosphere that's become home to me. However, it's not just the actual bar that makes this place such a delight to visit, but rather the eclectic group of regulars whom over the years have chosen to gather here. Intellectuals and working class philosophers, all varying greatly in wealth, interests, appearance, and personality. In fact, the only thing that seems to fully unite them all is a love of good beer and the idea that a person is inherently good unless he proves otherwise. Truly, a finer group of interesting, genuinely caring folk I have yet to meet, nor do I think I ever will.

Apparently, the biggest problem I seem to have come across in my early twenties is that I found paradise too soon and thus didn't have to search for it. Though I must say, it's nice to know where it is. I know that many people search their entire life to find what I have coveted for so long, each day as good as the last and bound to be just as well tomorrow.

However, while everyday was good it became impossible to tell one day from another, the sort of routine that prayed upon my youth and damn near took all of it!

I wasn't born rich, and can't say I've ever been close sense. Money has always been hard to come by despite working well over sixty hours in a week between my day job and whatever other work I could find. Hell, I barely made enough to keep a roof over my head and a beer on the bar. In all seriousness, I didn't ever really have money to spare for the latter, but by avoiding things like cable TV, quality food, or turning the air conditioner on I managed to find just enough. I'd like to say my circumstance was an unusual one, but I'd be lying if I did. I've met far too many people that work far too hard and have far too little, if even enough, in this day and age. Fortunately, I had made quite a name for myself as a finish carpenter, building everything from custom furniture to walk-in coolers, and by some small miracle every now and then I found a good side project that turned a decent profit. However, years of experiments proved that more money just meant that I could drink a few more beers in a week, but by and large I wasn't complaining.

At the time I was renting the first floor of a historic house on 6th street, with oddly painted walls and crooked floors, each room wildly different from the last in both appearance and pitch. In the winter my home was cold, in the summer I went surfing, on Fridays I'd drink wine down the block, and all other times I would be found enjoying a pint. I had many friends, and visited with them often, if not at their homes at the bar which I strongly believe I spent more time at then my own residence. I was comfortable, not thriving but surviving, I had good work, great beer, grand company, and an inescapable feeling of something being wrong.

Many times in life people are waiting for the big things, the sort of things that completely change a person's life around. Sometimes it's a promotion, other times it's the end of college, perhaps a marriage, or the kids leaving the house, or completion of a mortgage, or when the dog dies, or when my parents die, or something along those lines. I've heard so many times "Once this, I'll that.", and while it usually appears to be a sound argument it never seems to work. Trust me, if you're always waiting for something you'll never do anything! If it's not one thing it's going to be another, and the big things will never be enough to get you going. Strangely, its the little things in life that can push us over the edge, and get one moving after their wildest dreams.

My first step on this adventure may not have even been a step at all, but rather the simplest of conversations, the sort of one we skip over next to daily. Sitting in my North Carolina, beer slinging home, sipping pints and taking it easy as always, yet I just couldn't feel at peace sitting still. It's like an itch you can't scratch, or that feeling you get when you know you forgot something but can't remember exactly what. Though I do believe the true cause of this restlessness ran far deeper than any of that. What was I doing with my life? Why wasn't I doing more? Should I just have two beers and still try to do some work today or just hang productivity and stay till close? Should I call Mom this weekend? It's been awhile. Screw it I'm having another!

Today it was just me and the bartender, Ashley, in the place, chatting like we sometimes did when she had time. Must admit she's very easy on the eyes, long, curly blond hair, lips always painted bright red, brown eyes and the sort of short, sexy, curvy figure that can't help but make one think "Damn, that woman could kick my ass!". To this day I have no idea what stirred the memory, perhaps the stress of taking to a beautiful woman that causes men to act like fools, but years before I had watched a documentary on the Appalachian Trail (AT), a two thousand mile footpath through the mountains stretching across the east coast of America! I had since always secretly wanted to attempt this big bad mountain motherfucker, and this day I somehow came to the realization that at the moment I really had nothing keeping me here that I couldn't replace. I remember bringing all of this up to Ashley and her response hit hard and stuck with me. She didn't say something like 'That's so cool tell me more!, or 'I know what you mean I've always wanted to...", all she said before going about her business was "You should." Whether it was the beer or the soft smile on her lips after she said it I'll never know, but I couldn't shake the thought: Damn, I should.

I didn't grab my pack in the next instant and take to the earthen path, old stick in my hand, singing a song of myself, but that's where I feel the journey started. In the days that fallowed the bar stools that I had grown accustomed to seemed to have a little more spring in them, the floor must have been freshly waxed, or perhaps the walls had found a way to lean back. Whatever the reality, I began to wander in my home town, taking streets I had long forgotten and others that had never before been burdened with my footsteps.

Wilmington is always changing and evolving, bigger and better by the week it seems, and tonight was no exception. There was a new building being built along the river in what had somehow managed to remain an open field over the past three hundred years of human inhabitance. I'm not entirely sure what this building turned into, but at the time there was nothing but three floors of open iron work and a metal roof a few stories above that. Unable to fight the urge to explore I soon found myself over the eight foot fence and running across loose sand in the middle of the night hoping no one would notice me. After reaching the building I quietly, and carefully, made my way to the roof via some scaffolding and a lack of concern for possible second degree trespassing charges. Coincidentally, such a charge is the only blemish that managed to stick on my record after twenty five years of life, but I digress.

A bare metal roof is a bit of a familiar sight to me as I spent my first two years in Wilmington putting material over them. Roofing was one of the harder ways I've ever earned a living, but that's not to say the work came without its own rewards. Not only did it make a gym membership completely unnecessary, but whenever I needed a chance to reset all I had to do was look around for a minute.

Every town is different, and while one can somewhat get a feel for how things are by walking the streets to truly see what she looks like one really needs to climb higher. I won't forget looking down on the place I so fondly call home, a soft cool breeze coming off the Cape Fear river as the city lights danced on its rippled surface. The old narrow streets glowed softly and rested peacefully, their day's work done, and her churches stood illuminated like ancient guardians making a last show of strength. Beyond the river lie miles and miles of marsh land and woods making my little town seem great and yet somehow homey, nestled against the wilderness. The stars above made their best effort to be seen in the night sky, and all was quiet in my home town.

A thin smile appeared on my lips as I immersed myself in this moment, and yet I couldn't help but feel alone. It's a feeling I have long coped with, and while I have many to call friends some sort of deep longing had always kept me slightly distant from them. It's like I was just going through the motions of life but never really living, the little hindrances always seems so important at the time. I had noticed that entire days would slip by where nothing worth remembering had happened, days I would never get back.

One's days are numbered, those in our youth doubly so, and life is to short to simply let slip by. While there is nothing on this earth I value more than friendship, I found myself far more satisfied to sit on this roof alone than to sit in my bar feeling alone.

When I left the roof that night the world felt different. Not in the holy-shit-I-drank-too-much different like I'm used to, but more like I was now just a traveler passing through as opposed to a permanent fixture of this place. It's not the last time I felt something I couldn't find a word for, but it may have been the first. The only word that seems to stick is Freedom, freedom to do things the way I wanted, to go and to see wherever I chose, to be without fear of judgment or the need for approval. It was as if I was given a new set of eyes to see with, a new pair of feet to walk with, and ears to finally hear the call to wander, and wander I set out to do. Appalachian trail, why not? Couldn't find a reason. It was settled, right then and there--I was going for it!

2 PREPARATION, OR SOMETHING LIKE THAT...

To be perfectly honest I certainly had my doubts about the whole thing. Just uprooting and moving out is quite an undertaking, and it'd be a lie to say I didn't reconsider almost daily. I had never done more than a weekend camping trip on the beach to catch some early morning waves--what business did I have trying to hike the mountains of eastern America?! I knew my physical condition was good enough for it all, and my mind had become pretty tough in recent years, but this just isn't the sort of thing people in their right mind set off to do. However, it was time for a change, and seeing as I've never been more than a working class surfer this is really the only change I felt I had the ability to make.

Collecting gear was harder then I thought it was going to be. There aren't a lot of hiking supply stores on the beach, nor are there a lot of hikers for that matter. I don't believe the local surf shops could help me out at all other then tell me the waves suck in the mountains, so I was relatively on my own. I did know a few hiking enthusiasts however, and with the help of my buddy Nash, a shorter, avid hiker with a beard that Tolkin's Dwarfs would envy, I managed to find the Outdoor Provision Co. in Wilmington, NC. Like most outfitters in urban areas, there was a lot more apparel in the store then actual hiking gear, but that's not to say they didn't have some great stuff. The back half of the store was lined with hiking shoes, lightweight hammocks, tents, sleeping bags, water filters, hydro packs, camp stoves, expensive packs, gadgets and gizmos the world over, all of which I knew absolutely nothing about! First time I walked into the store I felt about as out of place as a Junebug in December, but after poking about a little bit I managed to get a feel for what I was looking for.

Step one was definitely to find a good pack seeing as I didn't really want to drag a little red wagon the whole way. To be honest, it's hard to think of anything more important; your pack is your lifeline, without it you can hardly carry more than a bottle of water, and good luck making that last for days between towns. Logically, I needed something just big enough to carry what was necessary to survive. Everything weighs something, including excess pack, thus the lighter the better. After trying out a few I settled on an Osprey Kestrel 48. I was real happy with it, the pack fit me well and I have a strange back to say the least, seeing as I was born with an extra set of ribs. No joke, most people have twelve pairs, and I have thirteen!

While this strange adaptation allows me to collapse my bottom ribs several inches into my abdomen without discomfort, which had saved me a fair amount of pain in previous car crashes, it also bends my lower back in the way scoliosis would, making a slight S shape. This pack hit me just right, and so I made it mine. Leaving the store with that bad boy strapped to my shoulders, I fully realized that this was going to happen. Too late to turn back now it seemed.

Training was one of the bigger challenges to face, so I didn't. Not in any sort of specific way at least--no gym, no short hikes, no cycling. However I did walk, a lot. Seriously, a lot. I had taken to walking to work long ago, although I'm not too proud of why. A few YEARS prior I got caught in a police checkpoint driving a few friends home from the bar. I was the most sober so I took it upon myself to get behind the wheel and next thing I know I'm staring down red and blue lights with nowhere to go but jail. Blew a point zero nine, indicating that my blood alcohol content was exactly one percent above the legal limit to drive. I was shocked! Not that I was going to the joint by such a small margin, but rather that there was that much blood in my alcohol stream--it's hardly ever that watered down! I came away from the whole thing with a suspended license, twenty four hours of community service, and a peanut butter sandwich courtesy of the New Hanover county jail, so not a total loss. In the aftermath of it all, I had to drive illegally for more time than I care to reflect on until finally realizing that the risk just wasn't worth it. Having two options, either to give up driving or to give up drinking and get things back in order, I decided to sell my truck. Not only was I then free of temptation, but also gifted a healthy sum of beer money and the chance to really enjoy the wonderful, temperamental, coastal Carolina climate. Things were looking up!

I liked where I was living, walking distance to the bar district, fair price, didn't leak, however when it came down to either renew or travel, I obviously chose the latter. The only problem was that this happened in early November and the peak start time for the AT is March/April. While my rent payment became only a fraction of what it was, having only to pay for a storage unit, I couldn't access the thing after ten PM, and they sort of frowned upon people sleeping there. Fortunately, with a lot of help from my friends and no fear of the outdoors, I was able to find a place to sleep every night. Sometimes it would be at a local theater I volunteered at, other times I would make my way to the front porch of one of my many drinking companions in the area where I could sleep on an old couch. On such occasions I would greet my friends in the morning when they left to go to work. It's nice when you're good enough friends with someone that it's no big deal to just show up on their porch. Must say though, these sort of sleeping arrangements made for some interesting, if not flat-out humorous mornings. Being woken up by everything from doors opening to complimentary hot coffee, but never with hard feelings, is truly something to be thankful for. There were many nights that I simply enjoyed the cool night air and night sky; it's not so bad having no set place to be and while most would have fallen into despair I rather enjoyed it.

If nothing else, my friend Maaika always had a couch open for me, provided I didn't mind sharing it with one to three dogs, and I didn't. Maaika is honestly one of the best people I had ever met, and I feel I will more then likely go my whole life without ever finding a way to repay her for all of the kindness she had given me, but that doesn't mean I'm not currently trying. Shes one Hell of a woman to say the least, not to mention fully capable of raising said Hell should she choose to! Stands just a little shorter then me, when not in roller derby skates, covered in tattoos from head to toe, red rock-a-billy hair, and better curves than '57 Chevy. Needless to say this Canadian beauty turned every head in town, including mine a time or two, and for some odd reason she had taken to looking after me. Not sure exactly why she put up with my frequent drunken shenanigans, but she did, and I'm more than likely still alive because of it. This wasn't the first time I was stuck outdoors, though last time I had little choice in the matter. Maaika had given me a place to work, a room to sleep, and even helped me out with some expenses I otherwise had no way taking care of until I was back on my feet. Even after all of that, if I ever had the need, all I had to do was find a way to her front door and I could find a safe place to sleep.

The hardest thing to prepare for actually was the thought of leaving my friends. Even though I frequently did things alone I could always find someone I knew rather quickly if desired, and the idea of not being able to was hard to come to terms with. Some people would ask why it is that I wanted to go--was I off to find the meaning of life or something? Actually, I had already found the meaning of life and it's rather simple actually. It's foolish to ask why life is, or what life is, just know THAT life is. To me, there is no great purpose to it all, nothing I'm meant to do or specific task I'm placed here to complete. While many I have shared this with find the notion rather depressing, I actually find it incredibly encouraging. By not wondering what I have to do or where I have to be I'm free to choose both! While I like to believe there is a guiding hand out there somewhere in the universe, I also believe that my purpose is based off of my decisions, not the other way around. Wherever I am, there is bound to be some good that I may do there. Seeing as I find myself to be the only entity to have control over my life, I still had one last major decision to make before it all began: when to leave.

It was starting to get a bit cooler out, and I was currently homeless, so it became not so much of a matter of when to start but rather where! Either that or I had to find a stable place to live, which, strangely enough, I really didn't want to do. I kept feeling that if I signed onto another place, even if only for a short time, I'd be stuck here again. So, almost as a joke, I typed 'Florida hikes' into my smart phone in hopes of finding warmer places to wander. Within pages I found the Eastern Continental Trail (ECT), which, apparently, is a ridiculously long foot path spanning from Key West Florida to the coast of Canada! My days in Wilmington were pretty straight forward: work till there's no work left to be done, and then drink till there's no time left to drink. Furthermore, I never strayed from work long enough to do anything other then take a piss or grab some pizza, so when do you think I found out about the ECT? There's a great chance that it was the booze thinking when I finalized my decision to undertake the trail, but damn if that beer-bred bastard isn't persuasive! Eighty-seven dollars later I had a plane ticket booked to Ft. Lauderdale, Florida, leaving December 4th, Two Thousand Thirteen at four in the morning, and thus the way was set. All that was left to do is find a way onto that plane and I was off!

Hiker-ism: Sleep System

(noun) People are not machines, and while the body is indeed an impressive tool it requires rest to function properly. With no proper beds set up in the woods one is forced to carry along a system in which to stay overnight in while resting tired bones.

Its crazy how something as small as an eighty seven dollar plane ticket can really turn an idea into a reality. I wasn't obligated to go, and if I chose not to the worse consequence I would suffer is the loss of barely two day's wages, but in a way I now felt as if there was no other choice than to set out. While it was impossible to know exactly what lay ahead I knew that there was a lot more needed before being ready to suffer it all, and so I began to amass the rest of my gear. It was about now that I came to the realization that I had next to no idea how to survive in the middle of nowhere for a prolonged period of time, and so I felt the need to prepare for the worst. I am actually a trained Emergency Medical Technician Basic in the great state of North Carolina, which pretty much means I'm barely qualified to work in a nursing home. Still, being ready for a medical emergency was in the forefront of my mind. My med kit swelled to an enormous size as I packed the little red bastard with gauze pads, rolls of gauze, medical tape, ace bandages, burn relief, anti-septic, anti-biotic, foot care ointment, benadryl, aspirin, Tylenol, Dayquil, triangle bandage, snake bite kit, hell, I even managed to get my hands on an epi-pen! With no help around for miles I was going to be ready, and though perhaps going a little overboard I figured it would be better to have it and not need it than need it and not have it.

The swelling of supplies didn't stop with medical, for I figured my needs in that regard would actually be rather minimal. In fact, while a proper med kit would indeed come in handy should I need to stop some severe bleeding it would do little good to keep the wind and rain off my back at night, and so I began to look into sleep systems. While I have heard rumors that some indigenous tribesmen have managed to sleep comfortably under the stars with little more than an animal skin to serve as a blanket, I was not accustomed to such a thing and preferred to not freeze to death. Sleep systems vary greatly from one product to another, while some people prefer to carry nothing more than a sleeping bag in hopes of finding a dry place to sleep each night others strike out with enough gear to survive a winter in the Arctic! Being far from an expert, I figured the best thing to do would be to ask around a bit on what would be the best thing to get, but soon disregarded that notion and purchased a three season, two person tent online. My boss had allowed me to ship things to my place of employment seeing as I didn't really have anywhere else, and within a few days my portable shelter arrived. It was a fine little green dome with the roof held aloft with a pair of aluminum poles and a rain cover to stretch over the whole structure if I wished it to do so. Even with very limited knowledge of such things this appeared to be a fine solution to my nightly needs, and I could hardly wait to use it out in the wild.

A tent is all well and good, but while it will keep the elements off ones back it does little to keep a person warm in the dead of night. Thankfully, there were several places in town where one could find a proper sleeping bag, which seemed to be a far more preferable method of keeping warm than to carry around a large bundle of blankets. Again, my knowledge was extremely limited on the subject, but how could one bag be all that different from the next, all I needed to do was pick one up right? I soon found that the world of sleeping bags was far greater than I had ever imagined, consisting of a nearly infinite amount of shapes and sizes, varying from pouches that are hardly the size of a football to massive rolls far bigger than my torso. While I didn't know much, I did know that I was going to have to be carrying whatever I decided to go with, thus smaller was undoubtedly better. That being said, I didn't want to pick up something that was not going to keep me warm enough in the cool mountain evenings. After examining my options at various locations I was able to find a bag that was supposed to keep a parson safe and warm in weather as low as fifteen degrees Fahrenheit that also happened to be on sale for half off. The price made it an easy decision, for theses things are surprisingly expensive, and I was still far from rich. Many places I shopped had sleeping mats for sale, but I didn't see the point, the earth was soft enough and I was unwilling to spend the extra money.

    With a sleep system in place it was time to move on to other gear I may need, though I had no idea exactly what that consisted of. Not wanting to be in need, I decided to cover all the situations one could think of. I was going to need to purify water, so I got a light weight collapsible pot in which to boil with. I was going to need fire, so I got a hatchet to chop wood with. If I was to have fire I was certainly going to need some way to make a safe pit to burn in, so I got a garden trowel to dig with. I got a flashlight to see at night, a compass to find my way by, a roll of hemp, a spool of forty pound test fishing line, fishing hooks, sewing needles and thread, binoculars, bandanas, duct tape, gorilla tape, seven lighters, magnesium fire starter, two can openers, beer bottle opener, and that's not all! I was going on a very tight budget, so I brought along a book about edible plants to use while foraging in hopes of keeping my food costs down. The world is simply full of wonderful things that a person can eat at no cost to them, except death if one eats the wrong thing, but other than that, completely free food is everywhere! I had a strong affinity for tools, having handled them daily for the majority of my life, and so the thought of bringing along just one knife didn't sit well. Thus, I brought along a good cooking knife with a leather sheath for preparing meals, a construction knife with a few replacement blades for detail work, a pocket knife to wear in town, and a military surplus KA-Bar for nearly everything else! Still not satisfied with my current level of protection I decided to invest in Bear-Grade mace, just in case I needed to fend off a pack of rabid wolves or a battalion of invading Canadians sick of simply being considered America's hat. It would appear that my initial concern for keeping my pack light had gone out the window, and with all this in tow, I felt that I was finally ready to set out on the trail.

Two final luxury items I decided to bring along actually turned out to be fine companions for the duration of my journey, though some would call them completely impractical. The less argued against was a notebook and pencil that I had brought along to record my daily trials in, and indeed I utilized it nightly. Of all the things that had been with me from start to finish, this is the most treasured and I truly find it to be irreplaceable. The second luxury I had acquired as a gift to myself in celebration of living for a quarter of a century: a good quality pipe, the likes of which I used to enjoy fine tobacco. In the time that I had possessed it I was rarely found to be without it, for I found the process of packing and smoking it to be far more enjoyable than cigarettes and with much better flavor. It made several appearances in my hike, though also spent long periods dormant in my pack; still, I found that some of my better thoughts came while softly puffing on a pipe full of quality tobacco.

With next to no time to spare, all the pieces fell into place. I had collected all the odds and ends that I believed I required and was ready to get at it. I had given my boss plenty of notice on my going away, yet when the time came she was certainly sad to see me go. With help from my friend Kris I was able to move all my tools into my storage unit, which I thank him greatly for. I also paid for over a half a years worth of storage all at once so as to not have to worry about about the thousands of dollars in equipment that I had gathered over the years. Furthermore, while I quit my main job about a week before my departure I still had plenty of work to finish up, and thus was working up until the day I left. In the midst of all this chaos there was still one major thing that needed to be done before bidding farewell to the port city, and that was to get really, really drunk.

Wilmington is not in the slightest bit short on watering holes and drinking establishments, though I certainly have my favorites. Of course in my mind there has never been a finer place to pound a pint then good old Cape Fear Wine and Beer, thus when it came time to see my last Last Call this is where I chose to do it. While I was certainly going to miss this fine city I chose not to make a very big deal about departing from it, though I did send word to those whom I figured would want to say goodbye.

Indeed, quite a few fine folk showed up to drain a glass and raise a toast. I promised to write, though I made it clear that I was not going to be using my phone for anything other than a camera, I honestly hate what it's done to social interaction in the modern age. The idea seemed well-received, or at least acceptable, seeing as I was indeed steadfast on maintaining 'radio silence' as I liked to call it. I made a valiant effort to drink the bar out of a specific brand of Extra Special Bitter that night, and before it was all said and done I had slugged down nearly twenty four of the little bastards, though this left me just slightly short of my goal. Still, beers and good times were had by all, and when the evening was over I felt ready to take on my travels.

I awoke the next morning on a park bench out back of the bar, hardly five feet from the door that the entire staff would have exited through and thus passing by my passed-out person before heading home. I wondered if any of them had tried to wake me, but I suppose that really didn't matter for there really wasn't anywhere else for me to be, and so I simply went to a local diner to get some breakfast. My plane took off in less than twenty four hours, and it's hard to describe the feeling of being on the verge of something that could prove to be potentially monumental. In all honesty, there wasn't much time to think about it as I spent the day walking from one place where I had stored equipment to another, packing and arranging everything in preparation to take off. My friend TC had been incredibly kind by letting me use his spare room to store much of my gear, and furthermore he sent me off with about two weeks worth of military grade rations. Granted, a military issue Meal Ready to Eat (MRE) is far from appetizing but they're lightweight and well designed to keep a body moving. However when I went to load this influx of food stuff into my pack it became rather apparent that I had nowhere near enough capacity to carry everything. Not to be deterred, I simply decided to clip my tent and my sleeping bag to the exterior of my pack with a few carabiners seeing as the each item had it's own carrying case, and while it looked a bit awkward the system seemed to be functional. I threaded as many things as I could onto my belt including my KA-Bar, binoculars, compass, cooking knife, bear spray, and hatchet, thus my trusty utility belt was born. The final piece of gear that I decided to bring along was a full brimmed leather hat that I had gotten nearly a decade prior while traveling through the Dakotas with my family. I had bought it from an old Indian fellow at the Crazy Horse monument, and while at the time it was only meant to be a keepsake I figured it would keep the sun and rain off my back better than anything else I had.

With my gear fully assembled I set off downtown for one last pint, which I imagine must have looked rather silly seeing as I was nowhere near a hiking trail of any kind. Just walking through a populated street with enough gear to take on the East Coast strapped to my shoulders, knives and all. Regardless, I needed to be at the airport by four in the morning and figured I could find a ride from someone in the area. I stored my things in the coat closet at Cape Fear as I enjoyed a few final glasses, and indeed I found a person who was willing to take me on my way after last call. So it seemed the dice were cast, that I was actually going on this crazy adventure. I didn't know where I was going to sleep, I didn't know how long it was going to take me, I didn't even know if I was going to live through it, but damn it all I was going to make my best effort! I had about five hundred and fifty dollars to my name, which I knew was not going to be nearly enough, and a pack full of gear. It was now or never, and so I raised a final glass to the bar I had come to call home, and set my sights on the road ahead.

Concerning Gear:

I would like to take a moment to say that the way in which I went about gathering my gear was completely impractical and in many ways flat out wrong! In hind sight I really wish I would have taken the time to research things a bit more before making assumptions and purchasing things that in many cases turned out to be useless. That being said I did actually get a few things right. One thing that I got a great amount of use out of was my KA-Bar, and I do strongly believe that all who venture into the woods should have a good, dependable knife on them at all times. This particular beauty boasted a six inch long blade with section of serrated edge, leather sheath to thread a belt through, and steel good enough to survive a tour of duty in the hellish climate of North Vietnam! Thankfully, I didn't have to use this tool to hold off a possible communist threat like it was designed for, but every time something needed to be cut, trimmed, scraped, smoothed, or pried this was the thing I did so with.

Another thing I got right was a supply of good, wool socks that were designed with hunting trips in mind. Many people I came to know preferred to hike in lighter, more current options, but I couldn't be happier with the performance I had gotten out of these tried and true classics. I forget who said it, though I've hear tell that the first rule of war is to take care of one's feet. I would like to fully agree, but I believe this fine fellow's opinion to be slightly flawed. Taking care of one's feet isn't the first rule of war, its the first rule of life! It didn't matter if I had enough water, food, or other supplies to last a life time, its impossible to take a single step with one's feet out of working order. Also, on that note, my choice of footwear was another decision I feel worked out wonderfully, though I don't believe many share my thoughts on the matter. I decided to hike in a pair of eight inch Danner brand hunting boots, and while they were indeed a bit heavy they were also waterproof, supportive, comfortable, durable, well made, and guaranteed against defects, a fine product indeed. While many of the people I came to meet along the trail preferred lightweight footwear all of them had blown through nearly ten pairs before the journey was over while I myself made it the entire way with just two.

 I have often thought about what I would have done differently if given the chance to gather all my gear again with the knowledge I now have of hiking. For one, I think I would have gone with a hammock instead of a tent for hammocks are lighter, more compact, and when one deploys the rain fly this type of shelter can keep a hiker just as dry. Also, I would have brought far less smalls. While I did use many of the things I brought in many cases I found that I brought far to much and would have been just as happy with a small bundle of good cord as with an entire roll of sturdy hemp. Though the most important change I would make is that I would have brought along a light weight water filter. A good filter can be purchased for under thirty dollars and I would have saved myself nearly an endless amount of grief along the way if I had been able to drink the prevalent, stagnate, bacteria filled water along the way instead of having to carry out large quantities of water from town or between mountain springs.

 Should one wish to fallow in my foot steps I would strongly encourage them to take the time and research their gear before purchasing anything. Know what sort of climate you're going to be hiking in and what sort of things are necessary for survival in said climate. The big three items one needs is a pack, sleeping bag, and shelter, spend a lot of time looking over various options before selecting what works best for you. Again, also be sure to have a water filter, rain gear, a sleeping mat, and quality footwear. I would recommend fifty feet of para cord, a good knife, bug spray, a pair of lighters, a hydro pack that fits into your backpack, note pad and pencil, a small roll of duck tape, a small roll of toilet paper, hand sanitizer, 3 pairs of quality socks, a lightweight change of clothes, and a good quality compression sack to carry food in. There are thousands of little gadgets that will be advertised to potential hikers, but nearly all of them are useless. Don't get overwhelmed by such things, just keep your gear simple and of good quality. Also, a simple med kit is essential! Mine was far over stocked, but a long distance hiker should at least have a snake bit kit, an ace bandage, anti bacteria cream, no more then five gauze pads, a days worth of day-quill, and white tape. Of course, one should always plan for any specific medical conditions they have as well.

Many of those that I've known to hike long distances like to carry a camp stove, though I managed just fine without one. Granted, a camp stove makes carrying dehydrated food a lot easier, and a hot meal at night is indeed a nice treat, but it's an extra expense, extra weight, and keeping the thing fueled can be a nightmare. This is a particular item that I don't condemn, yet don't embrace, and leave it up to the individual to make a personal decision to carry one or not. Also, tracking poles are another thing that many hikers are insistent on having, but I found an old stick to work just as well and at no cost to me. I had seen many days ruined by a bent pole while a broken stick is easily replaced.

Furthermore, those that hike frequently may want to invest in a bear canister for food, but only if one is to hike in an area where they have a good chance of encountering something bigger then a black bear. In the mountains of the east there is really no need for such a thing, but for those out west or farther north it may be a smart investment.

While its easy to look back on the hike and see many ways in which I could have been more piratical I'm not entirely sure I would have changed a thing. I had gotten a lot of use out of the things that I brought along, and while many of them sat in my pack unused for long periods of time I was glad to have them when the time came. The extra weight required that I use more energy, and made big mile days a real strain, but I'm happy with the way things went. I can make many suggestions, and I assure you they are offered honestly, but when it comes down to it, a person will carry what they wish to carry and that's that. There's no one hundred percent perfect way to hike, each trip is unique to those who venture and thus it is far better to be happy with ones own choices then constantly worrying about doing things someone else's way.

3 TAKE FLIGHT

So, it's two in the morning, and my ride to the airport had just fallen through due to a medical emergency. I should have been freaking out a bit, but thanks to last call and my friend Joan of Art, a lovely Michigan immigrant in the land of North Carolina, I managed to get to where I needed to be in time. I got one last picture taken outside of the bar in full gear and waving to set the profile picture of my social media account, and as of that moment I swore to abandon the app until the walk was over.

On the ride out I started to realize that Joan was going to be the last familiar face I was going to see for quite some time. It was strange to think of it like that, and while I was wide eyed with excitement over my journey I couldn't shake the nerve racking, stomach churning urge to call the whole thing off. I don't think the sensation has a name, possibly because those who experience it don't care to acknowledge it, but I think it's the base for words like no, wait, stop, and hold on. Hesitation is close, but it's bigger than that for it's not the product of rational thinking or an adverse reaction to something we're taught not to do. It's some sort of primal instinct put in place to keep the herd together, an outdated gene responsible for survival of the masses in the past and resistance of the individual in the present. For lack of a better term I've decided to call the emotion 'anchored' because I feel it could stop one dead in their tracks, literally feeling like there's a weight in your gut holding you in place. I had been feeling more and more anchored everyday as my departure date grew closer, but had managed to fight through it by drinking or simply not thinking about it. Now I was out of a job, no place to stay, and on my way with no vice to sooth me or other thought to distract me.

Pulling into the airport I was starting to shake from all of the built up emotions--joy, excitement, fear, anchoring, wonder and many others all rolled into one! Not knowing what to do exactly I turned to my final familiar travel companion and started to sing Hank Williams *Jambalaya*, a catchy, old country tune about going to party in a swamp, though I chose to replace the word 'Joe' with 'Joan' due to present company. Joan and I were known to dance together at local rock-a-billy shows so she knew the tune and joined in, putting my mind a bit at ease. In a way, I felt like I was giving a proper good bye to grand old Wilmington, and she in return offered a bit of a send off. Thanks Kitten, couldn't have done it without you.

The change in rides forced me to arrive at the airport a few hours before my flight, but by now I was feeling pretty good about things. Too emotionally discombobulated to sleep, I leaned up against a post and wondered what lay ahead, far more excited then anything else but still quite nervous. All I knew for sure is that the weather was sure to be a bit warmer than coastal Carolina and that when it was all said and done with, the trip was sure to be something to talk about. Made it through security with no real problems, even managed to check my several knifes and other gear without much of a fuss, and before the sun rose I was standing in Ft. Lauderdale, Florida, ready to go! Now I just had to figure out how to get to the trail...

Hiker-ism: Trail Head

(noun) The place where a nature trail meets a road, or the starting point of a section of trail. Some hikers have found a very different definition for this term, but I don't feel like explaining some of the dirty things that happen on trail just yet.

I suppose I should have planned things a bit better, for it seems that the troubles of this venture weren't wasting any time in showing up. I had hopes of starting my hike in Big Cypress Wildlife Reserve, which is the head of the Florida Trail, but wasn't sure how to get there. At the time, I was far too exhilarated to waste even a single moment, and with no better way out of the city I just started walking from the airport. Airplanes flew overhead and traffic zipped by as I made my way towards the heart of the city; the sun started to rise before me, it was the first day of who knows how long, my humble beginning. Made it to a greyhound station in hopes of finding a way into the infamous, alligator infested swamps of south Florida only to find that the closest I could get was Napels, clear across the state and no closer to my goal. Not wanting to waste money to get to nowhere, I thought about taking a cab to the center of the everglades, but at the price they run such an option was soon out of the question. Not really knowing anyone in the area that could give me a ride was the final nail in that coffin, and I decided that again the best course of action was to just keep walking. I studied a map of the Florida trail and a road map of south Florida and soon found that the most practical way of meeting the trail was not to travel to Big Cypress

Reserve in the Everglades, but rather the southern bank of lake Okeechobee, a large lake close to the center of south Florida, a good eighty miles from where I stood.

In a way it didn't feel real walking through the city, like I was dreaming or just on a short vacation or something. This was supposed to be a grand adventure into the wild and my mind simply could not grasp the grandeur of what was at hand being so confined by well lit streets and concrete walls. Still, I made my best effort to break out of the metropolis by walking until the sun went down, and a little further even for not really having any other option. I certainly didn't have money in my extremely tight budget to stay in a motel or anything, but since I hadn't really slept the night before, I certainly needed to find some way to get some rest.

Looking back on the many times I had passed out in strange places in Wilmington, it appeared best to take a page out of my own book and just sleep wherever I could, which in this instance became a grassy spot behind a park bench most of the way out of the city. Gateway Park was the name of the place, and it seemed sort of fitting to stay seeing as Fort Lauderdale was to be the gateway to my grand adventure. It worked well enough to get to sleep thankfully as I lay on a tarp designed to go beneath my tent, resting under the soft, artificial light of the city, hoping that no one would bother me in the night. Thankfully, no one did, and the park stayed empty the entire time I was there, but I soon found out way.

Sleep was hard to find that night, being awakened at every little noise and then cautiously nodding back off after figuring out what the source of said noise was. Until all of a sudden at roughly two am I heard a loud "POP" followed by a persistent hiss whose origin was hardly a foot away from where my head lay resting. Half awake and rather confused I tried to figure out what was going on, then it hit me, literally. The parks underground sprinkler system had just gone off spraying everything with water, and there I was with all of my gear at ground zero! Now fully awake and in quite a frenzy I snatched up all of my belongings and tossed them onto a near by walkway that seemed to be staying dry. Thankfully the tarp I had put down to sleep on magically covered the closest sprinkler head keeping the worst of the spray under control, truly an odd bit of luck in the whole situation. Mostly dry and rather annoyed I started to pack up to find a better place to try and sleep, in hind sight it was pretty funny.

I walked for another hour or so that night before finding another place to sleep. It was nice in an eerie sort of way, the once busy streets were now quiet and empty, and the night air was cool and pleasant to walk in. The street lights were still on allowing me to see where I was going though my pack began to weigh heavy on my shoulders as they struggled to embrace the fully-loaded weight. I found another park to sleep in, this one with a large, sandy, grass-free area which I felt would provide a far more pleasant, water-free slumber. Such was the case, and I awoke with the sun a bit more rested than before, ready to take on the day.

Along Highway 85 I passed a sign that said 'Next Services 30 Miles,' and I considered this to be the point of no return. With Ft. Lauderdale now fully behind me I stared down the seemingly endless strip of pavement outstretched before me, jutting out into the Florida marshland that I was about to call home. I smiled as I went along my way, and the miles fell easily. As I turned north onto Highway 27 the sun began to set and I found a small cement building with a wide area of elevated dry ground around it. The place didn't look like it was visited often and thus I decided to set up the first camp there beneath a large, solemn tree whose pronounced profile stood out against the marsh.

Sitting there as the sun went down, I prepared for my first real night away from people while looking over miles and miles of tall reeds ahead, and the road running through them. As far as I could tell, where I sat was the only dry ground around for ages with little but swampy water stretched before me. Everything glowed with a vibrant golden hue, and a soft breeze rustled the reeds as I looked down at the small, green hut that was now my home. Suddenly I was struck with a sense of fulfillment deep within me, my mind felt clear and my heart felt full. A thin, honest smile began to show upon my lips. So this was it, this is what I had been dreaming of for months now, and I was actually doing it!

Hiker-ism: Take Nothing But Pictures, Leave Nothing But Footprints

The idea that nature is to be preserved in its natural state for all to enjoy. It is not for man to haphazardly take from the bounty of the wild without purpose, nor should he leave anything that had been brought in from town, mainly trash, for such things have far more consequence then an individual may perceive.

Packing up the next morning I found that I had made a new friend. A small turtle had crawled under my tent and remained motionless as I loaded up my gear, and so I began to talk with him. He looked like a Fredric, so that became my new friends name, and he was indeed very good company for breakfast, very attentive to what I had to say and didn't check his smart phone the whole time! Part of this insanity was due to the relief of finding this harmless little guy nestled amongst my gear as opposed to an alligator or snake, which I'm sure were closer during the night than I care to think about. As I made for the road I went to move little Fredric closer to the water's edge seeing as I'm sure he wouldn't like to be roasting in the rising sun and I had already rudely removed his covering. It was then that I found that I had made two rather large mistakes in less than an hour of being awake. One: I had given my new companion an improper name for her gender, and two: she was in the process of laying eggs. Feeling terrible about moving her a little I hoped that she would be able to continue laying after I covered her with a few leaves from the surrounding area as I offered my deepest apologies.

This was my first real lesson about nature: man had once come from the wild, though he has evolved to the point where he is no longer really a part of it. One can choose to either destroy nature in a primitive and reckless advancement of his own species, or to preserve it so it may teach us the simple and yet profound things that we have all but forgotten. I am only a visitor to the wild, and I have no right to take or disturb anything I don't need to. Such was the case with Freddie, I renamed her, for I wish I would have had the foresight to let her be instead of disrupting the natural order of things. It was a good lesson to learn early.

I had thought that by taking highways to Lake Okeechobee I was going to regrettably deprive myself the opportunity to experience the Everglades, but that was hardly the case. Surrounded by reeds twice the size of a man and very little else I set off down Highway 27, soon to be known to me as the Highway to Hell! There was forty miles of smoldering black asphalt between me and the lake, and my skin began to suffer as I walked along in the relentless Florida sun that, back in Carolina, I had been so eager to be in. There was water on both sides of the road, but not the type that one would care to swim in as it was muddy and dark in color, certainly not suitable for drinking. It's strange to see fresh water, the absolute essence of life, and know that it could kill should one partake of it. The only thing this water did was reflect the sun's rays back upon me as I went along my way, making the intense heat all that much more of a burden. I had the ability to carry three and a half liters of water, and it was obvious that I was going to need every bit of it for this stretch.

Not far along the way I came across a good sized shack that stuck out in the middle of essentially nothing with several cars parked in front of it and a wooden sign advertising airboat rides. I'm not to sure how many morons waiting to sit in front of a giant fan while being pushed through murky, alligator infested water it takes to keep this place running, but apparently there's enough of them in the world to keep the lights on and, more importantly, clean water in the bathroom. I filled up every container I could with as much clean water as it would hold, knowing that I wouldn't have an opportunity like this till I reached the Lake, and set back off down the road.

By midday the sun was bearing down with full force upon this God-forsaken stretch of blacktop without a cloud in the sky to shield me from it. Whats worse is that I was really starting to feel my left knee ache from the stress of carrying so much weight. I took breaks were I could find a patch of reeds that was thick enough to offer a little shade to try and eat something to keep my energy up, though my main problem was still the constant threat of dehydration. I knew going into this that it was going to be an overnight affair, so it was really important to watch my water intake; too much or too little and I wasn't going to make it, with possibly grim consequences. Let me tell you friend, a liter and a half of water is not enough to get a man through a day like this, and I couldn't ever sit in the shade long to cool off due to high populations of biting ants. As the sun started to get a bit lower I was about halfway to my goal, already tired, struggling to keep my water rationed, and was beginning to wonder where I could pitch my tent and not potentially get run over. The thought of hiking through the night crossed my mind, stay out of the sunlight, get to where I was going, but I was already beyond tired and didn't think I could have made it. Hopefully by using whatever strength I could muster, and every prayer in the book, it would be possible to make it through this somehow.

The answer to my prayers came in the form of a beat-up white pick-up truck with a profoundly oversized hood ornament and a bunch of shovels in the back. The driver looked like one of those old biker types, long gray beard and thinning ponytail with a few faded tattoos on his forearm that I doubt even he could decipher what they were anymore. His name was Brian; he was thin, seemed to be in his early fifties, a hard working man through and through, and kind enough to stop and offer a wandering young man like myself a ride to town. I had never hitchhiked a day in my life before then, and normally wouldn't have accepted such an offer, but was in far too much need to do otherwise at the moment. Turned out to be one of the better decisions I'd made in the last few months! I still had about twenty miles to go at that point, and as we passed through the endless swamp and marshlands I didn't see a single place I could have camped. Brian was a kind soul, despite his rough outward appearance, spending most of his days driving about doing work for Sutton Homes and taking care of more animals on a small farm then I can even begin recall. He dropped me off at a gas station in the town of South Bay on the south side of Lake Okeechobee, wished me well, and took off without accepting a dime. I smiled as I filled up again on clean water from a spigot on the side of the gas station, thinking about the ride in and how lucky I was to have been privileged enough to meet Brian. I've been saying it for years, but it's the rare times like this that really affirmed my belief that sometimes good guys don't wear white. Sometimes the best of men have the roughest appearance.

It was only the third day but it seemed like I had already come so far, and was now about to take my first step on the Florida Trail! Exhausted, and yet strangely energetic because of being so close, I walked up the pathway to the Lake's edge, laughing like a mad man after making it through such a rough day. While standing upon the top of the bank and looking down upon Lake Okeechobee I raised my hands in victory, shouting for joy at the first of what hoped to be many accomplishments. Here I was, central Florida, alone and empowered, at long last on a nature trail that would bare my footsteps for God only knows how long! Then the bugs started to come out. Oh dear God how they came out! About halfway into setting up my tent there must have been about ten of the bastards trying to bite me at any single moment, relentless in their pursuit, willing to die for a taste of fresh blood! As soon as humanly possible I dove inside my barely erected hovel, not even bothering to put the rainfly over my tent, zipping in for the night as the onslaught continued. There seriously must have been over fifty mosquitoes hovering around me at all times, and making quite a racket I might add. At one point I must have been only a few pests short from my tent being carried off to some sort of muddy, blood-sucker infested hell hole to be served for dinner, but thankfully that never happened.

As the sun fully dipped below the lake and the night set in I looked through the bug net at the night sky above. The insect kingdom had called its warriors back to base as the stars began to show one after another until the dark was painted over with their light, bringing about a complete and surreal stillness upon the world. It was quiet, and for the first time in a long time without being drunk, so was my mind. This isn't so bad, I thought to myself, trying to find a way to rest that allowed my knee not to feel as if it was about to pull a full scale rebellion and burst out of the side of my leg. Not bad at all.

4 THE FLORIDA TRAIL

I awoke at daybreak, which wasn't terribly impressive as it was December and such an event didn't occur until well after eight o'clock. My body felt refreshed, knee and all, and I was in a good mood despite finding out that in my hurry to be safe from bugs, not putting my rain cover on had caused everything I owned to become damp thanks to the morning dew.

Looking out into the Lake it's hard to believe that there actually *is* a lake. For miles there's this strange sort of mess of shrub and reed that isn't exactly land and isn't exactly water, just some sort of barren swamp blocking any sight of open water. There's a channel running on both sides of the bank, but again it's not the sort of water anyone would want to be swimming in. The whole thing seems artificial and unnatural, and according to the locals, the fishing had gone to shit as well. These days there's hardly a thing biting worth catching, and you've got a better chance of pulling up something you don't want to be messing with!

That didn't mean there wasn't a good amount of wildlife still about; I can recall one time in particular when I encountered a playful otter while wondering the bank of the lake. The first time I saw the little guy he was a good thirty yards away, sliding between rocks and grass, in and out of sight, but always in the same direction I was heading. After losing sight of him for some time I again noticed the little bugger prancing up the bank towards me--seriously, prancing, there's not a better word to fit the motion. It seemed somehow the otter hadn't noticed me, and was simply making to cross to the other side of the trail, but that soon proved to not be the case. He emerged onto the path not more than five yards away, stopped, and just stared at me.

Completely at a loss as for what to do, I simply removed my hat and politely bowed to the native creature, and in response he playfully jumped on the path, spun in a circle, and then darted back towards the water's edge in much the same manner as he had come. It later occurred to me that people had probably been feeding this otter and he had raced ahead to meet me in hopes of asking for a free meal. Upon noticing that the answer was no, he simply went along his way just as merry as if he had not been rejected at all. In a way, I wish people were more like this. It never hurts to ask, who knows what may happen if one does, but if the answer is no there's no reason to be put off by it. I believe people would be far happier if we showed each other such courtesy, and so I decided for that the rest of the trip that this would be my model for traveling. If I needed, I would ask, which is something that I had struggled with my entire life. I'd always been too proud to admit my needs, always working through them alone, but now saw no reason to be so guarded and arrogant.

Jumping way ahead in my travels: I remember seeing an hornets' nest somewhere around central Florida that must have been twice the size of my head. Also it should be noted that I think quite highly of myself, so that's really saying something! Instead of being frightened by the chance of being stung more times then a nudist beekeeper, I had to fight a strange, yet powerful, urge to throw rocks at it. Not sure what would have happened, but I'm glad to have not found out. More often than not, its best to let a quiet nest of troubles rest.

Now, I told you that story to tell you another story, and for the sake of not throwing rocks at things that should just be left alone I'm changing the names of those involved. Why should become clear as the tale goes on.

Walking around the lake I stopped into a town to try and grab some clean water and find something to eat. It didn't take long to find a bar and grill where food was cheap and the water was clear--exactly what the doctor ordered. Sitting down and placing an order, I couldn't help but notice the guy working there, staring at me from the back of the kitchen as if he had never seen another human being before. My pack was surely out of the ordinary, but people have been known to hike around the lake often enough that this shouldn't have been too rare. After I ate, this guy came around to talk; his name was John Doe and despite my initial impression of him, he was actually quite pleasant. We shared a few beers, which he offered to pay for, he asked about my travels, and when I made to leave he asked where I was going to stay. Having not thought that far ahead and honestly having no specific place to be, I felt compelled to accept when he offered a room for the night, complete with shower, and at no charge. Why not? I'm no small man, weighing in at close to two hundred pounds of solid muscle at this point, and shouldn't have much to fear should things go south; though I did notice that this guy was quite a bit bigger than me.

Let me just say that we had a freaking BLAST! Next thing I know we're off on a beer run drinking cheap suds out of paper bags, talking like old friends. John got a bottle of cheap whiskey from a bar and some supplies from a local grocery store to make dinner for us both--things were shaping up to be a great night! I can't recall exactly how much John was drinking but it was easily a lot more than I was. Normally I would be trying to be keeping pace but, this being our first encounter, I didn't want to make an ass of myself, especially since he was kind enough to let me stay in his home.

I forget exactly how we got there, but at some point in the night we migrated over to his neighbor's place; his neighbor was a younger Cuban guy who lived there with his wife, daughter, and mother. Let me just say that they were, and still are, some of the most wonderful people I had met in my entire life! They had small birds flying freely through their living room, not many possessions, but were so willing to share everything they had. It was as if they knew my family from way back when and hadn't seen me in far too long. I truly felt welcome.

Not long after our arrival John had completely given up on trying to make dinner and proceeded to keep drinking while his neighbor's mother prepared the pork and rice John had gathered earlier. Hand prepared, Cuban style pork is one of God's perfect foods! I'm pretty sure proper Cuban style pork could single handedly destroy anyone's vegetarian-by-choice lifestyle if they gave it even the slightest taste. I don't think this woman spoke a word of English, but her cooking spoke volumes. Salted pork, rice and beans--so simple, and yet some of the most amazing food I can ever recall. I was beyond grateful to have it.

The five of us spent hours drinking a little, laughing a lot, and watching old Jean Claude Van Damme movies before I decided to call it a night. After thanking everyone for a wonderful evening I made my way back to John's place to rest. He decided to keep drinking with his friend for a little while longer, though said he'd be back before too long. Thinking nothing of it, I let myself in, made myself a bed in the spare room, and laid down for the night, very happy to have a warm place to sleep and a full belly.

I had just fallen asleep long enough to be more than a little tired when I heard John stumble in. Even without being able to see him it wasn't hard to tell this guy was about as drunk as a person can get while not succumbing to alcohol poisoning. After hearing him stumble around a bit and muttering under his breath, the door knob to my room began to rattle. At first it was nothing more then a slight rustle, as if to be sure the room was occupied, but soon the door began to shake, violently, as John began to throw his body weight into it, drunkenly cursing and making sounds I couldn't make any sense of.

Fully awakened by the sudden change in my host I sprung from the bed and began to pack everything as quickly as humanly possible, knowing that my warm welcome had suddenly worn out. It's hard to make any sense of the situation; he would scream things like 'You little BITCH,' and 'It was all FAKE,' banging against the walls and door so hard that the building shook! There was this strange sort of half-laughing half-crying noise in between outbursts that to this day I can neither emanate or be fully convinced that such a sound can be made by a human, at least not without some sort of demonic possession. What's worse, this guy was indeed a fair bit bigger than I, and should he manage to remember it he could become an incredibly lethal force by employing a massive, rusty machete that was kept by the front door. Furthermore, it seemed that my only way out was to open the flimsy door that currently served as my only protection from the raging drunken backwoods bastard and fight my way past.

I'm not sure what the consequences of failing to do so would be as I pulled out my KA-Bar, but I surely didn't want to find out. Nearly prepared to strap up and fight for freedom, I noticed possible salvation behind a small TV in the room: a window! Upon sliding out the table and pressing my hands flat against the glass the window opened with more effort than expected and made a terrible screech as it did. Being sure that my former host had heard it I paused, wondering if he was going to come around to intercept me, but an outburst of that horrible laughter from the other room insured me he was too drunk to notice. Damn good thing, too, as I was out the window, gear and all, within seconds, blowing this plastic, fifties-style external window cover nearly off its hinges before running down the street as fast as my legs would carry me!

I didn't exactly know which way to go for a safe place to stay. John knew that I was walking the trail making that direction an incredibly risky option for the night, and there was no hotel or other safe haven in the town. In hindsight, there may not have even been a police station in the town, at least not anywhere close for I don't recall seeing one. Running down the street and ducking into the roadside shrubs every time a car passed by, a church became visible in the distance--good enough for me! Upon reaching it and moving around the back, I found a place to set up close enough to the building as to not be seen from the road and dark enough to be hidden till morning.

Sleep didn't come easy that night; it seemed like every little noise warranted a full investigation and my knife never left my hand. As the sun rose I decided to stay put for a bit, for a bit of the previous night's conversation revealed that John was supposed to clock in to work that morning at nine, and with any luck he wouldn't be able to come looking for me after that point. Just then an old man pulled around the church and found me packing up, but he didn't seem to mind much, just wanted to be sure everything was alright. At that point, everything appeared to be alright for I had successfully and safely made it out of a real sticky situation and through the night. From this point on however, I deemed it best to keep one's whits close, and a good knife closer.

After finding my way back to the trail it didn't take long for the the night's events to feel like nothing more than a bad dream. The sun was shining, and it was just warm enough to hike shirtless. Still a bit shaken from the whole endeavor, I began to settle back into my rhythm, my worries and apprehensions seemed to be fall further and further away with every step. I looked ahead to see high grass dancing in the breeze, right to see water shimmering in the daylight, and down to look directly into the mouth of a snake ready to strike. I don't know if that snake made a hiss, or a rattle, or a noise or did anything at all, but I sure as hell did! Jumping a good three feet high and six feet over with the help of my walking stick! It seems that there would be no easy steps along the way, and it's best to stay alert and focused on the task at hand.

Traveling is not for the faint of heart nor the easily distraught, for things will always go wrong though it's impossible to tell exactly when. It was a hard lesson taught early in my travels; I had thought that I would be throwing caution to the wind, but suddenly it appeared I would need it now more than ever, just in a very different way. In all things there is a lesson to be learned. While I was indeed shaken up by a most hostile of hosts and a potentially poisonous serpent, I soon found the latter to be a little humorous--its amazing how high one can jump with a little motivation.

The rest of the day went well, and thankfully without any other life threatening events. However, the night seemed to come a bit too quickly as the daylight faded and I still stood a good three miles from the day's destination. It seems the late start was to blame, and to make matters worse I hadn't closed off my water reservoir very well last time I filled it, causing me to lose about half of what I had and leaving very little left at this point. Having no other choice but to keep walking until I found a good spot to stop, the daylight wore thin along with my patience. I had noticed a few fishermen in the channel that ran along the outside of the trail earlier in the day, and now they all rode their boats back to harbor, skipping along the water leaving me in their wake. Except for one: an older guy, more then likely in his early seventies, looking like he just stepped off the cover of a fishing magazine. Clad in a wide brimmed hat, oversized sunglasses and cargo shorts, he was still smoking a cigar as he slowed down and called over to me.

"Heading to town?!" he yelled.

"Trying to!" I replied, dehydrated, tired, and still getting used to the weight I was carrying.

"Want a lift?"

Gazing down at this older fellow standing on what looked to be an expensive piece of recreational machinery, the events from the night before still burned in my mind, causing me to hesitate. However, my legs burned a bit worse than my conscience so I decided to take him up on the offer. Besides, how often do you get to hitch a ride on a fishing boat?

"Sure, thanks!" I called down to him as he pulled the boat to shore, allowing me to jump aboard. "Name's Jordan."

"They call me Catfish Crawley around here," he said which brought up more questions than it answered--Why is that? Who's they? Am I to be included in this so-called 'they'? Is it different everywhere else--all of which I figured were better left unanswered as I enjoyed the chance to sit down for a moment.

He told me to hold on as he straightened out the boat and made to throw the throttle forward. I should have taken him more seriously than I did because when this old timer threw the hammer down he about threw me out of the seat and overboard as well! The nose of the craft shot straight up making it impossible to see past, and I had to hold onto my hat for fear of losing it as the stern plowed through the murky channel. In a matter of moments we planed out, sliding smoothly over the glass-like surface as I had seen the others crafts do, the wind whistling in my ears and blowing around my new-found facial hair. I had stopped shaving about a week before setting off and the sensation of a beard being caught in the wind was indeed a strange one, but I rather liked it and I laughed as we went along our way.

Arriving beside a bridge on the edge of town in what seemed to be no time at all, Catfish rested the bow of his craft gently upon the soft bank, bringing my ride to an end. He then gave me a Diet Coke and original Stogie before we parted ways while wishing each other well, which was indeed a far better parting then my last one. As I watched the old-timer ride off I began to think about the nature of men in relation to one another--are we born selfish and wicked, or good natured and caring? While I had indeed experienced both sides of the coin there seemed to be no clear answer just yet, though I believed I would find more help than harm out here. Still, I needed to be mindful that not everyone was not going to be so friendly. I settled in for one last night on the lake just outside of town, glad to have made it, and wondered what the next days would bring.

After stopping in Buckhead Ridge to resupply I made it to the Kissimmee river, bringing an end to the first major leg of the Florida Trail. Taking a moment to pause and gaze upon the great body of water that was soon to be but a memory I smiled, feeling as though I had already accomplished something. So many miles to go, but I had come much farther than most and I had a strong feeling the best was yet to come.

While walking along the long, narrow, grassy path that bordered the Kissimmee river I began to get acquainted with what were to be my long-term traveling companions, although quite unbeknownst to me at the time: free range cattle. Cows, everywhere! Across the river, on my right, all day, everyday just COWS EVERYWHERE!! However, along with cows, I now had access to a very vital resource that up until now I hadn't been able to find--firewood! Around the whole of Lake Okeechobee there were absolutely no limb-producing trees, just palms and shrubs, and while I know palm leaves burn wildly for a moment, building a fire that would last long enough for any practical purpose was until now utterly impossible!

The trail along the river was smooth and easy to travel, and my mind began to wander as I went along my way though it never landed on anything important. When I set out from Wilmington I had aspirations on solving all of life's great mysteries, but out here life seemed to make more sense than it had in a long time, making such questions obsolete. I felt almost childlike in a way, exploring a vast new world filled with simple joys I had long since forgotten about. I began to notice the smell of clean air, the feel of earth and the sweat upon my skin, the relief a simple cool drink could could bring on a hot day, and the value of every minute I'd been granted to live in.

At one point I stopped to rest for a minute, during which I made my way to the river to fill a pot of water. I had meant to bring the water back to boil, but instead via some grand impulse I leaned forward and dumped the entire thing over my head. I'm not sure what possessed me to do such a thing other than the fact that I had been walking in eighty-degree heat all day, but the feeling was absolutely incredible! It wasn't just physically refreshing, but also somehow spiritually, as if the water washed away all worries of normal life or some sort of burden that I had been carrying.

I started to think back to the first job I ever had at the age of sixteen where I worked with the men who became my greatest friends. We were construction grunts, that is to say that we did everything that needed to get done but no one wanted to do, and were paid in cash, off the record. I think were were listed as 'supplies' in the general contractors bill so we used to joke that we were the world's most versatile toilet paper, we cleaned all kinds of shit! The first week on the job however they had us in the middle of a parking lot chipping the mortar off of old bricks so that they could reuse them in the new construction. It was hard, hot, dirty work, and we would leave each day covered head to toe with a thick layer of white dust plastered onto our skin via a hearty layer of sweat. So rather then go home and annoy our poor mothers by tracking in more dust than a chimney sweep into their nice, clean homes, we would ride out to lake Michigan, just minutes away from the job site. Upon arrival we would race each other through the parking lot and down the pier that stretched well over a thousand feet into the water before diving off the end fully clothed and without worry. Its unusual for the water in Lake Michigan to rise above seventy degrees, and the cold, fresh water would always take one's breath away on a hot day. After a hard day at work however, nothing else has since felt so rewarding, or refreshing. Its amazing how something so simple like an after work swim or a pan full of river water can become so profound.

While I had originally planned to hike on, instead I camped where I had gathered the pot of water that night, taking advantage of the fact that for once in my life I had no place I needed to be and all day to get there. As I boiled a little water to purify it I smoked the cigar Catfish had given me, watching the night sky fill with stars again and a full moon rise above the river. In the distance I heard coyotes howling, and while I can't say I was glad about it I didn't feel threatened. My little fire burned at my feet keeping the bugs at bay and I couldn't help but feel like this is how men were supposed to live. Before settling in for the night I rose to put the fire out, the full moon at my back casting my shadow over the embers. To me, it looked like something was being forged, or rekindled within my shadow and I felt it inside of me, some sort of new passion for life, a binding of all my loose parts. I felt a bit stronger in that moment, like everything was alright for the first time in a long time, and I smiled.

As the trail parted from the river I came across my first orange blaze painted upon the side of a palm tree. What a feeling that was! Until then I had been relying on well-beaten paths, hoping that I was going in the right direction, and this was my first real validation that yes, I was going the right way. The landscape became very safari-like, almost as if I was traveling through some part of Africa. The grass was waist high and dried yellow, the trees grew short and thick with many branches in all direction, and only short palms and shrubs to break up the space in between. In fact, I may have believed that I was in Africa at times if it wasn't for all of the landmines my oversized animal companions were leaving about. Cows are not really known for their hygiene, and I spent more time looking down trying to keep my shoes out of shit then I did gazing at the natural surroundings. It should be noted that when I say 'shit' I don't mean it figuratively, I'm talking about actual cow shit! Not the most pleasant of things, but being outdoors is never a clean affair. I just figured that this was going to be the way things were going to be until I was out of Florida; none too adventurous, but easy to pass through.

After just over a week I began to be very confident in myself and my ability to travel by foot. My body began to feel stronger, and my joints weren't hurting nearly as much at the end of each day. It was then while passing through yet another cow pasture that I came upon Chandler's

Slough, an eight mile horseshoe shaped trail heading east from the Kissimmee river and then back to it. I looked at a map that I had picked up at a kiosk just off of the lake and noticed that it would only be about four miles if I followed the river northwest, which would cut off a good four miles of boring, uneventful cow pasture. I didn't come out to the wild to follow the rules, I came here to make my own bloody rules, to blaze my own trail, and here was the perfect opportunity!

Forgoing the trail I followed my compass north west through the high grass towards my new destination--piece of cake I thought, I'll be there in a couple hours. I passed by a few high shrubs, and then cut through some reeds, then a few more shrubs that began to grow closer and closer together. So began what I consider to be close to the worst twenty hours of my life! I'm not exactly sure what the word *slough* means, or exactly how to pronounce it though I have yet to find a way that sounds pleasant. What is fairly obvious, is that the designer of such a word meant it to be a warning in and of itself. It's the sort of warning that is easily missed by crass, young men such as myself sadly as I continued to foolishly push forward into the reeds as opposed to turning back. In less than an hour of travel into the slough the reeds became so thick that it required almost an hour to travel one hundred yards, having to push them forward with my forearms and then climb on top of them so as to have stable ground to stand on. Trying to weave left and right to find the path of least resistance while still moving north west I was now fully committed to making it through, after all it was only four miles, how long could it take?

What a maddening four miles it became! The reeds grew together so thickly that it was impossible to see more than ten feet ahead, and just tall enough that a full grown man couldn't see over them. Despite all of this, the reeds did nothing to block out the sun whose heat not only beat down mercilessly from above, but also reflected back off the mud and shallow water in the slough. There were no trees, just shrubs too thick to pass though and the occasional patch of vines weaving the reeds together like a natural fortress wall, taking massive amounts of energy to break though. Hours passed this way, the only relief I had was the rare moments that I could walk through black, thigh deep water in between shrubs and more reeds so dirty that I couldn't even begin to wash in it or dare think of drinking it. Not only that but I passed more snakes here than at any other time in my travels, bar none! I watched so many of them slide off their tufts of grass and reeds into the black mire that I still get chills thinking about it. Everything from small, harmless ball pythons to great, fat puff adders which I know could lay me low with a single bite! It was in one such watery section that I managed to make a good amount of progress before finally being able to pull myself onto dryish land through thick grass, or so I thought. Upon parting the grass I found myself hardly a foot from a great snake coiled up and none too happy about being disturbed. Needless to say I slowly backed into the muck and let him be, but I was still more than irritated about having to continue in these conditions.

The sun began to set and I had no idea how much farther I had to go. Keeping a steady direction was next to impossible, and I found myself having to turn around a lot more then I would like to admit. While I had no desire to spend the night in this God forsaken swamp, I was running out of time with each moment of the descending sun. A part of me wanted to panic--what had I gotten myself into? Thankfully I managed to keep my wits about me, and actually took the sunset as an opportunity for I knew that by traveling towards the sun I was going west, and hopefully to the river and out of this hell hole. I chased the sun like a drowning man swims for a life preserver, diving forward over reed and muck half crazy and in complete disregard for my own flesh. It was then that I found a small sanctuary, a lone maple tree that by some miracle had managed to take up roots here, and beneath it lay ground dry enough to stand firmly on. By no means was this a good place to camp, the ground was still very wet and full of roots, but the tree gave me a chance to get above the reeds and look ahead. From the top of the tree I couldn't see forward much more than a mile but could see far enough for my heart to utterly plummet inside my chest. There was no clear way out, I had run out of sunlight, and I was stuck here for the night unless I wanted to chance pressing on in the dark which really didn't seem wise. So here I was, not the Ritz, but regrettably my home for the night, and with no one to blame for it but myself.

It's hard to recall ever being so tired and yet so restless; sleep didn't come easy and when it did it never stayed long. In the distance I heard wild dogs barking and fighting one another, and seeing as I had spent an entire day blazing a path to myself I feared the worst. The morning did come though, none too soon, and I rose with it, never having slept long enough to have believed it all to be a bad dream. This day was more of the same, caught in the middle of this impassible wilderness trying to find a way out. It was hard to stay positive, hell it was even hard to not break down and completely loose the little sanity I still had. About midday I managed to find a grove of tall cypress trees with branches low enough for me to reach allowing me to climb up and try and find a way out. After climbing a good fifty feet up in this mighty tree a radio tower became visible, and appeared to be about two miles north. To the west however I could see moving traffic slightly closer, and so due west became my heading. If nothing else, I figured that the tower could serve as a reference point if ever being lucky enough to see it again.

    Not long after though, my worst fear became a reality: I was out of clean water and far from out of the slough. In this heat, and with no chance of purifying the water that was around, this could turn deadly real quick, and it took everything I had to not panic. I had to press on, there must be a way out, I got into this mess and damn it all I was getting out! The reeds never grew thinner or shorter, the sun never let up, and with every step my need for rest and water grew. Was I going to make it? I couldn't say for sure anymore, and finding a short tree whose branches grew thick and low I sat down and hung my head in exhaustion nearly defeated. It was this spot that saved my life strangely enough, the live oak that I was now resting on provided a dry place to regroup and more importantly allowed me to notice something very different about the surrounding water. Where everywhere else the water was stagnate, black, and muddy, the water here was clear and flowed quickly around the branches that dipped beneath the surface. I was too stupid to avoid getting myself into this mess, but smart enough to know that moving water had a far better chance of being safe to drink, and having no other choice that's exactly what I did. Cupping my hands and drawing deep from the current I drank my fill and filled my reserves halfway, hoping that I wouldn't be paying for it later with some sort of parasite or waterborne illness. Still, this was a do or die situation, and I'm certainly up for putting off death till a later date if I can. Sitting in this little oasis I looked around to see tadpoles darting in and out of the roots coiled beneath the water's surface, the sun became somehow pleasant again, and things didn't seem so bleak at that moment. Still being hopelessly lost and an undetermined distance from the road this was as good as I knew things were going to get here in the slough, so I took a moment to be glad in it. I was going to be OK, I just had to keep moving.

    Reluctantly leaving the tiny sanctuary behind it was hours before finding any sort of relief, and it came in the form of a waist deep, lilypad-ridden pool that was roughly seventy five feet wide and far from enjoyable to cross. On the other side however was grass that I could see over and clusters of dead, fallen branches that I imagine no human eyes had ever seen before. The branches broke with no effort at all, hardly even slowing my pace as I pushed through them emerging finally insight of the highway and beyond the slough. My joy was uncontainable while running through the pasture to meet the pavement and dropping to my knees to kiss it. Roaring in victory with my treacherous foe fallen behind me and dancing about with relief I rejoiced in what I had overcome, only cutting it short to kick myself for ever getting myself into such a mess! Still miles from any sort place to fill up on clean water I carried on, feeling better, but still worn thin from was most likely the roughest twenty-four hours of my life.

It was only days after that I remembered the words of a passage memorized as a child and long since forgotten. "The lord is my Shepherd, I shall not want, he makes me lie down in green pastures, he leads me besides the clear water, and yea though I may walk through the shadow of the valley of death I will fear no evil, for thou art with me". It was my mother's favorite bible verse, and it stuck with me through the years. I now realized that green pastures may be a patch of dry ground in an unforgiving wasteland, and clear water may be barely clean enough to drink, but the snakes and dogs were held at bay, and I needed to fear no evil. It's not for men to know exactly what they need in life, and a great blessing may come in such a small way that it can be skipped over easily. I now find it very hard to deny that there is indeed something greater then myself in this existence, and while I can not tell you exactly what it is I know it unto myself to be true. Believe it if you want to, or don't, but I do, and forever will.

The way was still mainly cow pasture at this point, but with the new addition of massive oak hammocks as they're called. Clusters of incredibly thick oaks whose branches barely grew more than twenty yards high but stretched an incredible distance from the trunk. At times they looked like great spider legs stretched across the plains, covered in moss and grass that grew upon their bark that gave them a very hair-like appearance. Many of the branches grew so thick that there's no way I could reach around them, and even at their farthest point from the trunk the limb could support the weight of a man, making them an excellent place to rest. I had never seen trees like this, and while I imagine many had grown accustomed to such things they made me happy--nature's quite a treat if you take the time to look at it. It was this sort of landscape that brought me to the border of an Air Force base set in a stretch of trail called the Road to Mico. Even at the end of the trail I never arrived at Mico, whatever that is, but I was forced to reroute upon finding a sign that informed me that the old trail was now in the active target range for bombing training. Was it actually? Couldn't tell you, and I didn't care to find out. All I know is that I was supposed fill out a permit upon entering the south end of the base and carry part of said permit to the north end, where once this bit of paper was dropped off the Air Force would know I was no longer a possible civilian casualty.

Much of the trail at this point seemed to pass by with ease, never offering much resistance or beautiful places to stop. It's hardly even a memory at this point, but I can recall feeling much stronger and very at peace with hardly a thought crossing my mind in a day. Although, one thing I always found perplexing was as to why this whole of central Florida wasn't constantly on fire?! There was nothing here but dead trees and grass so dry it seemed that if the wind blew it against itself too hard the friction might send it ablaze. When I wanted a fire at night it was effortless to start one, but many times I went without for fear that a stray spark would set the whole place up.

I do remember one night alongside a canal however, where I threw caution to the wind and started a small campfire to boil water. It wasn't the fire that made this night stand out though, but rather a full moon so bright that I could have wrote by it, and a cool breeze coming off of the water. I was thinking on how I had come to be in this place, and those that had affected my life the most. Many of my friends and family members crossed my mind but the one that stuck was my Grandad on my Father's side. I'd be lying if I said that I knew him well; he passed away when I was old enough to remember him but too young to have really gotten to know him. In fact, there's only two things that I can still remember about the man. I remember the sound of his laugh, partially because it's nearly the same as my father's, and a chorus that he used to sing with my Grandmother, something about a silvery moon. While the exact words escape me the melody rings clear, and I couldn't help but dwell upon it alongside of the canal that night, humming along as best as I could remember. It's the little things that make a person who they are, and I wonder, what it is about me that my friends will remember?

It's hard to believe how quickly time can pass, even when you're getting the most out of each day. Two weeks in the woods passed in what seemed to be no time at all, and yet I had gathered more stories in them then in the last two years! Hiking started to feel normal. Well, as normal as anything ever had to me which isn't saying much. I was still working a lot of things out, like what food to carry seeing as I was now out of MRE's, but people seemed to be very willing to help strangely enough, without even having to ask for it. For example, a hunter named Rod just randomly gave me twenty dollars to grab a burger after he stopped to chat with me for a few minutes which I was extremely grateful for. A lack of supplies did in fact force me to make a radical change in my course however, and in search of food I ended up walking twelve miles north from the end of the Kissimmee river section to the town of Holopaw. To say there's nothing in Holopaw would be a bit of an insult to things that align themselves with nothing--take major relationship problems for example-- but there was a gas station with enough stock to get me through the day. I had an unquenchable thirst for Mountain Dew which was odd seeing as I never really drank much soda, and I found myself sitting at a picnic table halfway through my second thirty two ounce cup of the stuff when a Sheriff's car pulled up in front of me. Well, here's my first vagrancy charge, I said aloud before the sheriff climbed out of his cruiser and made his way over.

Regardless of undoubtedly being in trouble I managed to offer a friendly greeting, and strangely enough was offered one in return. Rather taken aback by the whole thing we talked for longer than I can remember with the topic being not so much what I was doing here but rather what brought me here. He was honestly interested in the story of what I gone through so far, and about my goals for the days to come. I imagine it was a strange sight to see, a hobo and an officer sitting on the same bench smiling in conversation with one another, but at the end of the day neither a pack or a badge will prevent one from being human.

After about twenty minutes or so Mike, the officer, let me go on about my way giving me a protein bar as parting gifts before driving off. He also said that he would get on the radio and try and give the officers ahead a heads up about me in hopes of avoiding any further trouble. I'm not sure if he actually did, but I didn't have anyone stop me as I went along my way which I must admit was a huge relief. Traveling truly is a marvelous thing.

Hiker-ism: Hike Your Own Hike:

The idea that one's journey is uniquely their own, and there is no right or wrong way to do it. What works for one may not for another, and what some would consider completely out of the question others embrace as a new opportunity to explore.

It was the day before Christmas, and I had run out of water. That morning I had gathered whatever water I could by wiping the dew off my tent and wringing it out into my water bottle. A bit dusty, but enough to get me down the road and hopefully to Wilson, a town that lay about twenty country highway miles north of me. However by midday the water that I had managed to gather was all but gone and the future looked bleak. Despite being the day before what most Christians consider to be the most holy day of the year no one had stopped to help a young homeless looking man walking down the side of the road. I imagine they didn't want to keep Grandma waiting; they hadn't seen her since last year after all. That doesn't mean that help didn't find its way to this road weary traveler, though it came unexpectedly

I've always kicked trash along side of the road whenever walking down one--one would be surprised what can be found this way! More often than not it's just half eaten fast food or blown apart tin cans, which is really a sad sight to behold. I must admit that many times in my life I had allowed trash to blow out of my truck bed onto wherever it landed, what's one more bit of garbage among all this junk? Just another snowflake in an avalanche, which seems like no big deal until one takes the time to realize that an avalanche is simply made of snowflakes. On this particular day, at my moment of greatest need, it was that I stumbled upon something useful. There, on the side of the road just beyond the entrance of a hunting camp, I came across four unopened cans of Budweiser beer and a can of Sprite! "ITS A CHRISTMAS MIRACLE!!!" I exclaimed no no one in particular, overjoyed that one: I now wasn't going to die from dehydration, and two: I now had beer!

I can only imagine the series of events that led up to this, but in my mind they go something like this: some hunter is sitting by the fire with a few of his buds, sipping a few brews and talking about all the stuff they shot at when the topic of beer comes up. They then realize that they only have a few cans left and tomorrow is Christmas Eve--do they even sell beer on Christmas Eve? It's getting late, there's not much more time to buy beer so they need to act quick! With no one near sober enough to go for a beer run they do the only logical thing there is to do and draw straws to see who has to drive. Some unlucky bastard hops in the driver's seat of their souped up, four wheel drive pick-up truck, complete with shotgun racks and a CB radio, and they all shoot of to the gas station! Already breaking the law, the driver doesn't bother pulling out of camp and onto the road slowly, burning rubber and hollering like the Dukes of Hazard as they rush for booze before time runs out. Little do they all know that they left the tailgate open, and the few brews they had left sitting in the truck bed were not about to stay there. Falling out softly into the wet grass near the entrance to the camp, the beers manage to remain unbroken and ready for my arrival. The other thing I don't know is how they reacted to finding out that their remaining brew had suddenly, and mysteriously, gone missing, but I also believe they were too drunk to care. As for me, I now was ready to keep hiking and singing Christmas carols as I went.

Furthermore, in celabration of the Christmas season I decided to treat my self. I didn't have a lot of money to spare, but sleeping on the ground is evedently far less pleasant then I had anticipated. Thus I decided to buy a sleeping mat. For about fourty dollas I fould an inflatable hiking mat that strapped nicely to the outside of my pack, and what a differene it made! Sleep became far easier to find, my sleeping bag stayed dry as opposed to slightly damp from the ground, and I found that I was no longer cold as I slept. The ground has a way of sucking the heat from you while sleeping, and I know now that if I hadent made this purchase, theres a good chance I wouldnt have made it. Merry christmas to me, I wasn't going to die!

It had recently crossed my mind how South Florida wasn't constantly on fire, it's nothing but dried grass and dead limbs, though the answer soon became clear. They actually light sections of the forest on fire from time to time! It's hard to say exactly who, but apparently someone brings some heavy machinery out into the wilderness, tears up a whole bunch of trees and shrubs to clear a large path around a section of forest, and lights the fucker up! While this must be quite a sight, it makes for a very strange hike after this procedure, known as a prescribed burn, occurs over a section of trail. It's like walking on the surface of the moon; little puffs of dust flutter up beneath each step as they crunch down on the charred earth, and the scent of smoke is still heavy in the air. The once colorful landscape is replaced by an eerie portrait in grayscale, and some of the trees are scorched to the point of being completely black on the lower ten feet of their trunk. However, even in the areas that had seen the worst the higher branches were relatively unharmed, still fully green and thriving with their competition now burned away. By burning out the things that were stealing their energy these great trees were allowed to flourish, unburdened by the little things weighing them down, and thus we have a thriving forest instead of a tinderbox waiting to ignite. While the process may singe in the beginning, it's good to burn out that whatever leeches energy before some little things become a big thing, sparks, and burns everything down completely.

I noticed upon my arrival to Alexander Springs there wasn't much underbrush to be had however, which was very different from all of the other places I had been hiking so far. I had become accustomed to short and hardy oaks as well as a few other plants that appeared to struggle just to exist, but here they were replaced by tall, thin pine forests and sandy rolling hills. As the name suggests there were in fact several freshwater springs in the area, crystal clear and warm to the touch, thermo-regulating at a solid seventy two degrees year round. The earth is an astounding entity that can frequently serve as a thermostat and water filter all in one! In the spring small fish could be seen swimming to and fro, and the water was so clear that the few patches of seaweed growing on the bottom appeared to be floating on the surface via some sort of grand optical illusion. The strangest sight to behold about the whole body of water however was the rippled surface near the center where water was naturally being forced upward with such force that it's point of origin could be seen from the banks of the spring. Fresh water was a welcome sight seeing the trouble I had gone through trying to find it this far.

Alexander Springs marked the start of Ocala National Forest, which soon became one of my favorite sections along the entire hike! The pines grew tall and thin but all of them bent wildly in the same direction, to the point where it was a bit disorienting. I had never seen trees grow like this. If any single tree had managed to grow directly upwards it would have towered over those around it, and they grew so closely together that they looked like an old oriental painting of bamboo in the distance. The forests weren't all-encompassing of this area though. Apparently, a large wildfire had taken out a good amount of the forest in several parts of Ocala leaving strange sections of overgrown bushes and short trees among dead, burnt out trunks that were still standing. To me, it looked like some sort of post-nuclear apocalyptic landscape, quiet and eerie, the land still bearing the scars of a massive wave of destruction while starting to regrow. One has to step over charred logs and next to great gray pillars that were once trees, but it was interesting to see how the forest was rebuilding itself, though it felt very strange to wander here.

It was here that I ran into my first bit of real gear failure, which took me by surprise seeing as I wasn't even four hundred miles into my journey and expected to go the whole way with what I currently had. While I loved the freedom given to me by my little freestanding tent, allowing me to set up wherever there was flattish ground, the thing was completely reliant on a few collapsible metal poles that ran over the surface. While getting out of my tent one morning I foolishly pushed too hard against the rain cover while emerging, still half asleep, and stressed the pole to the point of snapping. Literally not a happy camper at this point. Being over-prepared, I had brought along a few different types of tape, and tried to repair the pole using them and whatever else I could find. Twigs were too fragile, tent stakes tore the tape when I went to flex the pole, but my spork had a fine channel bent into the center of it's handle that locked nicely over the pole. Success! Or so I thought. When attempting to use the newly bandaged pole I nearly had it in place when the pole suddenly gave way, and thinking that I had tore the tape again I went to repair it. I wasn't so lucky, for now I had a broken spork to match my broken tent pole. I had just rolled a 1 in the D&D of life. The tent wasn't broken to the point that I couldn't use it thankfully, so while I was a bit irritated at my sudden streak of bad luck I pressed on hoping for the best. Rest in pieces fair spork, you were the finest multi-purpose eating utensil I have ever come to know.

Things took a turn for the better soon enough as I passed through the town of Salt Springs, a charming little town stuck in the middle of nowhere.

There wasn't much to the place, just a gas station, grocery store, and most importantly a hardware store where I hoped to gather a few things to fix my gear. After looking around for a little bit I managed to find a quick drying epoxy which I expected to stick things back together with, plus a four inch piece of metal pipe to splint the pole with if the epoxy didn't work. Salt Springs was a nice little town, but I soon found that the best part of the area was just around the corner and back on the trail.

There are times when one is traveling that you just have to go check something out and see what happens, and thus, I found the 88 Store. While the Florida Trail is marked by orange blazes, side trails are commonly marked by little blue marks of paint not surprisingly called blue blazes, and they tend to lead to things just slightly out of the way worth seeing. Sometimes it's a waterfall, others it's a astounding vista, but in this case the little blue bastards led to a tiny little shack stuck in the middle of the woods a good ways away from anything worth mentioning. There's indeed a lot of words that could be used to describe the 88 Store, although I believe most of them would drive away more business then they brought in. However, it's here that I got my first taste of real hiker culture.

When I say it was a shack, it's because from the outside all that could be seen was an oversized porch covered with a tin roof and sporting a few benches to sit on, and the inside didn't boast much more. There's a small rack of candy bars and a few coolers with very little in them except beer, and a large bar that ran down the entire length of the building. It was easy to see that this place kept the doors open by selling cigarettes and cheap beer to the locals, serving more as a bar then a store, but despite being rather rough around the edges the placed seemed welcoming and homely. The bartenders were friendly and smiled as they welcomed this ragged young hiker, and as I took a seat at the bar the plywood floors and low tin roof somehow made me feel more at home then I had in quite some time. If I wasn't feeling at home when I walked in, a few rounds of dollar beers sure did, and I was chatting with the locals and staff in no time like I had always been there. Perhaps the greatest part of the bar wasn't the warm service or the fact that they let my drunk ass camp out back, but that they had kept a logbook with the signature of nearly every person who had hiked long distance on the Florida Trail. I proudly added my name to the book, feeling like I had joined the ranks of an exclusive group of highly regarded, bat-shit crazy individuals--quite an accomplishment in my eyes.

It was raining in the morning when I packed up, but the drizzle gave me a chance to rest my hangover away on the front porch as I attempted to epoxy my tent pole. The weather let up before to long, and while the epoxy proved to be a complete waste of time and money, the little pipe preformed wonderfully making my tent good as new. Refreshed and ready for the day ahead I left the 88 Store behind, but kept the memories of the place close by as I went along my way. It didn't take long to realize that it wasn't going to be just the woods that made this trip worth taking, but also the people I was bound to meet along the way.

My confidence in myself was growing by the day--I almost felt like I knew what I was doing at this point, but not really. My daily miles began to increase as well, and I was pushing close to eighteen miles a day at this point. However, the land was about as flat as a pancake, following bodies of water with barely more than a mole hill to break up the horizon. While the uneventful terrain let me get used to carrying the weight of my pack without much additional stress, the massive amounts of stagnate water provided their own unique sort of challenge. At one point there was literally a levy set up to regulate the water levels from one lake to another, with a walkway that spanned over the manmade channel that worked like a drawbridge. To get across, one had to arrive when the levy operators were on duty and press a large red button on the side of a chain link fence that subsequently caused a hellish buzzer to shatter the surrounding silence so as to alert said operators of one's presence. While it's always very satisfying to press a large red button it seemed like quite a hassle for just a few hikers, but nevertheless the button was pushed, the walkway swung across, and I was allowed to pass.

The section of trail after the levy proved to be one of my least favorite hikes, not because it was challenging, or because I got lost for over a day in a life-threatening situation, but rather because it was so bland and boring! The trail followed an a old jeep path through a mosquito infested wetland, keeping my boots dry soon became impossible, and there was never anything more to look at then a few dead trees and beat up old road. A matter of inches in elevation meant the difference between walking on old forest road or walking in water, with large puddles never more than one hundred yards apart. After completely giving up on trying to keep my feet any kind of dry I tried to walk through the center of one of these puddles and was forced to turn back after only my third or fourth step left me standing in thigh deep water with no sign of it shallowing. It took far longer to walk around the edges, but I had no other option and just kept moving along trying to find the end of it all.

It was three days before my feet would be allowed to dry off again, and I was worried it would cause me more trouble than it actually did. Just like it's hard to take a drink without water it's hard to take a step without a foot-- a simple truth usually only to be recognized by those no longer able to do so. Eventually, Rice Creek Plantation offered a fun bit of relief from the wet, squishy forest floor via Hofman Crossing. Hofman Crossing was a sight to behold; it was nothing more than a pair of narrow boards running next to each other and kept out of the mud by a series of supports driven deep into the earth to form a bridge. It wasn't the odd construction that made this crossing memorable, but rather the fact that it stretched for over a half a mile through what would otherwise be impassable swampland. It must have taken months to construct this crazy thing, and while I don't know the names of those who suffered through impossible hours in rubber waders in the middle of this yellow fly-infested hellhole, I thank them for preventing me from having to do the same. Seriously, it must have been miserable hauling every piece in by hand and driving it without any help from machines, for there was certainly no way to get a machine into this mire, and even if one managed such a thing digging holes in this muck was out of the question. However, their countless hours of toil, and I imagine enough DEET to drown a bull moose, proved that no matter how difficult Mother Nature makes it to pass, mankind will find a way to give her the finger and do it anyway

Hiker-ism: Hiker Hunger

(noun) The feeling a person gets after having to eat only what could be carried for long periods of time. Symptoms include: the feeling that eating an entire horse would not only be possible but also an excellent idea, reckless consumption of anything and everything especially at buffets, and still feeling hungry while physically unable to fit anymore food inside one's body.

I had been walking for thirty one days when I hit the town of Keystone Heights, stronger, more focused, lighter, and hungrier than I had even been in the last three years! I deviated from the Florida Trail to avoid a few days in a swamp, taking instead a long path that was paved and well populated by cyclists, a few of whom decided to stop and chat awhile. One such duo of women must have spent a little time in the mountains because not only did they know about the Florida Trail, which was uncommon even for Florida locals, but also of an all you can eat comfort food buffet just past town! I was already rather hungry and low on supplies, but in anticipation of this glorious, and highly recommended by complete strangers, dining hall I skipped lunch and all other opportunities to snack until I got there.

The Keystone Inn is a tiny place next to a car lot on the edge of Keystone Heights, and while the place does have a sign on the edge of the road, those who don't know where the place is could easily overlook it. Hell, I was walking and I almost passed by the unassuming little white cement building that looked to be more a part of the car lot then a restaurant from the outside. The inside wasn't much different, having only a few tables and a self serve buffet that ran through the middle of the building. The walls were bland, with only a few boring pictures hung upon them, and the windows had a sort of yellow, country style, farm house window treatment that one would only expect to see at Grandma's place. The wait staff wasn't outstanding though were attentive enough, but just barely, and I believe someone who had never eaten at this place would assume this sort of boring establishment would be doomed from the start. Those who have eaten here however know that the food is a-freaking-mazing! It's hard to make southern style comfort food wrong, but it's also equally hard to make it perfect, and what The Keystone Inn lacks in picture perfect, high class presentation it makes up for in flavor and enjoyment. A full plate of this sort of cooking is usually enough to fill the stomach of a full grown man, but I did my Grandmother proud and cleaned six. Cornbread, fried chicken, stuffed bell peppers, mashed potatoes, sweet corn, beans, beans, and more beans, carrots and green beans, and a thick homemade gravy to smother everything with. This place was a little slice of heaven to a wanderer like me!

It was getting dark by the time I left the Keystone Inn, meaning that I needed to find a place close by to set up camp. Honestly though, it wouldn't have mattered if it was high noon for I was so uncomfortably full that I wasn't going much of anywhere without laying down for awhile. Hard to say exactly how far I got, but I doubt it was more than three hundred yards from the front door before I found a spot in the woods to set up. I remember lying awake in my tent too tired to even write in my journal, but too full to fall asleep until my stomach settled a bit. Though the next day did fly by seeing as I now had more built up energy then at any other time in the last month..

I was approaching North Florida by this time in my travels, and things were starting to cool ff a bit. I stopped in Lake City to wash the few clothing items I owned but wasnt able to find a laundromat so I had to make due with the outdoor wash facility at a Holiday Inn. I didn't make it much farther that night seeing as twilight had already begun to set in, so I camped behind a small, thick tree just outside of a truck stop. One of the truck drivers had seen me walk by and offered me a place to sleep for the night in his cab seeing as it was going to get cold out, but I declined, feeling safer in my freshly cleaned bag. Yes, it did get cold that night, but I also slept very well tucked away inside my little tent and wrapped up like a newborn baby for the night in my nice, dry sleeping bag. In the morning I stayed tucked in a little while I had my breakfast, though I never ate enough to be full seeing as I constantly had to mind my rations, but it was enough to get the day going.

Honestly, if I had the ability to carry endless amounts of supplies, I would have preferred to eat like a Hobbit, that is to say a lot and often, and as luck would have it this morning I actually got the chance to. The truck driver that had offered me a place to stay the night before caught me as I was walking by and asked if I would join him for coffee and breakfast. Perhaps I'm just a sucker for a hot meal, but I couldn't resist the opportunity to partake of second breakfast, and soon found myself in the cab of this guys' truck sipping fresh coffee and chowing down a Jimmy Dean breakfast bowl. It's amazing the sort of stuff people can fit into the cab of a semi-truck--this guy had a microwave oven, coffee pot, TV, mini fridge, a pair of bunk beds, and still had room for the driver and passenger seats!

His name was Terry, a tall, thin, gray haired man who said he was in his early fifties though looked a bit older. He was traveling out of the hills of North Carolina, trying to find enough work to keep his truck running and a roof over his second wife's head. Good men are hard to find in this day and age, mainly because it takes struggle and hardship to make them, something many men in my generation seem to be a bit lacking in. Terry had seen more than his fair share though: he had divorced once while still in love with the woman who left him, he had a daughter in college whom he didn't see nearly enough of, he had jumped to truck driving after being fired from a manager position he had worked hard to get, and his new wife was very sick. She was sick enough to the point where it didn't look like she had much time left, and Terry said that the best part of driving truck and cab was that you could cry all day and no one would notice. Of all of the souls I had met in my travels, he seemed the most tortured, and yet while he was deeply saddened he did not despair, always maintaining strong faith and kept moving forward. There wasn't much I could do for the poor fellow, but I think in a way just sitting down to have a meal with him was helpful, and by the end of breakfast a few clever phrases and stories of my travels so far brought a smile to his face. Sometimes, the only thing that can make a rough life better is finding a quick reason to smile, just a moment to forget life's troubles and reset before struggling forward. I haven't seen Terry since then, and have no way to contact him, but I would like him to know that I kept him in my thoughts during my travels, and even now. While I don't think I can ever properly thank him for the breakfast I do hope that he's doing better, and if nothing else has at least found a few other reasons to smile along the way.

There are places in this world that will take your breath away, otherworldly paths that seem to have been lost in time and passed over by the whole of men. Such is the Suwannee River in North Florida. My hike through this prehistoric river valley started a bit off-kilter, just like everything else I've done I suppose, seeing as I didn't set foot in Big Scholes recreation area until after dark. It's not easy to walk through the woods at anytime really, having to dodge roots and shrubs while hoping not to run into massive spider webs or come across unexpected drops in the trail. With all that in mind walking purely by flashlight makes things much harder! Not only that, but I had decided to try and follow a blue blazed trail to a waterfall that was supposed to be less than a mile from the trailhead, figuring it would be a good place to set up for the night.

While trying to save as much battery as possible, I came upon a large, flat area where I could hear water rushing quickly, and decided this would be as good of spot as any though not exactly what I had set out for. Still, it was dark and I was tired so it was here that I started to set up camp for the night. Being too stupid to invest in a head lamp before starting the trip, I held a flashlight in my mouth while setting up my tent. Must have looked like a rabid werewolf by the end of it, slobbering and drooling all over the place as my mouth tried to digest the hard plastic light source. It worked though--I had set up my tent and even managed to start a small fire to enjoy the rest of the evening. It could be asked why didn't I start a fire to set up by, and I'll comment further on that when I think of a witty response. Until then it's to be noted that I'm sometimes a bit of an idiot.

In the morning I decided to leave my pack for a bit to search of Florida's only Class 3 rapids that were supposed to be somewhere in the area. The 'waterfall' that I did in fact manage to camp near was nothing more then about a waist high drop in a small stream, a bit lackluster, but any waterfall in the otherwise flat state of Florida is worth talking about. The rapids on the other hand were very impressive, as dark, muddy water turned white as it ripped over rocks and fallen trees. The torrent would have been difficult for an experienced kayaker to navigate unscathed and was far more then I'd be willing to attempt. To top it all off, there was a sign that said 'Beware of Alligators' ...though I must say this natural wonder was awesome to look at. However, standing next to water rushing with that much power will make even the driest of bladders suddenly full, so I stopped to take a leak. Here, I coined one of my catchphrases for the trip. "This is mine.." I said while peeing into the river. It's one of those things that I'm fairly certain women will never understand, but men in every species understand perfectly. What it breaks down to is essentially that whatever the place or object in question is, if I find it to be awesome then I want it, I need to show that I was here once, and therefore I need to pee on it. Thus, I was on my way to claiming my empire.

The biggest problem I encountered on this excursion was on the return trip to my gear. The path was well cleared and well blazed but the issue was that there were too many options! The path was intended more for people coming down the river who wanted to bypass the rapids as opposed to hikers who wanted to see them. After about an hour of trying to make my way back I finally ended up back at the waterfall, but on the other side of the river. Seeing as the stream wasn't very wide I managed to find a place to cross not far away, and made it back to my gear, and though I was a little wet and very confused I was back on my way nonetheless.

 It's days like these that I signed up for. The Suwannee River twists and turns naturally through the forests of North Florida, cutting a wide, deep channel as it makes its way. The water is black, and the current is strong and steady, but the surface looks calm and inviting on a hot day. For the first time in Florida there were rock formations of limestone, a bright white contrast to the river that let me know that I was finally standing on solid ground. Also, the rock is soft and chalky, thus washed away easily by the river and deposited as a fine white sand along the shore, making some of the most inviting campsites I've ever seen! Sharp banks, dropping over 40 feet at times, mark the river's edge and numerous small tributaries cut deep ravines on their way to the Suwannee making small waterfalls as they jump over rocks and roots. But the most memorable part of the Suwannee river valley is the trees, whose equals I've yet to see. Massive oaks lean over the river banks, knotted and twisted, their branches hang far above the water which indeed make spectacular resting spots for the adventurous. A thick, green moss covers everything, and just beyond the river bank groves of cypress grow smooth and tall, staining the water black as it rushes by. The most impressive oaks grow a little ways away from the river however, and are so wide that it would take more than five of me to fully reach around their base. They tower above the forest floor and their trunks raise a good three stories standing straight, thick, and limbless before finally breaking into a magnificent canopy with branches that would make even the stoutest of men feel small. I would stop and stare at theses trees for more time the I can recall as I passed by them, awestricken at the potential nature holds. While I hear that these trees are nothing compared to the redwoods of California, these oaks are unique and special having survived the worst of nature and worst of men, making the Suwannee river valley one of my favorite hikes to this day

 The Suwannee river regrettably became the last section of the Florida Trail that I hiked, though that isn't where the orange blazed trail ends however. The FT continues all the way to Pensacola, the westernmost point of the state along the Alabama border, but I had set my sights on the Appalachian trail and in order to make it there by my desired start date I had to be moving north. Making a very loose estimate based on my average speed at the time, I figured I was about a twenty day hike from the city of Atlanta, GA, and wanted to be at Springer Mountain on March 1st, which was thirty days away. So, on a lonely road, forty days after starting my walk, I bid adieu to the friendly orange blazes and made my own way, heading north to the city of Madison. It should be said that in no way do I consider myself a Florida Trail thru hiker, having only completed about five hundred miles of the possible twelve hundred, and much of it through cities instead of the wild, but it was a very important part of my travels. It was here that I learned the basics of long distance hiking without having to worry about pushing myself up and down massive mountains, as well as how to supply and ration. I learned to stay the course and that even in the worst of times there is a way out, that the bad times will come but won't last forever. I learned how to rely on myself, and trust my body's ability to travel. That and so much more set the groundwork for what had already become an incredible journey, and come hell or high water I felt ready for the road ahead.

5 THE ROAD TO SPRINGER

Of all the time I spent traveling, the road from the FT (Florida Trail) to the AT (Appalatchain Trail) must have been the strangest. There were no blazes ahead, no wooded trails, just open roads from one city to the next. There was no set way to get there, but rather than being overwhelmed I felt encouraged, for no set way, to me, meant no wrong way. Step one, go north, and so I made for the city of Madison.

Though I was nearing the southern border of Georgia, Florida felt the need to treat me to one last taste of its memorable weather mood swings, forcing me to take cover under a roadside tree for a few minutes until the rain passed. Well, that was the idea anyway, but while standing there trying to stay as dry as one could under the circumstances an older SUV pulled up and stopped just in front of my position. The driver gave a wave of his hand as he shouted out "Hop in!" and seeing as I didn't have much to lose I did just that, grateful for the ride into town.

The driver was a thin, older guy with a baseball cap and flannel shirt, more than likely weighed about one hundred and thirty pounds soaking wet but all of it muscle and he stood none too tall either if I remember right. His name was Clayton, an old veteran just trying to make a living here in north Florida and who had just caught a break being allowed to live in a trailer at a hunting camp in exchange for looking after the place. I didn't have the pleasure of knowing the guy for long but I imagine that kinder folk would be hard to find, though he also struck me as a man one wouldn't want to mess with should he be about fifteen years younger. Almost immediately he asked me if I wanted a beer and not long after asked if I smoked pot. I was honest, didn't want to be rude, and in less then ten minutes we're over at his place smoking a quick one and chatting casually, both of us grateful for the company. Eventually he gave me a ride the rest of the way into Madison, but before we left his trailer he insisted that I take a few packs of Ramen Noodles, a can of barbeque weenies, and a few packs of sardines. Like I said, nice guy, though I believe he may have gotten a few screws shaken loose upstairs while in Nam.

From Madison I decided to take I-10 to Tallahassee, I don't know with one hundred percent certainty if it's legal to walk down the side of an interstate, but even if it is I wouldn't recommend it. There's nothing like spending the day breathing heavy exhaust fumes, feeling like your left ear is going deaf due to the noise, and having to constantly hold your hat so as to not lose it thanks to the massive gusts of wind produced by a semi truck passing at seventy miles per hour. Then of course there's the chance that some absent-minded businessman checking his phone, drinking coffee while changing the radio station, planning his next affair from his failing marriage, and fixing his tie on his way to the day's third meeting will drift off and end one's hike, along with other things. Though I bet you'd hardly feel getting clipped by one of these overworked buffoons considering how quickly they're moving, just a flash of paint and a quick death.

Not exactly sure what I expected to happen walking down the side of a interstate outside a major city, but like anything else I guessed I'd just figure it out. At about midday a full sized semi truck stopped on the side of the road and the driver poked his bearded face out of the window to offer me a ride, which I was more than happy to accept. The driver was a heavyset guy with a full gray beard, bit of a southern accent and a heavy smoking habit. He asked me where I was going and agreed to get me there, not really saying much at first, but that changed after a few ice breaking conversations.

"You like pornos?" He asked in what I assume to be a poor attempt to initiate conversation.

"Yeah, haven't met a man yet that doesn't like pornos," I responded, trying to be honest.

"Got a few good ones in the back, we can stop off at the truck stop and watch one outside of Tallahassee. You like blow jobs?" He asked in a similar fashion.

"Yeah, what kind of guy doesn't like blow jobs?" I responded, again being honest although I thought it was a bit strange for people who just met to be starting off a conversation this way.

"Want one?"

It finally hit me. This dude was totally trying to solicit sex from me for the ride. At least he was being nice enough to try and get me off first before undoubtedly asking me to do the same, but lets just say that was on the short list of things that weren't going to happen today.

"Ahh, no I'm good man, thanks though, just looking to get along the way," I replied, somehow managing to keep my wits about me. I had always thought the truck driving, sex-exchange-for-rides stories to be more of a urban myth than actual reality, the sort of thing Hollywood liked to poke fun at for the sake of entertainment rather than fact. Learned my lesson though, and was grateful that I had learned earlier in my travels to keep a good knife close by. Thankfully I didn't have to use it, and by managing to be polite was able to switch the topic of conversation to women we screwed who then screwed us over, and as luck would have it he was an expert on the subject.

When we reached the off ramp into the capital city of Tallahassee I don't think I'd ever exited a vehicle so quickly. Would have much rather done so sooner but I wasn't too giddy to leave my pack behind and brave the pavement at 70 miles per hour. While I managed to dodge that--let's say, bullet--I haven't looked for any help from truck drivers since.

It didn't take more than a few hours of walking around Tallahassee to remember why I hate big cities. I had never cared to be in a metropolis or major city before I started hiking and now nothing here made sense to me. So many people rushing about, passing one another, and yet not a word to be heard among any of them. Busy one-way streets split apart the imposing structures of Tallahassee like veins in a concrete giant, there was very little that had been allowed to remain green, even less that seemed pure, and stuck in the middle of it was little old me, trying to comprehend it all. I wasn't here just to sight see--I had almost completely run out of money and needed to find a way to earn a bit more. Figuring there would be something to do around here, even if it was as simple as washing car windshields, I began to ask around a little just trying to feel things out. Now granted, I was a scruffy, unbathed, long distance hiker at this point, which in a major city equates to homeless, and most people would hardly make eye contact with me let alone offer some directions. Some people who were a bit down and out, holding signs on the side of the road begging for money, told me about this place called 'The Shelter' not far away where a guy could find a cheap place to sleep and, with any luck, a bite to eat. The Shelter was also supposed to have job placement assistance so this seemed like the perfect place for a guy to clean up and find some work.

There's no way to sugarcoat it, but neither do I have the desire to: I'm still rather appalled by the whole situation. The shelter proved to be three small parking lots, one of them unpaved, loosely converted into outdoor seating and hidden from the street by several small buildings. A chain link gate blocked off the entrance, and upon entry I was reminded of pictures of dog pounds and World War II concentration camps. People's belongings thrown carelessly in piles along side of the structures and a general feeling of bad fortune and hard times. The place was overflowing with people, but not a smile to be found on any of them, everyone staring blankly at their toes as if they thought death was upon them but coming slowly. A pastor stood in the center, preaching a message to deaf ears, apart from my own, not causing anyone to stir even when he asked us all to bow our heads in prayer. I thanked him nonetheless, assuming that this would be the best way to find out about some possible work. He was kind, surprisingly, and invited me inside to talk with an advisor that he thought could help me out. It finally felt like I was getting somewhere, and I hate to admit it, but I was more than grateful to be removed from the depressing, dismal lots.

I was itching to work really, it'd been awhile and I had never been so long without, so I was grateful for the opportunity to meet with someone about it. I was punctual, even looking as ragged as I did, and tried my best to appear and act both professional and enthusiastic. The man hardly looked at me. I couldn't tell you his name, I don't think he ever gave it to me, his sweater vest carelessly tucked into his slacks and his hair half slicked back. Any work ethic this man once had was long gone, it almost seemed as if he was shackled to his desk, forced to be there, and that the only thing he found joy in was the idea of clocking out for the day, though I doubt he ever really showed up for work in the first place. After explaining that I was looking for a bit of honest work he quickly referred me to this place called Labor Finders just down the street. Couldn't tell you if he ever listened to a word I had said, and the response seemed to be almost automated, but I thanked him anyway, promptly offering a handshake for the information. This man would have been better off just letting my hand hang there, but instead shook my hand with roughly the grip of a guppy, not even taking his eyes off the computer screen to meet my own. Very insulted, I was hardly able to bite my tongue as I went out in an attempt to find the place that he had told me about before having to report there in the morning.

It was easy to get lost along the way, which I did a few times, due to the horrible directions I had been given, but still managed to find the place after a little search, though I almost wish I hadn't. The place looked like a prison yard, with one small building surrounded by razor wire and more signs about unacceptable behavior than I could count. Just by standing outside this god forsaken place I was made to feel small, as if acting like a beaten dog trying to spare himself his masters belt would be the only acceptable behavior, and that even the notion of dignity would be punishable by death or exile. I just kept walking.

Let me be clear, at this point I was nearly out of money, I was cold, hungry, and by all means in need of whatever opportunities I could find, but

I would rather die than accept the god awful treatment provided by The Shelter! At our core we are all animals, and it's worth observing that we will at times act a bit wild and unruly, but it was not one man alone among beasts who built the world we now enjoy. It was a combined effort of mentally evolved creatures that perpetuated the human standard of living above all others. Through unity we prevailed, a combined effort towards prosperity, with each man pushing forward his brethren and not by each man squashing the next. We have forgotten. The people I was among this day had been treated like animals, looked at like animals, called every word synonymous with animal, and hence had become animals! I had seen more life in the eyes of livestock I passed on Florida trail! The people who now work with these forcibly devolved individuals had as well become part of the problem. I imagine that they had once had a heart for the downtrodden when they took the position, but after watching one mentally broken individual after another walk inline through the door of this human slaughterhouse they have become farmers instead of saviors. You want money? Here. You want food? Here. You can sleep there. NEXT! And every time someone tries to bring new hope into the system its is quickly, and quietly, driven out of them as poor people who had been enabled to survive without ever being told they deserve better drift in and out of the system. But perhaps the single worst part of the whole situation is that actual, living, breathing, human beings go through this everyday, hidden from view by a few rundown buildings. Hidden away so the rest of society doesn't have to see them. My heart was broken for these people. Where is the humanity? Does the word even mean anything anymore? Is it even possible to treat these people human enough that they can start to believe that they are? That I can't say for sure. What I do know is that it will take all of us to rebuild a functional society, much like it took all of us the first time.

I have never gone back to that place, not even that night in order to have a safe place to sleep, choosing instead to camp on the outskirts of town. It was dark and cold when I set up, and I had to be up early the next morning so as to not be found. However, even though I had chosen to sleep like a stray cat that night I felt far more human than I had the rest of the day.

Forty three days on the road, forty two nights in the woods, nearly empty pockets, and about five hundred miles of travel brought about my first taste of great accomplishment as I crossed the Georgia border on Highway 319 to Thomasville. There wasn't much there, just a road sign to mark the invisible line, but there are few things in this life that I have found more beautiful. It's hard to describe the feeling for it's not like this one step was any different in form than any other I had taken before it, and far easier than many others I had taken on the trail, but with this one step I had accomplished something that I had been wanting to do for ages. I was on the road and against all odds I was making it! When I crossed that imaginary line I knew that for the rest of my life, regardless of how far I went after, I could say that I walked across the state of Florida from Ft. Lauderdale north to the Georgia border. What a feat that was just in and of itself! I couldn't help but dance around a bit on the side of the road and I must have looked a bit foolish to those driving by, but I didn't care, this was too big a moment to not celebrate.

This particular line was less imaginary than one might think actually, for between Tallahassee and Georgia the land actually changed quite a bit. Palm trees disappeared almost immediately and were replaced by neat rows of long leaf pine trees, which made me feel right at home. Cotton fields started to spring up here and there while the earth became less sandy and slightly red in color. Even in the most remote parts of Florida it still never truly felt like the South, more like I was out west on a ranch or something, but that seemed to change instantly as Georgia welcomed me.

Wasn't really a warm welcome though, actually it was quite cold! Not that people weren't helpful or turned their noses up at me but more of the fact that I was walking around in forty degree weather with nothing more than a zip-up hoodie, a scarf, and a pair of light gloves. There seemed to be no warmer weather in sight either, and I wondered, how I could be so foolish to think that a sweatshirt would keep me warm in the dead of winter? Either way, I knew I had to do something about my current vulnerability to the elements, but what was even worse than the cold was knowing that I didn't have the money to buy warmer clothing. I camped in the pines as the sun went down, taking the little heat it had offered with it, hoping to figure something out in Thomasville the next day.

It wasn't all that much warmer in the morning sadly, but I managed to get packed up and on the way despite my fingers being noticeably weaker and stiff due to the cold. To those who have somehow managed to go their entire life without experiencing the cold, a streak I hope many are able to continue, there's just something about a cold hand that doesn't seem to work as well. Fingers lose their strength, they become more sensitive to hard impact, less responsive, and all things considered it's never a pleasant experience.

There was no work to be had for a traveling man, at least not for one who didn't intend to stay awhile, so I needed to swallow my pride and ask for whatever help I could get. I'm not about to say that I liked it in the slightest, but if I had to ask for money to keep me going I was at least going to be honest about it and never gather more then I needed. Also, I didn't want to say anything to people passing by, I would talk to them if they talked to me and would be overly polite whenever possible, but never verbally asked for change or whatever else so as to not disturb someone's day. Still having to somehow ask however, what I decided was to make a sign and smile at whomever would make eye contact with me. Using the little money I had left to buy a sharpie marker at a WalMart and finding some cardboard around back of the supercenter, I made a sign that said 'Need money for warm coat and warm blanket' before sitting back out front and close to the entrance.

One will never know what it is to truly need until having to beg for a coat. I didn't have to sit out there for very long thankfully, for if a few southern women see a young man shivering out in the cold they can't help but help, and when it was all said and done I had enough to buy a Dickies canvas coat and a emergency blanket for my sleeping bag at a total cost of roughly forty dollars. I learned a lot about humility that day, and also about my fellow man. While I still had a bitter taste on my tongue from Tallahassee, it's not all men that care so little for one another, and I began to think that perhaps people are truly good at heart and willing to help one another. It was something to think about as I wandered back out on the road, feeling like I owed it to those who had helped me here to make it to the end of the trail. I did carry another sign with me from this point on that I would strap to my pack while in town which read 'Walking to Maine, $ = Miles." I found out that this sign would help me in more ways than just monetarily, for it gave people an opportunity to start a conversation with me, asking if I was really trying to get to Maine. What can I say, if one is really passionate about something they will do whatever it is that has to be done to see it through.

The simple beauty of south Georgia was calming and comforting. The low rolling hills were arranged into a checkerboard of cotton farms and cattle range, covered in frost during the morning hours, and quiet. It's a strange thing to see frost on a cotton plant ready to be picked, at times the cotton would fall off the stem and blow in waves across the roads in the early winter breeze, and the whole thing felt like some sort of old painting become real. However, despite the peaceful ambiance, I was worried about how people would react to a young hobo walking down the side of the highway.

I wasn't anywhere near a long distance nature trail anymore and I was very aware of it, especially since I knew I looked like I had just come out of the woods and with a bit of a smell to match I might add. I just tried to be a pleasant as possible but also accepting of the fact that others would more than likely look down on me. I remember passing by Temple Baptist Church one Sunday in the little town of Murphy just outside the city of Moultrie, an impressive chapel in the middle of almost nowhere that looked both formidable and inviting. Growing up Christian and having been out of church for far too long I was tempted to stop in for a service, but as I spotted row after row of nice cars and families dressed in their Sunday best I decided it was best to just keep walking. A dirty young tramp has no business bothering a bunch of nice folk all dressed up on a Sunday morning, even if it would be to worship the son of a poor carpenter.

I would like to simplify what happened next into coherent thoughts and ideas, but it may prove to be impossible for there are things in this world that words are not able to describe, and feelings too obscure to even have a name. About a quarter of a mile past the church a car pulled up alongside of me and rolled down the window, and inside was a woman in her late forties with short curly brown hair and a kind smile. She wasn't a petite woman, but not heavyset either, dressed in a modest black and floral dress and obviously about to bring herself to worship. She asked me where I was going, and I told her I had my sights on Maine. She told me that she had one hundred dollars for me, free to take, and that God had told her that I needed it as she drove by. She also stated that if I wanted to I was welcome to come worship with her, but not obligated to in anyway. It seemed like too much to take from one person, and half of me though she was just being false for some reason, but my pack had felt overly heavy all morning and I just felt like this was what I was supposed to do. So we went to church, and along the way she proved herself true to her word as she passed me one hundred dollars in twenty dollar bills, rather insistent that I take it, leaving me awestricken. Her name was Patricia, but asked I call her Pat.

Still taken aback when we reached the church, I had almost forgotten my outward appearance and was now slightly embarrassed to try to fit in with all these fine folk. For the first time I was regretting not packing deodorant so as to save a few ounces on my back which seemed like a grand idea at the time, but now it meant I had to keep my arms down while around others. Never the less, I ran my fingers through my hair and ever growing beard in an attempt to look as presentable as possible, donning my hoodie seeing as it was slightly cleaner than the other shirt I was wearing. It was still obvious that I had just come off the road however and I apologized to Pat that she would be seen with me in such a nice place. She simply smiled and said "If they'll take me, they'll take anyone."

Can't say as I remember much about the service, but I do remember the welcome I had received. Having grown up going to church I knew some church members to be a bit elite, putting far more emphasis on how one showed up rather than if one showed up. In the years that followed I had found this kind of church mentality to be far more widespread than it should be, and furthermore that I wasn't the only one who had noticed it. In fact it was the sheer hypocrisy of Christianity that stopped me from practicing for so long, feeling that God's people should be caring and accepting but always finding them judgmental and concerned only for their own salvation as opposed to those around them. So to be welcomed so well in this Baptist church in the middle of the Bible Belt and south Georgia not only shocked me, but also restored a bit of my faith in the religion. They looked me in the eye, they shook my hand and smiled, welcoming me to their congregation, and they seemed legitimately happy to have a new face among them.

Pat stood close by me the whole time, introducing me to each person we passed, and after the service she insisted that we go out to lunch together. Hard to say exactly what made her so persuasive; she didn't speak loudly, nor posture herself strongly, didn't even insist on an idea without waiting for a response like so many people do these days, but rather just seemed so legitimately wanting to have the company that it was impossible to say no.

Speaking of not being able to say no: never put an all-you-can-eat Chinese buffet in front of a hiker who hasn't eaten well in over a week! Not sure if it was just the miles getting to me, but I swear the Chinese place in Moultrie, GA has the best damn egg rolls I've ever tasted and I couldn't help but put away about four plates of the stuff. All the while I talked with Pat, and in all honesty she has had quite the life raising four children and finding time to be thankful through it all. Her husband had passed away not too long ago and her children were all grown now, leaving her time to make children's books and help others in whatever small way she could. I had hardly known Pat for two hours when it was time to part ways, but the impact that she had made on me and on my travels cannot be measured. It felt like making it to Maine would actually happen, not so much as I was meant to do it, but more like the way would be opened before me and all things were possible, whatever it was that I felt I needed to do. I have thought of that day many times since, and not once have I ever been able to believe it truly happened.

The day's blessings weren't over yet though, and the second half came equally unexpected. As the sun began to get low, miles away from anything, it became clear that finding a place to sleep would not just soon be necessary, but also a bit tricky to find due to the abundance of barbed wire fences in the area. Deep in cattle country again, the only trees to be spotted were well within fenced off pasture and typically surrounded by livestock, making them rather undesirable to camp near. I had nearly accepted that I was just going to have to pray that I didn't have a full grown steer step on me during the night, or have to deal with a less than friendly farmer in the morning, when a small white pickup truck pulled close.

Having already accepted more help then I felt entitled to and starting this trip with the intention of WALKING across the country I declined the man's offer for a ride, but soon changed my tune when he offered me a place to stay. I can remember very clearly a man, named Tony, tall and thin with a short but full beard, dressed head to toe in camo work gear and with a knit cap to top it off. He said he couldn't offer much, but if I needed a place to sleep he had a barn that was both safe and dry, even had a cot out there if I wanted it. Remembering my experience around lake Okeechobee, it was the barn that saved this offer seeing as I was not overly excited about putting myself into another potentially dangerous situation, and I agreed to hop in and see what happened. Wasn't but a few minute ride before Tony pulled off onto a two track dirt road leading between pasture and farmland, and after stopping in front of a makeshift barbed wire gate he had to hop out of the truck and twist off a section of wire in order to clear the way through.

All things considered, this property was beautiful. Tony lived with his mother, son, and two daughters I believe, though I never met them during my stay here. He had two horses roaming free and a small barn, barely big enough to hold hay and feed, that connected his pasture to the road. It's hard to forget the joy he seemed to express as he showed me the place, being kind and accommodating the whole time despite just meeting this battered young vagabond out on the road. The barn was just as small on the inside, though more than big enough for me and actually rather clean seeing as it had just been built. Tony told that me his son would be along with a cot for me before long, and that he would be back by in the morning to feed the horses. It's impossible to recall how many times I thanked him before he took off towards his house, and as I sat in a folding chair outside the barn watching the sunset over farm and field I couldn't help but think that I could get used to living in a place like this.

Tony's son, Colby, soon came by with a cot as promised, and I helped him tend to the horses as best as I could when it was time to feed them. Honestly I was probably more in the way than anything but I felt like I needed to do something rather than just sit about watching this young man work. After the beasts of burden were tended to, he and I talked a bit while enjoying the last bit of the day. Colby had grown up here, and was just about to leave for Jacksonville, FL. He couldn't have been hardly over eighteen years of age, if even eighteen at all, and told me that he had never really been to a large city for very long before. The young cowboy had a look about him that I had only really seen in men much older, the sort of inner peace that comes from a lot of time thinking and accepting the world around them. However, he also had the sort of youthful energy a young man should, especially when about to set out and make his own way. I have a lot of faith in this young man, and I feel he may either go on to do great things or perhaps not much at all, but either way he will always do it the best he can. I just hope that wherever he decides to settle he remembers the humble, charming cattle ranch that can bring the sort of inner peace many men, such as myself, can spend their whole lives looking for and never quite be able to find.

I slept very well that night--warm, dry, and on the closest thing to a proper bed I'd had in some time until I was awakened by Tony in the morning as he went to tend to the horses. He told me to stay as long as I liked, but I opted to get a move on, thanking him one last time before packing up and parting ways.

There had become progressively less and less trees the farther north I went, and at this point there were next to none apart from a few between farms and those established on pecan plantations. It's an old farming legend that the winter will be particularly rough if the trees are producing a heavy amount of nuts, and if that's true such an occurrence would be very helpful for the small creatures forced to endure such a winter. Perhaps I should have taken warning on the off chance that this old wife's tale was true because the ground in the plantations was absolutely covered in pecans leftover from the harvest. However, instead of a grim warning, I took this as a great blessing, and stopped to gather nuts whenever I had the chance, thus helping both my stomach and wallet.

I thought little about the weather at this point; it was far from warm but didn't seem to be too bad as long as I kept moving. My new jacket and old gloves were doing the trick, and even though some clouds were settling in things didn't seem any worse than I'd seen before. Perhaps I was just high on adrenaline from the massive amount of exercise I was getting, or maybe I'm just young and stupid, but even a warning from a friendly Sheriff wasn't enough to make me take precautions for the weather. Hell, the guy didn't just warn me, he told me that if I was in danger to call *GSP (Georgia State Patrol) and ask for officer Whitaker, and he would be sure that someone got me to a safe place to be. In this age, people like to talk badly about the police, and I'll admit at times there's grounds for such things to be said. Corruption in some departments has run so deep that one of the major things that a traveling man has to fear are those who had sworn to protect and serve the public. I personally had never had a nasty run in with an officer of the law, more than likely due to my white skin and full set of teeth, but I have heard many horror stories from friends and relations whom were not so lucky. However, on the other hand there are many officers in service who honestly want to fulfill their duty to the people, and this was the second chance during my walk that I had the chance to find that out. Officer

Whitaker treated me with the sort of respect any human being should be shown, and rather than run a young hobo out of town he took the time to ensure that no ill would befall me should things turn for the worse. I wish I had a better way to thank him, but I don't sadly, and just hope that he continues faithfully his duty to the people of the United States, for the country greatly needs honorable policemen such as this. When it comes to dealing with the police, it pays to be polite, but also to know one's rights. Don't give up your rights, but don't give the police a hard time either--at the end of the day we're all just people trying to do the best we can and kindness tends to beget kindness.

In hindsight, someone should have slapped me across the face and made me listen to the weather report because if one has to make sure to frequently drink form a hydro-pack to keep the straw from freezing, it's freaking cold out! I had poured out my reserve water bottle to keep it from freezing and splitting in two, and I thought that I was being smart because the bottom had bulged out from the expansion of freezing water. I swear my own stupidity stuns me at times. Nevertheless I kept walking, and even as it started to rain I just figured I should set up soon but thought nothing else of it. To be honest, I actually did have a pretty good sleep system; between my sleeping bag and the two blankets I now carried stuffed inside of it I could keep really warm provided I kept dry. Keeping dry of course requires adequate cover, and thankfully after I had repaired my tent in Florida it caused me no future problems. That changed.

If I may explain, when water completely covers the outside of a tent and the the temperature proceeds to drop well below freezing the metal poles holding up one's tent become about as brittle as a ninety year old's hip, taking only the slightest misuse to break. Also, when the wind picks up in the morning and one hadn't staked his tent in place, don't remove all of the weight from inside the tent before taking the rain cover off. That is unless you're into really big, expensive kites that are essential for one's prolonged survival--just trust me on this one. Because it was on such a morning where my tent took off and landed not far away but directly on its roof and thus snapping one of the poles in two places before collapsing into a useless tarp covered in water that seemed to be existing in all three states of matter at the same time. It wasn't ice, it wasn't liquid, and it seemed to be both removed and replenished by the passing wind. Needless to say, this became a problem.

To fix my shelter I had to make an emergency detour through the town of Ashburn, which was well out of my way, but at the time seemed like a better option then backtracking four miles to the city of Sulvester. I'd like to say that things got better from this point, but I would also like to say that I'm a crime fighting superhero protecting the world from injustice and overpriced tire replacement. However I'm not, and they didn't. There was some sort of precipitation the entire day--if it wasn't rain it was sleet, or freezing rain, snow once or twice I believe as well, and the wind never let up. To make matters worse, about the only thing of any interest in downtown Ashburn is a giant statue of a fire ant, my mortal enemy from Florida, and the rest of the city is temporarily closed due to lack of business. Most of the buildings were vacant and those that hosted businesses were closed during my brief visit. The only stroke of luck I managed to come by was getting directions to a home improvement store on the edge of town which should have what I needed to fix my tent. They did, thank God, and five dollars later I was ready to fix my tent and even had a spare splint now in case my tent broke a third time. And while I had come to Ashburn to find simple supplies, it was at this store that I accidentally came across something that actually saved my life. The weather report was on and there were a few older men actively watching it, which struck me as very odd so I listened in. Apparently there was one hell of a storm coming into the area and was due to hit hard around seven o'clock that night, but now I had the supplies needed to fix my gear so I figured I'd be alright.

As I started out of town things just seemed to get worse and worse by the minute. The cold rain had turned to full on sleet and was blowing progressively more sideways with every step. It was getting dark, and I began to feel cold water soaking through my coat--obviously the tent wasn't going to cut it tonight and thus I needed better shelter. It's been said that there aren't any demolition companies in the deep south, people just let things fall over when nature decides it's time for such things to go, leaving many dilapidated barns abandoned where they stand. I started to scan for such a barn or building, anything would be a better option than braving this storm in a tent; furthermore even if I were to backtrack to Ashburn I don't think there was a hotel or motel in the entire city. I started to scramble as the sun began to go down, feeling like I may be in a bit of trouble this time, when I came across a sports complex containing several baseball diamonds, a few soccer fields, and a concrete concession stand in the middle. Out of time and other options, I figured setting up in a dugout would offer more shelter than anything else around, and I accepted my fate while entering the complex through a door in the fence surrounding one of the diamonds that by some miracle had been left ajar. Hoping for the best but expecting the worst I tried the doors of the concession stand, finding them all to be locked, still I figured it was worth a shot. The last door I tried was to the men's bathroom and I almost walked off before even trying it to find that it was actually open! Inside there were three sinks, four urinals, and three stalls, all of which were far from clean, but there were also four walls and a roof making this by far the best option.

    I was glad to have a solid building around me though it was still, in every sense of the word, a shitty place to spend the night. My pack was soaked through so I set it in a chair and under an overhang outside to dry off a bit as I scoped out my surroundings. My heart sank as I looked up to see a white pickup truck that hadn't been there moments before, obviously a maintenance truck and sure to be holding someone who didn't like the idea of company tonight. I wasn't disappointed, but accepted my fate and took off my hat while trying my best to be polite. The man's name was Mike, a middle aged white man, dressed mostly in camo and smoking a cigarette, not ever saying much more than he had to. He asked me if I was going to stay here tonight, to which admitted that I had planned to but now assumed I wouldn't be able to. To my surprise, he took pity on me, and rather then showing me the gate he laid out a few simple rules before parting ways. He told me the rest of the doors were rigged with an alarm and if I tried to break them the police would surround the place faster than I could blink. Also, the building was set up with central heating which should keep things about sixty degrees so I'd better not try and start a fire or anything. Lastly, he asked if I wanted a Pepsi before giving me two and driving off. Must say, I didn't see that coming.

    The stall doors proved to be a great place to hang everything I had been wearing, which were now completely soaked through, and while the little concrete room was never warm it was a fine shelter for the night. The next morning all my things were dry and so was I, so I packed up everything and made to hit the road. When I opened the door it made a loud cracking noise as I broke the thin layer of ice encasing its exterior to find the world around me equally frozen, shining slick and cold in the morning light. It wasn't till much later that I realized just how lucky I was; the ice storm that night proved to be one of the worse in the recorded history of Georgia, literally shutting down the city of Atlanta and several others surrounding it. People were stuck on the highway for over eleven hours just trying to get home, and children were kept overnight in school because it was too dangerous to attempt to take them home. Had I tried to camp, the chances of my poles freezing and subsequently breaking would have been excellent, thus wrapping me in what would become a cold, wet coffin, the elements promptly soaking through my bag and causing me to freeze to death. Life's not always full of sunshine and rainbows; storms are going to come, and storms will pass. Try and chase the sunshine the whole time and all you're going to get is tired, but with some effort and a little luck, one can get through even the worst of times.

It didn't warm up much that day, never rising about thirty five degrees, which made the miles hard to travel and caused the air to bite at any exposed skin. It was so bad that when I stopped in the village of Arabi I got a cup of hot chocolate and put a pair of socks on my hands to serve as makeshift gloves in an attempt to them warm. Almost out of town I paused for a moment after I thought I heard someone calling out to me. Thinking I had gone crazy and stopping to look around I soon noticed a pair of young girls that were indeed actually calling me back for some reason. Thankful I wasn't hearing voices in my head I went to greet them, when they asked me if I wanted a cup of coffee and you can be quite certain I did! They took me back to their grandfather's house and invited me inside where I was introduced to three generations of a family living under the same roof. I can't for the life of me remember any of their names sadly, and it's been a source of endless frustration trying to remember anything that would allow me to be able to thank them, but alas nothing has come to mind so I just remain ever grateful to have met them all.

In the kitchen we gathered to talk as they poured cups of coffee and warmed up some chili and sausage for me, despite not have known me for more than thirty seconds. Apparently they were slightly used to offering this sort of hospitality, seeing as a previous man had, by some miracle, managed to find and stay with them while he was cycling across country--truly they all had a real heart for travelers. This was the first time that I had ever tried maple syrup and sausage, which is awesome by the way, and I'll never forget this crazy, spontaneous act of kindness. I didn't stay long, but left full and warm which made the next eight miles fly by in high spirits, feeling grateful to know there are still such wonderful people in this world.

People in south Georgia might be about the kindest people on the planet! It seems that everywhere I went someone would stop along the road or in town to talk, many of them making a small contribution to my walk. While I greatly appreciated every dollar gifted to me it was the help that I received in other, sometime very strange, ways that I really enjoyed. There was one time that a man stopped on the road and said that his mother had seen me walking the day before so he picked up a box of oatmeal cream pies in case we ran into each other, which he then gave to me and drove off. Also in Georgia, this guy who owned a small barbeque joint walked over and gave me a sandwich and a flyer asking only that I tell someone about his place. Great sandwich I must say and if you're ever in Eatonton, GA, check out Kinorhook BBQ, they're good people--but that wasn't the only meal I was lucky enough to have in Eatonton.

Just south of the city there's a breakfast house, and while it's nothing special and actually a chain restaurant, there's just something about a good old fashioned diner that I just love. While I may love a good diner, the money I had at this point I could hardly call my own seeing as it was gifted to me so that I could keep walking, and a hot breakfast just didn't seem like the best way to use it. As I was passing by, the smell of average coffee and greasy potatoes filled the air and like a siren's song they called to me to try and lure me in. It was only by pouring beeswax into my nose and tying myself to my walking stick that I managed to row past, sparing my ship from the financial rocks. Well, perhaps it wasn't that epic, but nevertheless I did make it past with difficulty and was well on my way when I heard someone call to me. Looking back, there was an older man outside waving in my direction, and after checking to see that there was nothing beyond me I walked back to inquire what this was all about.

He had thin, white hair, and stood just slightly shorter than me, but well built for a man his age and asked if I would like to have some breakfast with him. The right price changed everything, and my strong desire for second breakfast was at last fulfilled thanks to my new friend Charles. Inside I tried to straighten myself up a bit as I joined a table with Charles, his wife, and two other women before enjoying a very nice meal with the four of them. Charles was a Vietnam War veteran and we spent most of our time talking about his tour of duty. He had volunteered because he had his sights on marrying a young woman and didn't want the draft to tear them apart, figuring it was better to get it out of the way so she could move on in case he didn't come back. Turns out that his service did in fact stop them from getting hitched, but he had been with his current wife for many years and was grateful for the way things turned out. His job in the armed forces was to drive food and supplies from one place to another, keeping the boys fed and fighting, and was constantly having to fend off what were known as the Cowboys of Vietnam. They weren't necessarily Vietcong, but rather teams of men who would steal things off of moving trucks using only motorcycles and a complete disregard for their own skin. After eating we all took pictures together, and they sent me along my way with a full belly and sixty dollars they had pooled. It's encounters like this one that made the days of walking in ice and rain well worth it, the simple pleasures of life taken for granted everyday seemed so profound now, and I will ever be grateful for those whom I was blessed to meet.

    The trees were back, and in full force, and at times the pines were grown together so closely that I would have trouble finding a way into them to camp for the night. I began to feel like I was finally in the foothills of the Appalachians, and that I was starting to build up to real mountains as the land rose and fell more than anywhere else I had been walking. Here, nestled among ridges and valleys, lay the city of Athens, boasting the University of Georgia, an extensive downtown shopping district, and many places of historical importance. The reason that Athens was known to my friends and myself wasn't for any of those reasons however, but rather because of one building on the outskirts of town that had provided us with nearly endless good times and cheer--Terrapin Brewery! Not only had this superior suds supplier been on my list of places to check out for years, but thanks to Georgia state laws, tasting at the brewery was FREE, making it a great place for my hobo ass to pass through.

    I arrived in Athens rather early in the morning which meant that I had a few hours to kill before I could visit the brewery, so I decided to walk through the University of Georgia campus. I had tried attending college right after graduating high school, and all the more I can say is that it was by far the most expensive party I'd ever been to. I could have done so much more with the money I threw at this endeavor, and after a full year of attendance about the only thing I had learned was that I had no idea what I wanted to do with my life. Needless to say I didn't do very well, although if I could have majored in ultimate frisbee I would have graduated with honors in the first semester! However, a walk through this campus got me thinking, what it would be like if I had stuck it out? Many of those I graduated with were just now getting their degrees, and I could have had a doctorate by now, but where would that leave me? I would have a very expensive piece of paper, no job experience, a nearly unsettleable debt, and still no idea what I wanted to do with my life! While my peers were about to be climbing mountains of student loans with compounding interest, I was about to be climbing actual mountains. All things considered, I believe that I made the right choice.

Terrapin was everything that I thought it could be and more! At the door one has the option of either getting eight individual four ounce plastic cups, or for ten dollars buy a sixteen ounce pint glass which one was allowed to collect eight individual four ounce samples in. After investing in a pint glass I was given a wristband with the numbers one through eight on it, which were to be marked off as I gathered my samples, and it was off the the races! It's a shame that the bartenders would NEVER think to fill the pint glass with more than four ounces at a time, ESPECIALLY not if they were tipped after every pour. Also there's no way that an interesting story about walking across the country could possibly make them forget to mark a number off a wristband. They were all very professional and seeing as this is all in writing I would just like to stress just how perfectly legal and within the state's guidelines their operation was. I stayed until closing time, sampling beer and touring the facility, even picked up a sticker to put on my water bottle, all the while not noticing just how intoxicated I had become. I found out in a hurry after leaving, and not long after walking out the doors I found a safe, well-hidden place to set up for the night.

As I emerged from my tent the next morning I couldn't help but to start laughing. Not only was I set up with my tent completely exposed on three sides to a parking lot, but the cover that I thought had hid me well the night before only blocked me from sight of people traveling in one direction on the nearby road, while those traveling in the other would have noticed me instantly. To make things even more amusing, I had made it about two hundred yards from the front door of the brewery and could clearly see it from where I stood, but I had slept well and so hit the road, a little embarrassed, but well rested and thankfully unnoticed.

Even after spending the night in Athens I was still very ahead of schedule and needed to find a way to kill a little more time seeing as weather in the mountains this time a year could turn deadly quickly. After looking at a map for a little while and noticing that Stone Mountain was only a few days hike away, I decided to go see the great Confederate Monument, thus changing course back west towards the city of Atlanta. Also, after making a quick phone call I found out that one of my childhood friends was now living close to the mountain and would very much like to see me should I have the time.

When I arrived at the base of Stone Mountain there were well over seven hundred miles that had passed under my boots and I was by no means a new hiker. That being said, this was one of the hardest miles of the trip! The base of the mountain is easy enough, comprised of pine and oak forests with natural stone steps worn smooth by years of foot traffic and rain water. Twisted and tangled roots fought to gain ground, forcing cracks into the moss-spotted granit, and a thin layer of leaves and needles provided just enough soil for some smaller shrubs to take hold. The light vegetation soon gave way leaving nothing but a few patches of trees and vast, exposed stone continuing ever upward towards the summit. My knees began to hurt again for the first time in weeks, and I was soon out of breath as I struggled up the mountainside. I began to wonder why the hell I was doing this--was this honestly going to be my life for the next two thousand, three hundred miles? I kept my head down, focusing only on the next step, for each time I tried to look up not only did my energy level drop but also my self confidence as the top never appeared to be in sight. It appeared shortly after the trees disappeared completely, leaving nothing but stone forever rising upwards, and quickly enough to where I felt the need to walk at an angle to the summit, zigging and zagging in a pathetic attempt to triumph over nature. By what felt like the grace of God alone I managed to reach a point where the earth began to flatten out and after looking up for the first time in a long time I found that I was in fact at my destination, the Stone Mountain Summit.

There are questions that are easy to answer, there are questions that are hard to answer, and then there are questions that have no answer. I don't know how to categorize those that I was asking on my way up the mountain, but I do know that they ceased to exist as soon as I saw my first mountain vista. What a view; the world never looks so clear as it does in the few hours before a storm and a very large one was on the way, the sun was low, and it made the summit shine like fire in its last remaining rays. The whole of Georgia stretched before me, and the Atlanta skyline stood like a tiny broken comb stuck amongst the otherwise endless sea of trees. I could see for the first time the Blue Mountains to the north, and I was overwhelmed with a sense of awe, bewilderment, and accomplishment. It was hard to believe that this existed, and even harder to believe how far I had come to get here! The only question that was left to answer was how much better is it going to be just ahead?

The way down Stone Mountain was far easier, and I even sang a little along the way, still riding the wave of confidence I had just gotten. This was far from the tallest peak that I would climb, but remains one of my favorites simply because of what it symbolized. I now knew that I could do this, that it wasn't going to be easy, but as sure as I was standing it was possible.

I decided to make good on seeing my old friend who lived in the area, but where exactly I had no idea. I hadn't planned on getting this far until at least two days from now and there was no way he would be expecting me, but that's what cell phones are for. I had allowed myself to use my smartphone for navigation purposes through the state of Georgia, but had remained true to the idea of remaining completely out of contact until reaching out to my buddy. What can I say, it had been too long since I had seen a familiar face, and so there on the summit of Stone Mountain I unknowingly made one of the best decisions of the entire trip. Not but five miles from the base of the mountain my long time friend was renting an apartment in Norcross, and after a quick conversation I was on my way off and over to his place. Welcome to stay as long as I like were his words, and it's a good thing--no sooner had I started my way out of the park did the storm that had been holding off all day hit. The rain was light at first but with every passing minute it fell fuller and colder, and before the sun had fully set it had switched to some strange sort of freezing rain and snow mixture that was anything but pleasant to be out in.

There are many words that could be used to describe my long time friend Nick, but pansy isn't one of them. In fact, ever since I met the guy in grade school I knew that I would rather stand in the path of a raging volcano than stand in a fight against him, and I believe many others share this opinion. He stands about about my height, and I have seen his figure carry everything from a 145 pounds of lean muscle to a 190 pounds of raging beast, this time being on the heavier side of the scale, and boasting a beard fierce enough to make Edward Teach think twice before engaging in combat. While he has always had the presence of a pissed-off bull, those who knew him know that he was as loyal as they come and a good man to those who had been good to him--a finer friend I may have never known. It was always good to see Nick and this time was no exception as I embraced him like a brother and he welcomed me to his home. Roughly a year earlier he had been released from the his service to the US Navy and had come to stay with me in Wilmington to decompress from the overly-regimented life of a sailor, staying for about a month before moving south. Even though not much time had passed, it's always too long between visits and I was thankful to be able to stay here with him.

To digress, I had mentioned that choosing to stay here was one of the best decisions I had made on the trip, and here's why. The storm that began to settle in as soon as I wandered off Stone Mountain turned out to be a six day long shit show, dropping several inches of snow and with temperatures never rising above freezing. If there was ever a good time to be lounging on a couch watching kung-fu movies and drinking beer this was it, and while I had next to no desire to do these things when starting my trip it seemed to be the absolute most amazing thing to do at the time! I want to say that I wasted a week there, but it was definitely not a waste as I managed to stay dry and warm through the storm with a good friend. Nick and I would go wander down the the nearby grocery store daily to pick up whatever we felt like cooking that evening, also to restock the fridge with cheap beer and grab a few cheap movies if we could find some. We would talk most of the day in a way that almost felt like thinking, the other's response to every statement seamlessly flowing back and forth, and it became apparent that by having known each other for so long that we had both been shaped the same way.

When the snow had melted away after six days of covering the ground, I was eager to get a move on but decided to stick around one more day to hike back to Stone Mountain with Nick, seeing as it was only four miles away. Things went well and the ascent proved to be challenging even without my gear, but that was mainly due to the fact that the thawing snow kept the smooth granite wet and therefore as slick as a greaser's pompadour. I'll admit, I ended up on my ass a few times but we made it and the view proved to be even better than before, with the Blue Mountains now clearly in view and the lighting far more favorable. I knew Nick had a mind to keep on with me at this point, but I felt that this was my journey, and while I would have liked a companion this was something I needed to do on my own. So the morning after my second go up the mountain we parted ways again, both promising to keep our doors open should the other ever come calling.

Hiker-ism: Trail Life

(Noun) Trail life is how one lives while on the Appalachian Trail and the word encompasses all things from interactions with people in towns to the various grooming habits, or lack thereof, in the woods. Hikers will often say the phrase 'back in the world' when talking about things that happened before hiking because life on trail is honestly that much different from the normal day-to-day.

It's amazing just how quickly a body can fall out of shape. I had only been sitting on my ass for about a week and I was right back to my knees being sore and tired after a day's hike. I had hoped to be out of the city by the end of the day, but the metropolis surrounding Atlanta is absolutely massive, and so that didn't happen. My first night back and I was urban camping again, but I suppose there are worse things, like fearing to travel if one can't stay in a four star or better hotel every night.

The Blue Ridge Mountains grew ever closer, and the visit to Stone Mountain let me know that this was not going to be easy. It was mid-February and I wondered if I would meet anyone attempting a thru hike this early in the season. So far I don't think I had met more than seven hikers in the whole of Florida, and while I had gotten quite a bit of help in Georgia no one had wanted to walk along with me. To be honest, I really didn't know much at all about the Appalachian Trail, or it's hikers, other than they existed, but I was ready and eager to find out more.

My first glimpse at trail life came sooner then expected. As I was walking down a country highway close to the city of Ball Ground, GA, an older gentleman came out of his home and called me over. His name was Steve and he offered me a glass of tea if I would like one and wondered where I was heading. Turns out that both his son and daughter had hiked the Appalachian Trail in years before and he was fairly educated about the whole thing. Before I knew it I was sitting in their kitchen sipping sweet tea and listening to the stories had been passed on to him from his children. He lived there with his wife Kath who was quite the woodworker and had redone a good section of their home, and she insisted I stay for a little to rest up. Having already been resting for so long I decided to put a few more miles under my boots that day instead of staying the night, but I thanked them just the same before parting ways. I can't recall exactly what many of Steve's stories were, but one that did stick in my mind was how his daughter had met up with someone at one point and soon lost track of him only to meet up again several states later. He had gotten sick at that point and Steve's daughter stuck around to help him out, which I found incredibly encouraging in many ways. I got the feeling that people truly would be looking out for one another on the trail, and that I would have the opportunity to meet some wonderful people along the way. Only time would tell for sure, but either way I had made it this far on my own and wasn't afraid to walk the rest of the way alone as well should I need to.

 I made it pretty close to the city of Ball Ground that night, and when I was starting to look for a place to set up a man pulled of the side of the road ahead and waved me over. I can't say I remember his name, but there could be a reason for that; all I remember is that he was heading my direction and to the city of Ellijay and so he offered me a ride. It was hard to find room for my gear in the back of his late 90s T-Bird, but we managed and were soon on the road to the mountains. I remember watching hills turn to full blown mountains as we passed them, now with ridges and valleys, far bigger than anything I had seen up to this point. I was amazed but I didn't have much time to stare at them as the sun went down not long after leaving the city of Jasper and I began to wonder how hard it was going to be to make camp without any light. This guy in the driver's seat was a trip, and I can't tell how much of what he said was true ,though have no cause to doubt him.

 Apparently, he had been in the US Special Forces and now did something with computers in the area, and if nothing else he sure as hell knew a lot about guns! He was driving his daughter's car today because he had either beat the crap out of the local sheriff, or one of the sheriff's buddies, and therefore he didn't want to drive the thing for fear of being targeted. Can't recall the whole story, and I only got bits and pieces of it, but despite him being a smaller guy I knew I didn't want to piss him off so I just tried my best to be polite and grateful for the ride. I did get a little worried when he pulled off the the side of the road, after he had just told me that the gun he was carrying had the hammer back and might have a bullet in the chamber so he needed to stop and pull the trigger to be sure that the thing wasn't going to go off in his pocket. Fortunately, after we ensured that the gun wasn't loaded with a comforting click of the trigger while the muzzle pointed out of the stopped car, we were able to get moving again without any risk of the old boy blowing off his balls.

I told him that I was here to hike the AT and was trying to make my way to Springer Mountain, just east of Ellijay and hopefully I would be there in a few days. He then insisted that he could drive me into the park pretty close to Springer and so, seeing as he may have a few screws loose, I didn't feel inclined to argue with the guy. I hadn't really wanted to take a hitch for such a long distance, hoping to complete the trip mainly on foot, but who am I to refuse such kindness from an armed and slightly insane ex-Special Forces gentleman?

Even after the several slightly uncomfortable conversations we had had, mostly just him talking and myself listening, the worst was yet to come as we started East into Chattahoochee National Forest, the home of Springer Mountain. I don't know if this guy felt like he was driving a Hummer through a war zone or something, but he sure drove like it. Also in all honestly I couldn't tell you if the car had brakes or not, seeing as he didn't use them even when the road changed from rough pavement into a one lane, dark, narrow, winding dirt road through nowhere. I don't think that he actually increased his speed at this point but it felt like it as the trees began to zip past just feet from the car and we started to bounce wildly over the incredibly uneven road. I have referred to it as the redneck version of Mr. Toad's wild ride, and I was very glad to hop out of the car as we reached a small campsite just a few miles from Springer Mountain.

Must admit that while very shaken up I felt invigorated and very alive from the ride in, and was glad to finally be here in the wilderness once again. All things considered, I liked the guy I rode with, and his knowledge of the area managed to find me a safe place to sleep for the night before starting the first grand leg of my adventure in the morning. We said farewell as he turned around his now very dirty car, and I started to wonder how we had ever made it here or if he was going to be able to make it out again. Either way, I was here now, and the real work was going to start tomorrow.

The road walk through Georgia was one of the most rewarding parts of the entire journey, and if nothing else uniquely set apart my hike from anyone else's. My faith in humanity was restored, and I now know for sure that no matter what is reported on the news, or what is said about the state of the world, there are good people out there just waiting for the chance to help. I felt like I owed it to all of those who had helped me along the way to make it as far as I possibly could, and I hope that in some small way I helped, or at least encouraged, all of them in turn.

CONCERNING THE AT:

Ah the AT, the land of enchantment, the golden road to self discovery, the route 66 of foot travel, but what exactly dose all that mean? By now I've talked a lot about it but have yet to really explain what exactly the Appalachian Trail actually is, and to be honest I'm not entirely sure that I can in a few pages, so I'll just lay out some basics.

The Appalachian Trail, abbreviated AT (Ay-TEE), is an over two thousand mile footpath leading from Springer Mountain in the northern part of Georgia to the great Katahdin at Baxter State Park in north central Maine. Year to year the actual mileage of the trail varies a little due to repairs, reforestation, and small re routes, but in 2014 when I hiked the official mileage was Two Thousand One hundred and Eighty Five point Three miles, passing through thirteen states and two national parks as it winds its way across the Appalachian Mountains of Eastern North America. Every year the trail hosts hundreds of thousands of people wanting a little breaks from normal life, some only venture out for a few hours, Day Hikers, some for a few days or weeks, we call them Section Hikers, while other crazy bastards, known as Thru Hikers, attempt the whole thing in one go! Needless to say, I was one of those nutty, nature obsessed, nomads whom decided to give the whole thing a go, and it is without a doubt my favorite story to tell.

These days about five thousand people every year attempt the whole of the mighty AT, but it may come as a surprise to hear that thru hiking was never the intended purpose of the trail. In fact, its origins are far more humble, and came to be thanks to a vision had by a lone hiker as he sat atop a tree overlooking the Vermont wilderness. Let me set the stage, Long distance hiking wasn't a thing, it didn't exist, there was no place to do it, nor was there any sort of gear designed to accomplish such a feat, but things were about to change for in 1910 work began on a two hundred and seventy two mile continuous footpath spanning the whole of Vermont. Dubbed The Vermont Long Trail, completed in 1930, it became the first of its kind in America, an extensive trail crossing rivers and mountains for no reason other then recreation! It was along this path sometime in the early 20's that Benton MacKaye sat atop a tree overlooking the Vermont wilderness and thought, can we do more? After a good amount of thinking he made his idea for a trail spanning nearly the whole of the country public via a news column in New York and subsequently gained enough support by march of 1925 to make it a reality! The AT was born, but far from existing. Originally, MacKaye had intended for the trail to be a sort of national icon, an idea of contiguity that people of all walks of life along the East Coast could partake in, hiking a bit in their respective regions and having a reason to venture further on vacations and such. By 1937 the two thousand mile way was set, marked by little white blotches of paint and ready for people to enjoy!

Until 1948 that's the way things went, people up for a stroll in the woods had a place to go for a few days and the world was the better for it. However the late 40's proved to be a time that some Americans need a little bit more then a few days alone to feel normal in civilized life, and the reason was WWII. In 1948, three years after leaving the bloody shores of Germany, a man by the name of Earl Shaffer still felt a bit off and decided to give the whole trail a go to "Walk the war out of his system". He decided to walk from south to north so the he could "Fallow the spring" as he made his way, and to this day most hikers choose to travel the same way. Shaffer became the first ever to successfully complete a Thru Hike, something the nation thought was impossible before then, and things have never been the same. There has been many colorful figures that have made it since then, from all walks of life, from a five year old whom hiked with his parents to a seventy year old woman clad in little more then denim jeans with an old canvas bag to carry food in. There has even been reports of a blind man making it all the way with help from his dog and a good supply of casts.

Despite the stories of overwhelming triumph that every Thru Hiker has well committed to memory the AT has always been and will always be an incredibly difficult, and sometimes dangerous, endeavor that should never be taken lightly. In any given year only about one out of every five thru hike hopefuls complete the journey (about 20%) and in years where the weather is particularly bad the ratio can be as low as one in ten (10%). Why people give up the noble pursuit is no mystery, along the way one is forced to deal with aching joints, bad weather, snakes, and spiders, and bears OH MY! Worse weather, hunger, one's own thoughts, solitude, sprains, twists, and bruises, heavy gear, crucial decision making, dirt, germs, zero starbucks, weridos, icy rivers, even worse weather, and thousands of feet of elevation change everyday! It's exhausting just to think about sometimes, but even those that don't make it but a few hours have a new story to tell, and those that make it the whole way will never be the same.

It's incredible how different life is on this simple dirt path stretching farther then any one person can comprehend. Thru hikers often adopt what are know as trail names which are nick names of a sort, and many of those whom I have met I do not know their Christian name. Everyday one ventures over ridges placed high along mountain tops, through valleys in the shadow of great peaks, over summits perched at the highest point around and near rivers cutting their way ever down to meet the sea. The entire way is maintained 100% by volunteers, many of which are former thru hikers themselves, and the path is legislated as such that no one can profit directly from it nor can anyone ever take action to destroy it. Truly, the AT holds some sort of magic that not even the wisest of men can describe, but I'll take the rest of these pages to try and give you an idea.

6 THE APPALACHIAN TRAIL

I awoke my first morning in the Blue Ridge Mountains at a backcountry campsite off the side of a forest road, ready to be hiking on the AT but with no idea where to meet it. The advice I had gotten from my ride in was to keep going east down the road and I would hit the trail sooner or later, and having no other way of figuring it out that's exactly what I did. Although I must admit: it's very frustrating to know your so close to something and yet have no idea how to actually get there. Nevertheless, once the pack was loaded and strapped to my back I was ready to begin what I hoped to be my greatest adventure, and so I took to the road the same as I had done so many times before.

Hiker-ism: Scramble

(verb) The act of moving up the side of a very steep mountain by channeling one's inner bear and using one's hands as a second set of feet in a very unique half-crawl/half-climb motion. Usually used by expert rock climbers or hikers that are beyond exhausted by an ascent.

I didn't even have to start walking to notice that I had not seen anywhere like this wilderness before. The trees were tall pines that grew close together and the road rose and fell quickly while winding wildly along side of a cool, clear river. Even the river was strange to me--it was not more than a foot deep but easily fifteen feet across, with a bottom of bare stones all roughly the size of a coffee mug and worn smooth by the flowing water. It's not as though there hadn't been rivers along the way so far, but there had been none so lively for being so small. I had to wonder how it managed to move so quickly but soon got my answer, for not but a few miles up the road I noticed a large amount of water springing from the underbrush in a manner that seemed very out of place to me. Upon closer examination I noticed that the water didn't start it's forceful flow at the side of the road but rather well over a hundred feet nearly straight up, and almost entirely hidden from the road by trees and shrubs. Having never seen anything like this before I had to get a closer look, and so decided that the best course of action would be to leave my pack close to the road as I attempted to ascend the steep ridge.

It was a lot harder than it looked! The dirt was slick and rose quickly and I had to scramble on my hands at times, grabbing every root and rock in my path to keep moving up the mountainside. After about a fifty foot climb I stood at the base of a forty foot waterfall, completely taken aback that this sort of thing even existed, let alone was allowed to remain hidden so well! The river jumped off the top of the ridge, turning slightly white before cascading down a massive rock face, disrupted slightly by a few downed limbs and a tree that had fallen across the water which made for an excellent place to stand while snapping a few photos. Even the Class 3 rapids of the Suwannee paled in comparison to this out-of-place waterfall in the mountains, and I then realized that in my 800 miles of travel thus far I had yet to see even the slightest fraction of the beauty embedded in the eastern United States. After taking a moment to wash my face in the crystal clear water I noticed that my beard had grown out quite a bit already; taking a moment to twirl my fingers through it I wondered, how I had ever gone so long without ever trying to grow one? Simultaneously and more importantly, I wondered what must be ahead if this breathtaking sight was allowed to be bypassed without even a marker on the road to show its existence.

Hiker-ism: Trail Register

(Noun) Some sort of writing pad, usually a spiral notebook (but not always), placed at various, frequently traveled points of the trail, serving the purpose of giving those that pass by something to record their thoughts in, or at least mark that they were there. They are also a great way to communicate with hikers that are not far behind, and the various comments and stories within their pages provide a nearly endless amount of entertainment for people who take the time to read them.

It's easy for me to forget my first steps on the Appalachian Trail, which is contrary to most other hikers I imagine. I soon found out that I was on USFS (United States Forest Service) 58, where the trail intersected with a few dirt roads before cutting its way north. There was a sign pointing the way to Springer Mountain Summit 4.3 miles away, thus my way was set as I made towards the great southern terminus. These were actually my first steps on the AT, and it was here that I came across my first white blaze. I wish almost more then anything I would have taken more time to appreciate just how far I had come to see the small, almost insignificant blotch of white paint that marked the start of it all, but my mind was set on getting to the summit and in some way leaving a mark of my own atop the mountain to show that I had indeed made it to the starting line. It just seemed more important to reach the designated beginning then to remark at my own, a folly I do not intend to repeat ever again.

The hike up the mountain was quite a challenge for me; I had come so far but all on flat ground, apart for my short climb up Stone Mountain. No one starts out as a good swimmer, but picture spending your entire life swimming in an indoor pool, calm and sheltered from the elements, in time the basics are learned and in this protected environment mastered until one can be confident in their ability. Now picture being thrown out into a raging ocean after knowing only peaceful waters, tossed about by the waves and pulled by currents that before now one had not even known to exist! That's what this first mountain was like for me. Stone Mountain had provided a taste of this sort of environment but even that was hardly a rippled pond compared to the torrent of Springer, and I knew that this was only the beginning and not even to be the worst of it. The air was cool on my skin, and at times a cool mist hung in the air almost as if someone had opened a freezer door quickly allowing the half frozen air to escape. I was far from warm, but with the amount of effort I was putting in to track up the mountain the chilled air pockets actually felt nice as I passed through them. The path was rocky and steep, but to my surprise it was actually well maintained, cleared of most overlying branches and even had a few steps placed along the way to make things more pleasant. Compared to the Florida Trail it was almost as if the way was paved in gold--easy to follow and well marked--and yet far more challenging.

While I may not remember my first steps on the trail perfectly, I will never forget the feeling of actually arriving at the summit of Springer Mountain. The trail begins to level out and becomes a smooth rock stair, allowing the boulder that marks the southern terminus to be easily visible from a ways off. On its face is a plaque depicting the fourteen states the trail travels through and behind it, inlaid into the rock, is a metal box holding a notebook and pen. Thus in the late afternoon of February 18 this the year of our Lord 2014, Jordan D Bearss added his name to the long list of those who had gone before him in hopes of joining the elite few who managed to traverse the entire two thousand and two hundred mile trail by foot and earning the title of Thru Hiker and Two Thousand Miler! An older couple arrived not long after myself, coming up what was known as the Approach Trail starting in Amicalola Falls, which I soon found out would have been a far superior starting point to my nearly random backwoods campsite. Regardless of how I got here, I had made it and had my picture taken by these fine folks to prove it. There was a break in the trees here allowing me to peer onward over the forest, and as I gazed over the seemingly endless wilderness that stretched before me I became grateful for all I had overcome already and eager to find what was ahead. I tried to think of how far I had yet to go, but found just the thought of it all to be very overwhelming and exhausting. Thus, I decided not to look any farther than the next step and to focus instead of how far I had already traveled. This moment set the tone for what was ahead--I had no plan, but I had a marked trail, little money, forty-five pounds of gear, a quiet mind. No place to be, and all day to get there.

Hiker-ism: Shelter

(noun) A shelter is exactly what it sounds like: a man made structure in the woods that usually consists of three walls, a roof, and a wooden floor on which to sleep. Great for keeping the rain off one's back in rough weather, though typically rather dirty.

Didn't make it very far from the summit of Springer by the evening, for I was running out of daylight and an opportunity arose that I couldn't pass up. Up until now I had been pitching my tent every night to sleep in, and had gotten quite good at it, but here on the AT another option was suddenly available. Thanks to the large amount of people who find time, and occasionally money, to keep the trail well-maintained and accessible to people of all walks of life, they had found it in their hearts to erect a multitude of shelters along the way. These tiny hovels along side of the footpath vary greatly in size and construction along the way, not to mention quality, but all provide a solid roof for hikers to sleep under for the night. Usually shelters consist of a roof, three walls, and an elevated platform for which to sleep on. If one is lucky, there's a few platforms to set up a sleeping bag on, but for the most part one is shoulder to shoulder with others sometimes just met that night, which let me just say, is one hell of a bonding experience. Many people have asked me why the shelters only have three sides as opposed to four, and I have yet to find an answer other than the build up of stench from long distance hikers could potentially become lethal.

My first run in with one of these partially exposed abodes was at Stover Creek, a whopping 2.8 miles from the Springer Mountain summit! After not having a solid roof for so long it actually looked a bit homey, and seeing as the day was wearing thin I decided to set up here for the night. I didn't know it at the time, but this was actually a pretty nice shelter, boasting a second story sleeping platform and quality metal ring outside to start a fire in. Because it was so close to the start of the trail the surrounding woods had not yet been cleared of firewood by previous hikers, and so I managed to start a small blaze by which to warm myself in the fading daylight. I had passed a few hikers on my way up to the summit, which was exciting seeing as I had been all on my own during all of my time in nature, and a fellow hiker had set up in the upper portion of the shelter. I hoped that the fire would have brought him out, but he must have worn himself thin on the way up the Approach Trail and so he remained hunkered down as I sat and puffed a pipe during my first night on the east's great trail.

I had hoped that the stars would make themselves known as I sat outside enjoying the last of the day, but a thin fog prevented their appearance and I soon retired myself to peaceful slumber in the shelter. Or so I thought. During what must have been close to the middle of the night I awoke to what sounded to be either a Norwegian curling tournament or a new multi-directional bowling alley that had just opened roughly six feet above my head. I resisted the urge to go check it out mainly because it was a bit cool out and I had made myself rather comfortable in my bag, but also because I had no idea who this guy was and didn't want to be rude. This activity persisted for a good twenty minutes before stopping as suddenly as it had started and I managed to drift back to sleep, though at times I did hear the occasional shuffle from what I assumed to be from the same source.

I awoke in the morning before whomever was upstairs and began to pack up in the manner which I had become accustomed to before starting the day. What was different though was the environment in which I awoke. The air hung thick with a blue fog, cool to the touch but also crisp and clean, almost otherworldly compared to anything I had seen up to this point. Most of the shelters on the AT have a trail register and this one was no exception, so I took a moment to make my mark and read over the other entries in the chilled morning air. At this time I was joined by the young man with whom I had spent the night with and introduced myself, happy to have finally met someone out hiking.

For lack of a better name I will from here on refer to him as Shuffleboard due to the previous night's events, and he stood a little shorter then me but was built thick and sturdy, with short black hair and a wide face. He didn't say much but before long apologized if he had made too much noise the night before. Apparently, he had just become acquainted with what were by far the most prevalent pests on the entire trail, mice, and they just loved to make their home in safe, dry shelters. I suddenly realized that several of the shuffles I had heard the night before had indeed come from either one side of the shelter or the other as opposed to directly above me, meaning that I had somehow remained blissfully ignorant to the infestation of these pesky little rodents for at least one night, but never again. Shuffle Board had managed to create so much noise the night before by setting up his tent in the shelter to shield himself from the hut's pint sized permanent residents, and informed me that I should be hanging my bag on the wall each night to keep them out of my belongings. There were indeed many thick pegs sticking out of the walls of this shelter and now I knew why; one learns something new everyday I suppose. Thanks to my early rising, and the fact that I didn't have a tent to pack up, I was on my way out before Shuffleboard, but we were heading the same way so I figured I would see him again.

Hiker-ism: Blue Blaze

(noun) A blue mark indicating a side trail or alternate route. The art of Blue Blazing is an interesting skill to hone; try and see them all and you'll never move an inch, but skip them all and you will have missed much of what makes hiking worthwhile.

The north Georgia mountains are a strange sight this time of year. Upon entering the trail, at no point are you any lower than 2600 feet above sea level, which is a solid thousand feet above the Stone Mountain summit, and the land reflects the challenge. It soon became clear where the name Blue Mountains came from, for when given the chance to stand and look from a place high above the mountain valleys, distant peaks lie quietly in a cool, cobalt blue the like of which I have yet to encounter elsewhere. While the path is lined with tall maple and oak trees, and weaves between waxy rhododendron shrubs and creeping vines, what makes hiking at this time of year intersting isn't the plant life but rather the lack thereof. Nearly everything save the rhododendron has dropped their leaves for the winter season leaving nothing but tall, barren trunks and low lying twigs, the likes of which have a nasty habit of grabbing one's boot and not letting go. The result, due to the lack of things blocking one's sight, is incredible vistas nearly every step of the way provided by looking between trees. The valleys which should be glowing a radiant green by spring now look vacant and peaceful, showing a greyish brown up close and fading ever more blue as they stand closer to the distant mountains. One of the main disadvantages of these sort of conditions is that there is now very little to block the cool winter air as it blows over the ridge line which, for better or for worse, is where the trail seems to be set. The best place to see everything is undoubtedly from the highest point around, but every now and then I would find myself hurrying to the next bit of lower elevation trail so as to be protected on one side by the mountain and be out of the elements. At this point I had taken to wearing a bandana over my nose and mouth in the morning in an attempt to keep them from the cold, which worked well enough until things warmed up a bit in the noon day sun, or the bandana got so full of moisture from my breath that the bit covering my nose would become saturated and let in more cold then it kept out.

    Even if it was rather brisk in the morning, by midday I would be hiking comfortably in a hoodie, partially because moving up and down the mountains was very labor intensive and thus keeping the body warm from the inside out. It was on such an afternoon that I came across my first blue-blazed trail, and while I knew traveling it would make no forward progress towards Maine, I had also heard from a passing hiker that the waterfall on this particular trail was worth the walk. I had come on this trip to explore and to see things I had otherwise been ignorant to, not to endlessly drone on like I always had in life, thus I decided to venture down the blue blazes and see what I could see. Some blue blazed trails are only a hundred feet long, others are over five miles in one direction, I've even heard tell of some being massive multi-day loops, but this one proved to be on the shorter side. After no more than a tenth of a mile I found myself at the side of a marvelous waterfall, at least twenty feet high and very wide, pouring heavily into a shallow, sandy pool with walls of stone and several trees hanging over it all. It wasn't the first time I looked at something and had trouble believing it was real, but every time is just as striking as the last, and always fulfilling.

Taking a moment here to rest my tired feet in the cool, clear water I started to notice my own smell for the first time in a long time, and trust me it was anything but pleasant. Realizing that I was all on my own, on a side trail, in the middle of nowhere, this was obviously the best chance I would have for a shower for who knows how long and it would be foolish to let it slide by. Not saying that I'm anything but foolish at times, and perhaps plunging naked as a jaybird into a cold pool of water in the dead of winter constitutes as more foolish than wise, but after a quick shower I felt much better than before, even if a little chilly at the moment.

It would appear that I had somehow managed to relearn the lost art of relaxation. Life was as simple as it had ever been, and I took time everyday to enjoy everything around me no matter how small. My journal began to reflect it as I now took the time to add an extra line through my 7s and 0s; even the words I used began to look neater and grew in length and detail. On the Appalachian Trail, all other things ceased to exist and the mind is free to wonder where it will.

Hiker-ism: Switchback

(Noun) The fabled switchback is a novice hiker's best friend and an expert hiker's biggest annoyance. By traveling to the summit via a series of winding trails cutting sideways up the mountain and nearly overlapping each other instead of blitzing straight to it, a person will travel ten times the distance but with one tenth of the effort.

It didn't take long to realize that my body had seen nothing like this before, and night after night I tried to sleep with aching knees, elevating them as I slept when I had the chance. I was pulling about twelve miles per day at this point, which is actually better than most, but was a big step back from the twenty mile days I had been putting in since central Florida. That being said, at no other place in my travels had the road risen and fallen a thousand feet at will, and having to keep my mind constantly aware of roots and rocks so as to not trip over them certainly didn't help my progress. Perhaps I wouldn't have minded the little ankle snares so much if falling didn't have such a dire consequence. The trail was so narrow that if two hikers met coming in different directions there would be a bit of a struggle to find away around each other seeing as it was not easily possible to step off. Actually, stepping off more than likely would be impossible seeing as falling off would soon take its place. The land to the side of the trail nearly always fell sharply on at least one of two sides, and at such a rate that I strongly believe a person would tumble for a good ten seconds before coming to rest and forced to hike a good hour to regain his place.

Every risk comes with its own reward however, and the rewards of these precarious paths were astounding! Large granite faces would shine like ice from a distance in the morning frost, springs, rivers, and waterfalls around every corner, endless forest with tree and shrub enough to make society feel like a myth from years past. The greatest thing at this point was the silence, pure, unabated silence, often without even a breeze, bird, or bug to break it. When I would stop, thus preventing my feet from rustling playfully in the downed leaves, I could hear my breath clearly and the space between my ears would strain in a desperate attempt to hear anything at all. I didn't know such quiet was possible, nor did I know the peace it would bring. It was almost like pieces I didn't even know were missing had fallen back into place, and any weight from my wrongdoings of old began to fall from my shoulders. I began to feel what trail life was all about, but was far from understanding it just yet.

What I did understand soon enough is just how nasty a high elevation storm can be as I was pinned down in one at Gouch Mountain Shelter for a night. Wind and rain ripped by with such force that even the most remote corner of the well-built shelter wasn't removed from the elements, and I was forced to spend the night wrapped in the footprint of my tent so as to stay dry. Necessity is the mother of invention, so they say, and I managed to get through with the only real repercussions being a severe lack of rest and a complimentary pack wash.

Another lesson soon learned is what it means to really climb a mountain, taught courtesy of Blood Mountain, Georgia. Being the first time a northbound hiker will break four thousand feet with over fourteen hundred feet of elevation change from the approach to summit, which is called its prominence, this big bastard has been known to knock out more would-be thru-hikers than any other particular peak. In fact, the legend of Blood Mountain extends far beyond the trail as even my buddy Nick had heard of it, and with good reason: this was no picnic. Winding back and forth up the rocky side of the mountain progress was made slowly. Trail maintainers had managed to arrange and break large rocks into a semi natural stair at times, making things go a bit smoother, and the vegetation got ever thinner as the summit approached. The earth gave way such as it had on Stone Mountain to reveal smooth granite, dotted with pink at times, which is rumored to be where the mountain got its name. A more educated individual would find that it's named after a monumental Native American battle that took place upon the mountain, but to those attempting to get up and over this oversized rock the name matters little.

What dose matter is the view from the top, and it was indeed one worth remembering. I arrived just before the sun began to set on a day as clear as clear could be, it was cold but no so much that I could not bear it, and perched upon the summit there was a unique shelter with walls made of nothing but stacked stones. To the right of the shelter there were several boulders, roughly the size of a small home, blocking any view that could be had but they were very easy to climb, and the sight from the top was far worth the effort. I could see more then I can begin to understand while perched atop the rocks and looking down from four thousand four hundred and sixty one feet, towering above the neighboring peaks and valleys. With my sight set due south I could see what looked to be a tiny broken barcode jutting upwards from the distant forest, and was taken aback by the notion of one being able to see the Atlanta sky line from such a distance! I took the time to enjoy a pipe of tobacco as I wrote in my journal, fingers seizing against the cold as they tried to work but my eyes were unable to peel themselves from the view, utterly perplexed by the fact that such beauty could exist. The sun began to fade and the stars started to show as the dropping temperature forced me to climb back down to the shelter and set up for the night. There was no use trying to go any further tonight, and this building was bound to be better than anything else close by, so I prepared to call it a day, and a grand one at that.

Shuffleboard managed to show up that night, and he set up in the shelter as well, although he did so further away from the door then I and was blocked from my sight by a wall dividing the barren stone room in two. There was no door to block the large entryway into the building, nor were there any means of covering the windows built into the sides, but seeing as it didn't look like rain I thought little of it and prepared to slumber till the morning.

    Or so I thought. I had learned early on that it pays to know where your flashlight is, and made it a habit to keep it close by when I slept. On this particular night I was rather grateful for the newfound addition to my nightly routine as I heard something rummaging around my pack that I was forced to leave on the ground at my feet due to the lack of pegs to hang it on. Fully prepared to meet and do battle with whatever rodent dared to defile my dwindling supplies I wielded my light and illuminated the unwelcome cat burglar where he stood. Well, CAT burglar is close, but not exactly right. Though such a description would have been greatly preferred for this thief in the night, I now looked directly into the eyes of a black and white striped varmint perched behind my belongings, looking very confused and slightly annoyed by my intrusion. To put it simply, there was a skunk in my pack, and upon realizing this I completely changed my approach to the matter. I had hoped to simply scare away whatever it was that was pestering me in the night, but now scaring my unannounced visitor was certainly the last thing I wished to do considering he had the potential to mark my gear in such a way that carrying it may prove to be impossible over the smell. Nevertheless, I had to do something, and so I did make some noise to urge it off, but far more nicely than I had intended to before, which to my intimidate relief worked well and without a 'gas-tly' reciprocation. However, it wasn't the last I was to see of this smelly swindler, as it made several attempts to sneak back in as the night went on, each time meeting me with whatever resistance I could firmly, yet kindly, muster. On one occasion the bandit made his way into the other room to pester my sleeping comrade Shuffleboard, whom I felt the need to inform before things turned nasty to say the least. He was just as happy as I was to see our new addition to the shelter but managed to send the bugger off as well, yet for the rest of the night neither of us slept well. Come the morning we managed to pack up tired but smelling no worse then when we had arrived, grateful, for once, for the scent of sweat and earth.

Hiker-ism: Trail Name

(noun) Thru hikers on the AT have a long standing tradition of adopting a nickname for the duration of their hike. While anyone can give a hiker a trail name, only the hiker himself can accept it, and while some names come from very distinct traits carried by the hiker many others come simply from one's strongest food craving.

Shortly after decending from Blood Mountain I came across something I had not seen before in my travels through the woods. The trail lead directly to a decent-sized stone and wood building, housing a small store, smaller cafe, and a bunk room where weary hikers could pay to find shelter for the night. I remained blissfully unaware of the housing potential of this place until much later, but I did stop at the store because up until now I had been lacking a crucial piece of equipment: a map. In all honestly, stepping onto the AT without a proper map was by far one of the dumber decisions I had made thus far, but I had made it through Florida gathering resources along the way and thought I would find the same thing out here. In Florida, people don't often attempt the entire state long trail, and each wildlife preserve provides its own map at the entrance for people to take with them as one comes across such trails. Springer Mountain had a similar kiosk set up not far from the summit, but lacked individual maps for hikers to carry so I had written down the distance between major landmarks on a piece of paper and duct taped the back side of it to keep it from disintegrating in my pack. This did prove to be a good ready guide for the rest of Georgia but would have been very impractical for some of the larger states, so I jumped at the chance to pick up something better.

The store referred to itself as an Outfitter, meaning that it provided many trail-friendly pieces of gear and also an excellent selection of dehydrated food and energy bars. Located in Neel Gap, Mountain Crossing's open year round, providing a place for people to view the color of changing leaves in the fall and barren trees in the winter. Being from a bit farther north and very used to seeing trees drop their leaves in the winter I had previously thought nothing of it, but apparently trees farther south can keep green year round. Such a sight is actually worth traveling to for native born Floridians who wouldent dream of living in somewhere this cold; a natural array of beauty not known in their native lands. Looking back, Florida was very green the entire time I was traveling through it so I can understand why people would want to travel to see such a sight as these woods, but even if I understood the idea I still found it a little weird. Nevertheless, I had more pressing things to tend to, namely finding a map!

Mountain Crossing's did indeed carry several trail maps but after talking with one of the employes I soon found that there was an entire guidebook printed and immediately available. Furthermore, the AT Guidebook not only listed the distances between various landmarks, but also provided a rough elevation chart, distance off trail to neighboring towns and what could be found there, and brief descriptions of nearly every shelter along the way! Priced below twenty dollars, I soon became the proud owner of AWOL's northbound guide to the AT, overjoyed at the wealth of information now tucked safely in my pack. Before leaving I was informed by the staff that as a hopeful thru hiker I needed to sign the logbook to make it official and to leave a record of having been there for others to see. Thus I put my name next to the number Fifty Six, but since I was lacking a trail name for myself I had to ask what to put in the information slot that would otherwise be left open. The staff decided to give me one, and since I had many small pieces of gear strapped to my belt they decided that my trail name should be Batman in honor of Bruce Wayne's most memorable equipment. So Batman I was when I left Neel's Gap, but I didn't go more than a mile before deciding to leave the name there because I had always liked the comic book villains of Batman far more than the hero, and the name just didn't fit well.

Batman did lay the groundwork for the trail name that stuck however. That night I managed to stay at a shelter with several other thru-hiker hopefuls, where we discussed what would be a good fit for me. Thinking of other famous utility belt wielders, names like Darkwing Duck and Dick Tracey came up, and the background character from the Goonies seemed to be a promising fit, though none of us were sure on his name. Straining to remember from the depths of our childhood we weren't a hundred percent sure on the name but we all somehow agreed it was Gizmo, and at this moment I was born anew. My mother was the trail, and my father the woods, all those who wander are brothers and sisters to me, and every daydreamer and radical my kin. In hindsight, the character's actual name is Data, but I didn't remember that until hundreds of miles later, so Gizmo it was, and I was happy to be called such.

The rest of the night was also one to remember, as I got the chance to finally sit and talk with other hikers about their past experience and their hopes for the trail ahead. I'll admit I was a little intimidated despite having already walked eight hundred miles to get here, but my longing for companionship well outweighed my nerves as I had slept far too many nights alone thus far. There was ten of us there in total, counting me, three couples and a few strays, plus a dog which was not included in my count. Two of the couples had brought flasks of bourbon and we stood around a small campfire sipping spirits and star gazing. Shuffleboard was there, as well as a guy who went by Quail Man, but the couple most worth remembering were a hearty, heavy set pair who had just graduated from Michigan State University and were looking to travel a bit before settling into real jobs. Their names became Margarita and Tree Beard further down the way, but they still had their Christian names here. Margarita had very pale skin, common of Michigan folk, a kind round face, and short dirty blond hair. She was a very kind hearted individual, and in the past had been known to carry things for other hikers when they packed a little too heavy. It was common for male AT thru hikers not to shave their beards while on the trail, but Tree Beard had gotten a running start on the idea and already sported a face warmer worth remembering. A large man, he had very dark hair and a resounding laugh, usually dressed in layers; he had the appearance of one who had gotten to know the woods and I found him a fine companion. They both had done several previous hikes and I was glad to see them whenever chance allowed us to meet.

The shelter was set to hold seven people but two of the couples had already set up their tents, so space was not really an issue for the rest of us. In spite of several offers to condense our sleeping arrangements, Shuffleboard decided to sleep near the fire under a picnic table seeing as he had decided to drop his tent back on the trail somewhere to save weight. I suppose I should have been wondering what possessed him to act in such a way, but I was more preoccupied trying to figure out exactly how a picnic table had made its way out to the middle of nowhere with no sort of motor vehicle access in the area. Rather than continue to bend my mind over the matters at hand, I instead crawled into my bag, shoulder to shoulder with people I had just met, yet I had hardly ever felt so at home. It was all new to me but didn't feel as strange as it sounds; it was just nice to have some company to share an evening with for the first time in far too long.

Hiker-ism: Rock Hopping

(verb) The act of moving through a boulder field like some sort of backwoods ninja! Sometimes it's as easy as stepping over a large crack in a rock, other times you nearly have to summon the spirit of a spider monkey to guide your body through challenging, and occasionally dangerous, terrain.

Before writing further, I'm going to go on record and say that one should ALWAYS purify their drinking water. I'm even in favor of purifying water that comes from your tap at home but that goes double for water collected from streams and rivers!

Up until now the biggest problem I had faced was finding clean drinking water; on the trail in Florida it had been an impossibility. Stagnate, bug infested water everywhere and not a drop to drink. On the roads in Georgia things got easier as I could fill my reservoirs from spigots on the sides of gas stations, but I always felt a little dishonest doing it even though I needed the water to survive. In the mountains though, I found a solution to my problems in the form of natural springs. A spring is an area where water emerges directly from the ground--some are little more than shallow pools but others literally spring from the earth forming free flowing streams of water ever growing in size and speed as they descend down a mountainside.

How exactly water forces itself from barren ground at high elevation is something that has been, and will remain, a mystery to me. While I'm sure there's a wonderful wealth of science that describes the phenomenon in detail I'm not entirely sure I want to know it, leaving the spring as a sort of natural miracle in my mind. That being said, the real miracle of a spring is that because the water is flowing directly through the earth before emerging onto the side of the mountain, it's naturally filtered and if the water is collected from the source of a flowing spring it's generally safe to drink. Pathogens don't have a chance to form in the earth for a multitude of reasons, nor do they have the chance to contaminate the head of a spring because it is constantly new water. The Georgia mountains are so full of springs that they didn't even attempt to diverge the trail from them, often allowing the water to flow directly over the foot path. I was hesitant to collect the water from these natural wonders at first, but now there is no other water I would rather drink than that from a cool, clear mountain spring.

Many times springs would emerge in a huge area of barren rocks that varied in size from tiny pebbles to boulders the size of a small home. Called boulder fields, the earth had been washed away from the stone leaving them exposed, bare, and typically a real bitch to pass through. Forced to leave the flat, level ground, hikers attempt to make their way by stepping from rock to rock, occasionally having to backtrack if a path proves impassible or backstep if the next rock proves to be unstable. Like miniature teeter-totters a rock can be very stable until someone puts their weight on one side of it where it then breaks free from its resting place. It's best to avoid rocks like that for the sake of your skin, but sometimes the chance to test them isn't presented and the only way to reach them is to leap down, up, or over to them with nothing but a prayer that they'll hold in place. I honestly loved the boulder fields, they would remind me of the beaches I had know all my life where boulders had been piled to either keep the sand in place or waves from eroding a pier. Many times in my life, much to the chagrin of my mother, I would hop along the shoreline boulders as some sort of childhood game. Even as an adult I would sometimes let myself work my way through the semi-natural jungle gym, reminiscing simpler times.

The highest point in Georgia is Tray Mountain, a noble climb to say the least. Perhaps it was that I was finally starting to adjust to hiking in the mountains, but I didn't find the climb overly strenuous, and I enjoyed the rocky summit for a moment before pressing on. While perched atop the rough and jagged peak I looked again over the woods, immense and void of human disturbance, and though my view was slightly obstructed by a thin mist that lay over the mountain I sat still and satisfied until the curious figure of a man came wondering up the trail. He was dressed entirely in vibrant blue that couldn't be missed, a thin and older man who lacked only a scruffy beard from looking like the quintessential gold prospector of years past. We greeted each other and it didn't take long to know for sure that this old kook would have been right at home digging gold straight out of 1800s San Francisco. The Florida native called himself Penguin Man, a name given to him back in the world due to his tendency to spend literal weeks setting up an elaborate Arctic display around his home every year at Christmas time.

We parted ways on the Tray Mountain summit but met up again later that night at a close by shelter, along with Shuffleboard and another older gentleman called Turtle. I was tired, it had been a long day, and so I opted to set up my tent instead of utilizing the shelter, but I did enjoy staying warm by a campfire that Turtle had gotten going until the time the stars came by. It's a strange thing really, everyone on the trail is so happy to see the stars but as soon as they show up nearly everyone leaves for bed--I hope that the stars don't feel like they're not welcome, I had become rather good friends with them.

I only saw Turtle the one night on the trail, and I was grateful for it. He was a nice enough guy but didn't share my desire to be technology independent. In fact, it was long after I had set up in my tent before I could fall asleep because Turtle had decided that this was the best time to make a series of four phone calls to his friends and relatives to talk about being in nature. He didn't take the hint that perhaps phone calls weren't meant to be made in nature as he had to call several people back when the call was dropped due to lack of reception, and he went on and on about how great being away from everything was. Sometimes people just need to stop and listen to themselves and think on if that's really what they believe in. I'm not saying that every person who walks in the woods must be disconnected from the outside world, everyone is entitled to hike the way they see fit, but a consideration for other hikers is important and consideration of one's self is doubly so. Integrity is a trait every man is capable of, but few hold. To me, there is no more important quality in a man.

Even though my body was aching and complaining in the early next morning I soon hit my stride, stopping only to munch some trail mix or take in a pleasant view where the trees broke. Although it wasn't always the lack of trees that made for a pleasant sight, for many of the downed trees were a sight in an of themselves, as they had become hollow in their years of resting on the forest floor, some big enough around for a full grown man to climb inside. I was learning that being here, nearly lost in the woods, I felt very at peace. Back home, my mind was always racing and I had thought that being out here would give me the chance to solve all the great mysteries of life, but what actually happened is that, for the first time, I would have large periods of time where I would think of nothing at all, my mind completely silent. It's a strange feeling to know that you literally haven't had a single worry, care, or even a pleasant thought pass through your mind much of a day, but I was beginning to realize that the greatest things in life weren't in the complex bits many obsess over daily, but rather the simple, ever present, and taken for granted.

Hiker-ism: Hostel

(noun) Oh sweet Mary mother of Jesus Christ if there is a greater place on earth then a warm hostel on a cold day I have yet to see it! A hostel by definition is a place for weary travelers to rest, but what that translates to is a cheap place to stay with other hikers, under a solid roof and usually with a warm shower.

One thing I had largely taken for granted in life was the chance to be warm when desired, but after so much time in the wild I had become very aware of just how nice it was. The weather had not been terrible in the last few days though far from enjoyable, and there appeared to be a good storm attempting to roll in. According to my hand-dandy guidebook and several other hikers, there was a hostel called the Blueberry Patch in a nearby town, which was supposed to be a fine place to rest for a day if needed. It was a good three miles off the trail, so when the trail crossed US-76 I made my way on foot to hopefully find a proper nights rest in Hiawassee, Georgia.

It's hard to judge distance sometimes when walking, but thanks to the guidebook I was able to calculate a rough rate of speed by timing myself between landmarks. When hiking over hills and valleys in the mountains I was traveling at roughly two miles per hour, but what my average rate of speed was on flat, paved roads I had yet to figure out. I had hoped to hitch at some point along the way, but it wasn't for miles until someone actually stopped. Walking around to the driver's side I asked if he could get me to the Blueberry Patch Hostel, and if he knew where it was. Turns out that the guy was working at the moment and had only stopped to check on some wire boxes close by. Despite feeling quite embarrassed, I did manage to find out this way that the area I was in had long been called the Blueberry Patch and that I should be close--no harm no foul. However, what proved to be even more embarrassing about the whole endeavor is that once I made my way around the bend in the road not more than a hundred yards ahead, I spotted a small wooden sign at the base of a driveway clearly, and proudly, displaying the words Blueberry Patch Hostel. What can I say, I had arrived.

I was met at the driveway by a thin, older man with a full beard of white and a quiet but cheerful demeanor. He seemed rather small to my eyes, almost like a plant that hadn't seen enough sunlight, but I had no idea just how great of a man Gary actually was. After introducing himself he let me know that he needed to run into town to pick up a smaller flag for his sign, the one he had intended to fly proved to be a poor fit, and that I should just make my way to the bunk house and settle in until he returned.

I had stayed in a hostel before but I always had an enclosed space of my own, so I wasn't sure how much I would like the experience of paying to stay in a shared environment. Having not been in boy scouts or the military I had not seen too many bunk rooms in my life, but even with my limited experience I could tell that this place was very different then most. The front door led into a small kitchen complete with a microwave oven, working sink, refrigerator, and a single long wooden table in the center of the room. Through another small entryway was the actual bunk room, boasting two bunks with three single beds each and one bunk comprised of a pair of stacked queen sized beds, all with clean sheets and soft mattresses. Being the only one there I chose the lowest bunk on one of the single beds, and after having suffered several months of cold I very much enjoyed the chance to warm myself by a small wood burning stove in the corner of the kitchen.

It wasn't long before Gary returned and proceeded to show me around the place. A short walk out the side door revealed a path of roof shingles leading to a small shack that housed a toilet and more importantly a shower, complete with hot running water! He asked that I stay on the shingles so as to not tear up the surrounding earth, a problem he'd had trouble with in the past due to the popularity of his hostel. I thought the request a bit strange seeing as I was currently standing in the middle of a pasture with the guy's livestock, but it was his place and I wasn't about to question what he deemed best for it. Gary let me know that I was a bit early in the season compared to most hikers, arriving here February 24, and that it would more than likely be a little lonely in the bunkhouse tonight, but I should put my dirty clothes in a basket soon so they could be washed and also not to keep them waiting once the breakfast bell sounded in the morning. I had expected nothing more than a place to stay and was floored by the idea that my stay included not only a free wash but also had the potential for a hot meal! I honestly thought it a little too good to be true, but I did as he asked, hoping that things went as well as he indeed said they would.

The kindness of Saint Gary didn't end there however. When he came to collect what needed to be washed, and trust me it NEEDED to be washed, he also asked if I needed to pick up any supplies in town, which I surely did. He said to check the boxes in the corner first to see if there was anything I could use out of them before we went, seeing as whatever was there was left by other hikers and was free to take. First off, box of free shit? And second, WE!? This guy was going to give me a safe place to stay, a hot shower, a free wash, a hot meal, and a free ride to town!?! I don't think there are words that can describe just how amazing this whole deal is to a person who hadn't even seen a car or running water in a week let alone thought of riding into town. That being said I did check out the hiker box in the corner and was indeed able to pull out several things before heading to town to pick up the rest of what I needed. After a short ride in Gary's Jeep, he dropped me off in town and said he would return around six to pick me up outside the store. What a nice guy!

Hiawassee is a nice little town, relatively flat and open but with a lot of places to pick up supplies or grab a quick bite to eat. I had never really cared for fast food, for it hardly ever seemed like food at all, but I couldn't help but find a place to grab a greasy, fatty, more than likely over halfway comprised of beef-like filler, hamburger. I swear I felt like I died a little inside, but in the most enjoyable way possible! If the last few moments of my life were the only thing keeping me from that blissful, semi-solid patty of fried lard I consider it a fair trade, life in our old age looks a bit too long as it is anyway. Also in town I stopped at a grocery store to grab what I needed for another nine day batch of trail mix, and it was here that I noticed an unfamiliar face pushing around a cart laden with oats and a large, hiking backpack.

He was about my size, just slightly heavier and with short brown hair and a round face, clad in clothes that had obviously seen excessive wear in the woods. His name was Vegemite, a name the Australian native had gotten due to a peculiar type of sandwich spread popular in his homeland, and he was also staying at The Patch with Gary. After supplying up we talked a bit outside as we waited for our ride back, no topic in particular, but I realized that I felt an immediate connection simply because we had both hiked here. It's hard to explain, this connection that thru hikers on the AT have--it's a sort of brotherhood, an all inclusive private club, possibly even some sort of spiritual bond that connects us. AT thru hikers, upon meeting, are either instantly best friends or instantly in a mutual agreement to tolerate each other for as long as they're together, sometimes one leads to the other, but regardless I was always happy to meet another!

I soon further cemented the theory of Thru Hiker Relations as Gary returned to collect us. He was a little bit late, which seemed out of place because he had been so on point all day, and even though it didn't bother me or my new friend in the slightest he still apologized for the delay. Apparently, a group of hikers had called from the trailhead and he had made to get them before heading back to town. At the hostel, I noticed a few familiar faces; Shuffleboard and Penguin Man had made their way here in hopes of dodging the storm that still threatened the area. Along with them were four others whom I had passed not far out of town earlier in the day who had set up their own camp and had a small fire going by the time I passed, and I recall waving as I passed them but didn't care to stop. They called themselves The Friends of Sasquatch, a four person team consisting of Nomad and her significant other Mountain Man, whom had both had made uncompleted twenty thirteen thru hike attempts; a tall, thin man called Free-J, who was new to the trail; and a younger hiker who was called What's-it-to-ya, I can only imagine how he got that name. Whether a new friend or an old favorite I was happy to meet them all, and they in turn seemed to be excited to get to know me. After a short while Gary had returned with my fresh laundry, a blessing in and of itself, and the rest began to send out their own as quickly as possible so as to let the Saint soon get to bed.

The Friends were great to talk to, and I learned much from them. Not just about what's ahead from the previous experience of Nomad and Mountain Man, but also about what this trail was all about. They, instead of trying to push as far as the day allowed them, would hike until they found a pleasant spot to spend the day and set up, sometimes going as few as three miles in an entire day! In sharp contrast, a conversation with Free-J detailed an encounter The Friends had with an older German fellow who had flown to America so as to see the great eastern trail. This guy had a laminated notecard for every day that he was to be on the trail, with everything from daily miles required to when and where he would break, resupply days and points, side trails and landmarks--I almost wonder if he had written down when to wipe his ass or blow his nose! He had such confidence in his schedule that he had even booked his plane ticket home, a good five months in advance! An interesting night, surrounded by interesting people, with many interesting conversations to dweal on as we drifted off to sleep.

We were all hardly awake and half packed up when we heard the breakfast bell ringing from the side of Gary's house the next morning. I almost couldn't believe my ears, but went along anyway with the rest of my brethren in hopes of finding a hot meal, and did we ever! Gary and his wife had not only prepared a practical feast of pancakes, but also biscuits and gravy, hash browns, eggs, sausage, hot coffee, fresh orange juice, and a homemade blueberry syrup so good that it demanded to be poured over everything! Our gracious host said grace once we had all settled, and we made short work of what had been laid before us, cheerful and in high spirits, chatting about the day ahead. The table had been set in a large covered porch where the mountains could be easily seen from where we sat. One large peak in particular caught our eyes, standing strong against the gray sky and looking over the pastures of Saint Gary and his neighbors. Shuffleboard looked to it and remarked at how awesome it would be to have such a sight in one's backyard, to which I responded that for the next six months it is, prompting a round of raised coffee mugs and cheer from my new friends.

It was here, gathered at a table with people I hardly knew and a host that I had just met, that I began to really understand what the trail was really all about. On the surface, it just looks like a challenge, a chance to test yourself against the earth using all the resourcefulness, perseverance, and determination one can muster. A chance to see America from the eyes of our ancestors when they first landed on her virgin shores, and the mountains that had remained untouched through years of expansion and industrialization. However, while it is indeed all of those things, the greatest bits of the trail lie in the little encounters that occur almost haphazardly each day. The chance to slow down, to look at oneself without the chaotic pace of normal life. To sit with your fellow man in a place close to which our kind had first divided themselves from apes, unbound by class, creed, or nation and united as a species. It's a chance to explore not only the untouched earth but also the deepest, most remote parts of the human condition, a grand social experiment where the researcher is also the subject, without control or conditions. And above all else, the trail is a place to be happy, to be simple, to be free.

Back in the woods I began to think of what I wanted to get out of the trail, and of the conversation with Free-J the night before. I felt that long ago the thinking man had first observed the need for a balance between order and chaos, to embrace all things in life, but not to favor either side too strongly. I thought of the difference between The Friends and the German fellow they had met, and concluded that either route would not suite me, that my way was set somewhere in the middle. The German would surely make it the entire two thousand miles if he managed to avoid an injury, but to me it seemed as if he should have just stayed home and worked. Why throw five months of one's life into a trip exploring a different country that allowed no opportunity to explore? Why on earth would one want to wake up each day, labor tirelessly, then set up base camp in a militant fashion for nothing more than to be half a year older?! On the other hand, I don't think The Friends were any better off. At the rate they were going they were never going to make it past the halfway point before the weather shut them down. To wander is to learn, but to spend time so frivolously in the woods as to simply exist just to party the days away, or relax constantly, not only lacks meaning, but also brings a life to lack purpose. If all one wants to do is party, just stay home, work until the weekend, and then go camping for a few days, trust me a man can buy a lot more beer that way.

As for me, I wanted to make it to Katahdin, I wanted this trip not to be just a relaxing walk about, but carry with it an air of accomplishment, and triumph. More importantly though, I did want to unwind, to enjoy this year away while I still possessed the youth to do it. I wanted to see things I had never even heard about, to walk where few others had the chance to be, to know the world and those that walk upon it, and hopefully in turn know myself. I do strongly believe that one can not legislate a man into freedom, nor can one party to prosperity, understanding the balance is crucial! The trail was sure to be full of chaos, and only by keeping order within myself would I be able to make it through.

7 HOME, BUT AWAY FROM HOME

Hiker-ism: Fire Tower

(Noun) Originally built for some lucky bastard to hang out in all day overlooking endless acres of forest for signs of fire, but most are now sadly retired due to more effective technology. Fortunately, many of them still stand atop some of the nation's greatest peaks, providing height insensitive hikers a chance to gaze over the grandeur of nature.

    I won't ever forget the feeling I got when I noticed that the trees had started to shift more and more towards being the longleaf pines that I had known for many years. After over three months of travel, the mountain path finally led me back to North Carolina, my home sweet home. Well, almost as far away from Wilmington (my dear city) as I could possibly be while in North Carolina, but still in my home state damn it all! It was a wonderful feeling seeing a tiny wooden sign bolted to a tree with hardly room enough on it to display the letters GA/NC, but that tiny plank in the middle of nowhere let me know that I had successfully made my way through the entire state of Georgia on home! Shuffleboard had made it there just before I did and was taking a break on the border, thus he was able to take my picture upon my arrival. I've tried to think of a time that I had seen him after that moment, but I cannot think of one. Not everyone makes it all the way to Maine and it's no surprise to lose people early. However I wish him well, on whatever path he chooses to walk in life.

    Out of pure joy from being reunited with my wonderful state I turned to the woods and shouted "Lucy, I'm home!" in remembrance of the TV show which had occupied many hours of my childhood. I felt like if I managed to find a way to smile any wider the corner of my mouth might be able to sip a beer at Cape Fear, or at least back up traffic from here to Raleigh. Seeing as traffic is always horrendous in the Raleigh Durham area it's probably good that I didn't, though my feet did fall rather easily the next few miles due to my good mood.

    February was running out quickly, but wasn't taking the winter with it. The ground was frozen solid, and in fact it had actually gotten cold enough to freeze the chocolate bars I was carrying, snapping one clean in two while in my pack! Many of the large rocks had icicles on them yet, and I spent entire days hiking clad in my heavy coat and scarf. Things got worse before they got better, especially since the temperature drops the higher above sea level one is and I was ever climbing at high elevation. On top of Standing Indian Mountain the trail had completely frozen over with large sheets of ice, which made hiking a bit tricky, but not impossible. I would simply have to slide from one exposed stone or root to another and try like hell not to fall on my ass as I made forward progress in this slow, cumbersome manner.

One of the mountains here in early North Carolina I will never forget as long as I live: Albert Mountain. The approach to the summit trail wasn't really anything special; actually it followed an old road and crossed it several times, which I was none too fond of. There's nothing like a paved strip of earth to ruin the solitude of nature. That being said the last 0.4 miles to the summit were the hardest to date! I remember looking over my guide book and completely missing it the morning before, seeing as a quick four hundred foot spike wasn't something my eyes were trained to look for just yet. However, what my eyes had missed my body sure noticed as the trail accelerated upwards at such a rate that it would have been impossible to pass if it was not for foot holds literally chiseled into large rocks. It was the sort of thing where one would have to reach over a rock as best one could, attempt to grip the earth on the other side, and carefully place one's feet in such places as to finally press over the obstacle just to find another one waiting beyond it! It was late in the day and I was already tired, making the short, but strenuous, climb up Albert Mountain toting over fifty pounds even harder.

What made the mountain memorable wasn't the effort needed to climb it, but rather what was waiting on top of it. The US department of agriculture had set up a tower to observe the surrounding area for the effects of forest clearing on soil erosion, with much success and very little damage to the natural environment I might add. Whether or not the tower was still used is unknown to me, but what I do know is that after pressing so hard to reach it there was no way I wasn't climbing the damn thing. It was an impressive structure to say the least; it stood higher than I care to think about, raised by four massive metal poles with cross braces in between them. It would have taken at least five lengths of my body to stretch from one leg to another, and inside of them all was a large metal staircase winding it's way to the top. Leaving my pack behind I braved the cool, windy steps which turned so many times I lost count as I tried my best to not look down. I had never really cared for heights, but years before I decided that my very rational fear was inconvenient and ill founded and took a course in rock climbing to remedy myself, which worked, but only after several knee shaking attempts.

Even previously breaking my internal desire to not be in a position to possibly plummet to my doom didn't make it easy to keep my nerves steady while climbing ever higher, not looking at anything but the next step until reaching a door cut into the uppermost platform and, sadly, blocking my entry. I had just thought of turning about and heading back down, but since I was here I might as well look up, and am so glad I did. I was well above any of the surrounding trees, and the view was astounding to say the least! It was cold, and the light wind caused my nose to run, but there was not a cloud in the sky and I could see for countless miles in all directions, gazing over where I had been, where I was, and where had yet to travel. What I remember most about this mile high sanctuary is the distant peaks visible for the first time. I had looked over some simple incredible vistas and views the entire time on the AT but never had I been able to see so far! I felt like I was completely lost in an untouched section of time and space, the very heart of nature. No homes, no farms, no roads, just mountains, trees, rock, and silence. If ever a prayer of peace on earth had been answered, it had settled here once the rest of the world ignored it.

I sat atop this metal work of man tucked away unnoticed in the middle of nowhere, gazing over it all as long as my freezing body could bare it. The sun started to cast a golden hue over the valleys, so lovely that even if I had frozen to my death there it wouldn't have been the worst of deaths--in fact, it would have been far more preferable than many I had heard of. However, there was more to see, and far more to do, so I finally pulled myself from my frigid perch and back to my gear to hike another day. To make things even more significant, the tower marked one hundred miles traveled on the AT, a milestone to be reckoned with, in my book. I felt accomplished, but didn't dwell upon my recent success, for as I said, there was still so much more to do.

The night after summiting Mount Albert was one of the coldest, if not the coldest, night I had spent outdoors. I felt it coming as I set up in a nearby shelter and thus utilized both of my blankets, tucked my head completely into my bag, and even covered my sleeping bag with my coat as best as I could. Hard to say how cold it got exactly, but even with all of that I was far from comfortable during the night. Needless to say I made it through, but come the morning I was in need of a hot drink and a warm room. On a related note, I was running low on supplies and the town of Franklin was not far off, and hopefully it would be the perfect place to unwind from a rather strenuous night.

The trail to Winding Stair Gap, where I intended to hitch into town, was not too difficult, and I arrived before noon. At the Gap a pair of hikers had just been dropped off from town, and while I didn't recogonize them it was obvious that they were in it for the long haul. Their packs were large and looked heavy, they were bundled from head to toe in cold weather gear, and the farewell they had given to the folks kind enough to drop them off was indeed a warm one. As I walked onto the road we greeted one another, although a bit hesitantly for some reason, if I recall right. The most likely reason is probably because I was a solo male hiker and they were a female team, barely a hundred miles into it all and still green, as we like to say on the trail.

Of the two the slightly shorter one with a bright, round face and unkempt curly hair went by the name Ibex, named after a breed of goat said to live in New England and given to her by her brother. She was remarkably high in spirit and one of the younger hikers I had met, seeing as she was only seventeen and had somehow managed to convince her high school to give her course credit for hiking the AT--a clever girl! The other was about my height, with pronounced cheeks and smiling eyes, her hair in a long braid hanging over one shoulder and a Russian style winter hat holding it all back as well as it could. I couldn't help but notice her ears; they were sure to already be quite pronounced but with her being as winter-ready as she was they were pushed forward and out, giving the appearance of either an alert deer or a wayward elf. She was called Moxie, a southern term meaning one who has drive, determination, and a will to persevere even in the face of overwhelming odds. They were heading north like myself, but had just come from town while I was intending to head in. However they offered me an apple as a parting gift and we hopped to see each other again soon.

Sadly, I didn't have much of a chance to enjoy the fruits of our introduction because no sooner had I stuck my thumb out on the side of the road did a car pull over and motion me closer. First try, first car, an incredibly rare event I like to call a 'Golden Thumb.' My new northbound friends stood dumbfounded at my luck, but who was I to ignore the kindness of a fellow North Carolinian?

The town of Franklin had just what I needed to restore my spirits, a nice warm cafe, piping hot coffee, and a place to stock up for the next week. My ride into town , a woman named Donna, actually paid for my lunch that day, and once back on the trail I survived another cold night warmed by a little coffee and the kindness of strangers.

Hiker-ism: Trail Angel

(noun) There are still saints that walk among us--many of their selfless acts will never be known, and even fewer of their names. Trail Angels practice random acts of kindness along the AT, usually in the form of snacks, but occasionally offer far greater help such as a place to stay, a hot shower, or some have even set up entire barbeques in the woods for hikers!

While wandering through trees so heavily covered with moss that they still appeared green though rendered leafless, I came across a man carrying absolutely no gear other than a walking stick and a bright orange hat. It seemed a bit out of the ordinary, but I didn't think much of it until we crossed paths and chatted for a moment. He told me that just up ahead some Trail Angels had set up and were offering a quick snack and a hot drink to any thru hiker who passed by and that I was welcome to come join them all. It seemed like I couldn't go a day without something awesome happening, but I wasn't complaining.

Not but a few minutes walk up the trail I encountered what I had been told of--only it was even better than what had been described to me! Not only were there a few kind souls passing around snacks but they had set up a large canvas tent which housed a few places to sit down, several propane burners to heat drinks with, and even a full blown wood stove to heat the place! It seems that I was a little late to the party and the tent was already buzzing with other hikers. There was Crash, a 2013 thru hiker at it again, Mudder Finger, Cool Story, Italian Stallion, and June Bug, all from the Philadelphia area and heading north. I was beginning to feel that being a solo hiker was the way less traveled and more people had opted to go with a group or at least a partner, though previously I had figured it would have been the other way around. We all managed to find a place to rest and enjoy each others company for a time in the large, warm tent, and I even managed to snag a cup of coffee and a few snacks to refuel my weary legs. The Trail Angels told us we could stay for the night if we liked, but that they were leaving soon and would be back sometime tomorrow, an opportunity everyone but me took them up on for I felt they had done enough for me. That and I felt a little alienated by this group of friends; I'm not sure exactly what it was that I didn't really care for about them, but they seemed a bit stuck on themselves I guess is the best way to put it. They had been telling me about a pair of hikers they were trying to lose, unsuccessfully, the last few days because they found them odd and annoying. I wasn't sure, but I almost felt as if I may like those that they were trying to lose better then present company.

    I didn't have to wonder long, because low and behold the other two showed up before I set out. One stood a little shorter then me, thick build, with a bit of a belly and a short but full beard light in color and curly; his name was Doc. The other was tall and thin, with long arms and legs and a smile ten miles wide. It's a bit hard to describe this young man at the point I met him--he had this youthful look about him, almost like he had just spread his wings and was off to see the world for the first time. We called him Mountain Mime. Mime had grown up Mennonite in Lancaster PA, and had gotten his name for miming the crucifixion of Christ outside a grocery store in one of the trail towns not long ago passed. An odd naming to say the least, but the kid's heart was as good as gold.

    I left them all at the tent and made it a few more miles to a lonely little shelter up the trail. It was an old one to say the least and had fallen into disrepair, but the roof was solid and its sides still bore the names of bored, knife wielding hikers from as far back as 1978. I was full of energy still, despite the setting sun, and decided to build a fire so as to attempt to enjoy the night a little. I wouldn't consider myself an expert fire starter, but I'm far better than most. That being said it proved to be a bit tricky today for some reason. I had ample amounts of wood, though none of it perfectly dry, and plenty of dry leaves to try and kindle a blaze. After several attempts I finally managed to get a small, steady flame burning in the center of a mass of sticks and began to blow softly on it in an effort to keep it alive. At this time Mime and Doc appeared, and without hesitation Mime dropped his gear and began to fan the flame with me. I hadn't really expected his help so it came as a bit of a shock, but between the two of us we soon had a good blaze burning strongly in the young darkness, keeping us warm and well lit. I asked if they were going to stay in the shelter tonight, to which they responded yes and no. They were staying in the immediate area, but were setting up their tents, and no sooner than they had arrived they went to it, disappearing just out of sight. It all seemed strange to me, but I tried not to think about it and just enjoyed my little fire which managed to burn softly most of the night, rekindled every now and then by a gust of winter air and softly lighting the little shelter where I laid to sleep.

In the morning I awoke to find that it had snowed the night before, a sight I hadn't expected. It wasn't much, but enough to cover the ground, making the trail appear clean and new. I had gotten used to being up and at it early, thus leaving the other two hikers in the area behind as my feet broke through fresh frost. It was fun really, I knew that no one had walked this section of trail before me today, and in the trail's present state it looked almost like no one had ever hiked it at all.

One particular vista stopped me dead in my tracks as I tried to take it all in. A dense fog had settled over the mountains due to the frost, but at this elevation the peaks of other mountains could still be seen in the distance, almost like islands in a sea of mist. The one that held my interest for a moment stood alone in the distance, its base completely covered and a light, billowing cloud appeared to break like an ocean wave upon its side. Another cloud wrapped around the summit in a sort of ghostly embrace, picturesque, powerful, and yet somehow so simple, it brought a tear to my eye for the first time in far too long. The snow faded before the day was out, but I will always remember the brief renewal inside me that occurred on this old trail.

Not making it to a shelter one previously planned to doesn't seem like too big of a deal from an outside perspective, just find a camp sight and add in a few more miles the next day, or readjust the next night's destination, right? Well, yes and no. I never planned my trip farther then the next resupply point, normally three to four days at a time, thus allowing me to adapt quickly to a setback, sporadic blue blaze, or something that caught my eye and deserved a little more of my time to be looked at. However, to paraphrase Newton's first law, nothing is without consequence, the biggest one in this scenario being supplies, or rather the lack thereof. Every setback requires food one hadn't planned to consume and therefore doesn't have, and while I did try to carry an extra days worth at all times it can easily be lost for one reason or another. After suffering several setbacks in one such section a quick assessment of supplies concluded that I needed to resupply by the end of the day or go without breakfast tomorrow. I almost could have concluded that just by picking up my now pathetic deflated foodstuffs bag, but nevertheless I now had no other choice this day than to press forward to Fontana Dam, over twenty miles away.

Having done plus twenty mile days in Florida and south Georgia, it didn't seem impossible to pull off; I had gotten used to hiking in the mountains and was feeling strong and up to the challenge. That being said, if there was one thing I wish I could have taught myself before setting off to hike, it would be how to read a fucking guide book! The first nine miles of the day were none too easy, many ups and downs to keep things interesting, but it was nothing compared to what was to follow them. Later in my travels I learned that if a section of a trail carried a specific nickname which had stuck well enough to have it documented, it's going to be anything but ordinary. In addition, the more formidable the name the more difficult it was bound to be, and such was the case with Jacob's Ladder. When I hit this particular stretch of trail my rate of travel was cut by more than half, not even making a mile's progress in an hour. The first ascent was so difficult that I could barely move a hundred yards without having to stop and lean upon my walking stick in order to regain some of my strength. The greatest victories come after the hardest challenges however, and the view from the summit rang hearty with calls of victory as the mountain fell in my wake. Though worn and dripping with sweat I felt suddenly invigorated as my small conquest resonated within me, and I was northbound again after only a moment's rest to look over the mountain vista.

Whether I was tired or not, there was no way around the ten miles that still needed to be traveled before I could rest. It was far from easy going, but due to the sense of accomplishment I was carrying my pack didn't seem quite as heavy, and I made good time. Sadly, the sun was nowhere near as invigorated as I was, and made to call it a day at its scheduled time, forcing me to go without it with four miles yet to go. In the last rays of the day I considered setting up--I wasn't going to be able to resupply tonight even if I did make it into the village and breakfast was now a long forgotten dream. It's the principle of the thing however that kept me going, I had nothing to prove to anyone or anything but myself and yet I had to make it tonight simply because I said I would. Perhaps the fact that the promise was made to myself is what caused it to be so important. For years I had stopped short of what I set out for, or avoided making goals all together so as to not fall short of them, it was easier to not try and not feel bad about it than to risk failure and disappointment. Nothing ventured nothing gained I would say, but lived nothing ventured nothing lost. Not this time.

    Forgoing a struggle in the morning and transferring it onto this evening, I abandoned the rational decision and pressed on into the last of the day's natural light. By the time I hit Walker Gap, three miles from Fontana Shelter, all sunlight had been lost, but I waited as long as possible before reaching for my flashlight--it only had so much juice and on my budget I needed it to last as long as possible. The path became rocky at times, with large natural rock stairs cut into the mountain side, and the well beaten path became nothing but a faint shadow against the dry, dead leaves surrounding it. It was time to switch the light on before I got hurt.

    One problem: my flashlight is gone. It was a crushing discovery-- had I'd of known that I had lost my light this morning I would not have been nearly foolhardy enough to hike well into the dead of night! Further more, while I did know my gear inside and out, setting up with zero light would be incredibly difficult if not impossible thanks to the makeshift repairs I had made, even if there was flat ground in the area in which to pitch a tent on. Undoubtedly out of options, I had to keep going, I had to find a way.

    To this day I'm not entirely sure how I managed to make my way, but I do know that I used my sense of hearing and feel far more than my sight, contrary to what I had become accustomed to. Hard earth and a low, thumping noise meant my feet were still on the trail, while a soft step and a loud crunch meant I was now off the trail and should take a step back. Using my walking stick as a blind man would I miraculously avoided large rocks and roots, and traversed the still present stone stairs the same way. Even in the dark I would sometimes make out a white blaze when I passed about three feet from it, and there are few things on this earth I had found more beautiful at this time. However, if they did have any competition it would have been the dam I was hiking towards, Fontana Dam to be specific. The top edge was lit brilliantly with a series of soft white lights, with brighter lights at each end. Standing like a beacon against the night, I poked, shuffled, and stumbled towards it, ever astonished at my own ability to make progress in such conditions. I traveled for over an hour like this, hardly able to see my own hand at an arm's length, before finally emerging onto a paved, lit road, and the way to Fontana Village!

There was a shelter a mile further down the trail, but I had achieved my goal, and felt no need to go any further. There was a bathroom here at the road, which was not only spacious and well lit, but also warm with running water, and so it became my shelter for the night. I was beat, my shoulders were bruised, my legs were dead, and my feet were swollen, but I was also at peace, satisfied and proud of myself for the first time in ages. This wasn't the first time in my life that I fell asleep next to a toilet, but it was the first time I was happy about it.

The next morning was rough, but the success of the day before carried me through. I did indeed have to go without breakfast, but not for long as I managed to find a convenience store that served hot food. After a plate of the most amazing, grotesque, sloppy, heart stopping, disgusting and glorious gas station jalapeno chili nachos covered in some sort of synthetic goop that one would have to stretch the imagination to truly call cheese, I was ready to go. The whole time I partook of this gelatinous tub that even the hungriest of racoons would pass up, my mouth cried for joy while my stomach wept at the damage it was about to endure. In the end my stomach was right, but I'd do it again in a heart beat!

Fontana Village is a seasonal town, only open during the height of hiker season, and I was about a week early. What this boils down to is that the store at which I had hoped to resupply was now closed, but between the convince store and a bait shop on a lake close to where I had spent the previous night, I was able to acquire what I needed. I decided to stay at the shelter in Fontana that night; even though it only meant progressing a mile on the trail, I needed the rest. Not only that, but the shelter in Fontana is called The Fontana Hilton, and it's rumored to be one of the nicest on the trail. Indeed, the waterfront, two level, wooded shelter is a beautiful sight, but the real reason it was so appealing is the fact that there was a free hot shower in a proper bathroom just a hundred yards from the shelter! After cleaning up and a day of rest, my strength was regained, and I now felt sure that I had conquered the last thing that would have stopped me for good during this trip: myself.

Smoky Mountain National Park: one of the most remote and well kept treasures of the American Southeast. The day that I crossed Fontana Dam into this sanctuary it was cold, but calm, and the air hung thick with mist from the man-made reservoir, patchy and mysterious. The fog hung low but was very broken up, and at times from the tops of distant peaks were visible but only for moment as they were soon hidden again in the swirling haze. It's not very often that I am made happy by hiking in cold, wet air, but the sights outweighed the burden ten fold and actually provided me with an incredibly unique, and nearly indescribable, experience. The reservoir was just warm enough to allow the water to mist instead of freeze but the air was cold enough for the fog to freeze upon whatever it touched. The ground kept itself warm, as it tends to in the spring, and thus resisted the air's icy grasp, but the trees were not so lucky and stood covered in ice crystals protruding a solid inch off of their branches. Not just the branches mind you, but the trunks, the needles, the entirety of each tree, from mature pine to freshly sprouted sapling, completely covered in ice. It was a marvelous sight; the trees were painted white and still, while the path still stood firm and visible giving the forest a truly otherworldly feel. A dense, smoky mist still hung in the air, keeping my visibility under fifty yards and making it feel as if I was truly walking in a dream. In all of my winters I have never seen anything like it, nor do I believe I will again. I was simply awe stricken to be wandering in that which poets and novelists had tried in vain to describe since the invention of writing. The mist stood thick until roughly midday, where it then retreated from the advance of warmer air, taking my enchanted forest with it. It was at this time that I found myself under aerial bombardment as the ice lost its grip and the trees flung it from their limbs with a loud crack and a youthful spring. Can't say I was complaining though, I would gladly trade a hundred impromptu ice showers for just five more minutes of walking in the frost covered Smokeys.

    The Smokies are considered to be one of the more challenging sections on the entire AT, and it is a reputation well earned. However, it's also said that if one can make it through these majestic mountains, then one can make it all the way to Maine. The range follows the NC/TN border so closely that at times it's impossible to tell exactly which state one is currently hiking in, but when looking over the topography from one of the many stunning summits, such as Rocky Top, it was easy to see why the line was drawn there. Looking east into grand old North Carolina, the mountains stood strong, shrouded in mist and rising and falling as far as the eye could see, while a look to the west into Tennessee was so dramatically different that it almost didn't look natural. The mountains stop nearly instantly and the low, flat, smooth Tennessee river valley stretched ever onward, with settlements here and there by those lucky enough to have staked their claim. The trail was narrow and winding along the ridges, but well beat and easy to follow, a challenge well worth the effort.

Perhaps one of the most wonderful things about the Smokies is the fact that it is not only a National Park but also a Nature Preserve, meaning that no hunting is allowed within its boundaries. As a result of this, the wildlife was virtually fearless of humans, so much so that I would almost swear that songbirds would perch upon one's shoulder when resting and snakes would smile when passing by them. I'm of course exaggerating, but I do know for certain that the deer were particularly bold in this part of the country, acknowledging hikers as a potential food source instead of an enemy. While the deer were aware of the long standing truce, I however was not, and when I encountered a few on the trail I quickly grabbed my camera and tried to be still so as to not scare them off. They wandered ever closer and I couldn't believe that they didn't see or smell me, and I sat there overjoyed to be taking pictures of deer closer than I had ever been to one before. Then one walked within ten feet of me and I now knew that these nimble, strong, elegant, yet rather dumb creatures simply didn't mind me being there and probably saw me as more of a nuisance to walk around than anything else. It really was an astounding thing to witness, to see such blatant disregard for what I thought should be a natural instinct. I couldn't help but wonder, if even wild deer can learn to live and trust in men, why do we have so much trouble living with each other?

The crown jewel of the Smokies has to be the tower at Clingmans Dome. At 6,655 feet above sea level Clingmans Dome is the highest point on the entire AT, towering over even the great peaks of Mt. Washington and Katahdin! Atop the summit is a large cement tower unlike any I'd seen before or since, with a large concrete observation platform that sits on top of a massive concrete pillar and a large walkway leading up to it. It's the walkway that is most impressive actually, it starts near the base of the observation platform's pillar and loops over the trees, raising ever slightly upwards until it crosses back over itself and connects with the platform. It was a very cold day when I arrived here, and the wind was blowing hard, but I'd be damned before I not see the view from the top of this intriguing structure. It was well worth it to endure the elements, for the platform stood well above the surrounding trees and while the air was cold it was also clear, and I felt as though I could have seen all the way to Wilmington if I would have strained my eyes hard enough. The distant mountains, still cobalt blue, completely surrounded the tower, and while I felt small and lost in the middle of such grandeur I also felt strong and empowered knowing that I now stood as a part of it, and in turn it began to feel like part of me as well. To be surrounded by such raw and untouched beauty pulls strongly at the very heart of a man, face to face with the humble origins of his creation and the earth that provided the means for his advancement.

Because Fontana Village was still closed for the season I was, again, nearly out of supplies, but I had rationed well and therefore had made it to Newfound Gap in fair condition, where I hoped to find a ride into town. It was a good spot to hitch from, the road was busy compared to any others I had crossed in the park, and traffic still moved slow enough here for me to catch their attention. It didn't take long at all really until a nice Hispanic couple pulled over and offered me a lift. The gentleman driving the vehicle didn't say too much, I don't think his English was very good, but the woman was very able to hold a conversation and we talked the whole twelve miles into Tennessee. She had just recently lost her foot, and nearly her life, to a nasty spider bite, but was surprisingly upbeat and thankful for another day of living. I'll say again that I swear the happiest people I've ever met are the ones with far less than most--it seems a little struggle does wonders for the soul.

It was a very interesting ride down the mountain, the road wound and twisted its way ever downward, at one point looping under itself when there was no other way to safely descend, until we arrived in Gatlinburg, TN. The first view of the town is a little strange I must say, like some sort of tourist trap with nothing but odd shops, arcades, half assed sideshows, and a few bars. I didn't know what to expect when I decided to come to Gatlinburg, but it was bound to be an experience. My new friends dropped me off right in the middle of this bazaar, and I thanked them for the help. It's always interesting to see who can be met when hitching a ride.

Suddenly inspired by a Johnny Cash song, I had just hit town and my throat was dry so I thought I'd stop and have myself a brew. A quick wander about revealed that there was no place on the strip that fell within my budget, so I decided to walk to the closest grocery store and ask around as I gathered the things I needed for the days to come. The cashier was a little young to know anything about the local bar scene, but her co worker knew a place just around the corner called 3 Jimmys that he thought would suit my needs, and so I set out to find it by street light as the evening set in. I figured I'd just settle in and have a beer before setting out to find a nice church to camp behind and hitching back to the trail in the morning.

I found the place easy enough, and it was indeed my kind of place. It was well built, with lots of wood grain, but not too much, and the bar is a classic horseshoe, two toned, with just the right amount of lighting, being dim and casual. They have several taps of craft beer, but that wasn't my speed this night, I was just after something cheap and simple to sip on after going so long without. I had always known the South to be friendly, and the patrons of 3 Jimmys were no exception. In next to no time I was talking with a few folks about my travels and life out on the trail, and many were so interested they insisted on buying the next few rounds! I started to feel like I was right back at home, chatting with a handful of good folks, knocking a few back--I even got suckered into a round of karaoke--and I began to lose track of time while just enjoying being there. A middle aged man walked behind the bar as the night went on; his hair was thinning, stood about my height, thin but hearty, and with a sort of kindness about him. He walked up to me and asked if I wanted a shot of something, so I said I'd like a shot of gin, a liquor I had grown a fondness for even though I knew of few others who shared it. He seemed a little surprised by my request and brought up a bottle missing roughly seven eighths of its contents and set it on the bar before me.

"Finish it off!" he said. "No one orders it and I'm not even going to restock it once this is gone."

Feeling blessed, I began to do as I was told, and asked him for his name in return. I soon found out that my new friend James Woods was part owner of the establishment, and from word of mouth I heard that he was by far the more active of the partners. It's hard to recall exactly where the conversation went from there, most likely due to a sudden influx of alcohol, but we both thoroughly enjoyed one another's company, so much so that James even offered me a place to stay. Who was I to refuse such charity? A warm place to stay seamed like a Godsend after slipping and sliding over the ice-covered

Clingmans Dome all day. And so after a short James, his Girlfriend, and myself were loaded up and driving over to his place just down the road, with a few beers and high spirits in tow.

James' place was simple, yet elegant. It stood on the banks of a wide, quick moving stream that was apparently quite good for fishing. The house had two stories and a large deck on the second floor for entertaining, and the interior was a cozy, retro, closed floor plan that seemed to be built sometime in the early 70's. James had a roommate, Kirk, a man just slightly older than myself with short, curly black hair and who made his living playing music wherever he could. He was a bit eccentric, but a kind fellow, and we all became friends close to instantly.

I forget who first said that they were hungry, though I don't think it was me for once, but that didn't mean I wasn't thinking it. Either way, Kirk started rummaging through the cupboards and refrigerator to see what he could come up with, and soon settled on jambalaya. So there I was, with three people I had just met, chopping onions, drinking beer and joking while half drunk and trying to come up with a halfway decent pot of jambalaya at nearly three in the morning. I don't think there is anywhere else I would have rather been. I must say that things turned out quite well, ending the night with a hot meal, good times, and even a warm bed next to the fireplace which served to heat the home.

In the morning I restored the fire, scored a hot shower, and was soon greeted by my host who was still glad to have me about. James' lady friend had to be getting to work, so we all rushed out of the house to ensure she wouldn't be late and arrived just in time. After that he asked if I'd like some breakfast; 3 Jimmys was also a restaurant and he assured me that his stuff was the freshest around. Frankly, a warm PopTart instead of a cold one would have seemed like heaven to me at this point, so I decided to take him up on what ever he felt like serving. James took great pride in his establishment, and had actually built a fair amount of it himself--from the outdoor seating to the bar to the booths to the stage, this was his place. There was a large meat smoker in the back that had just been installed and I got a brief tutorial on how to properly smoke bacon, and it's quite a process! I also had the pleasure of meeting the kitchen staff and a few waitresses, after working in the service industry I always like getting a quick look behind the scenes, and James seemed to treat his employees well. We then sat down for a few cups of coffee and waited for whatever the chef felt like serving up, and this way got to know each other with sober minds.

James was a very interesting person to listen to. He had studied religion and had even spent several years overseas studying in the Far East. He was a very spiritual person, yet claimed no major religion, and was very focused on practicing meditation and consuming wholesome food. One thing I'll never forget him saying was how it hard it was to meet someone who had spent a lot of time in nature who wasn't spiritual in some way, and I found it a statement nearly impossible to argue against. I had been wandering for roughly eighty days at this point, and felt profoundly different. I didn't stress about little things, or even big things for that matter, I smiled all day everyday without even trying, and I did feel connected to something greater then myself. It's impossible to describe the feeling, to be completely in control of one's own self but also feel as though there is something meant for you to do or see anywhere and everywhere you end up.

After an exchanging of ideas and a phenomenal omelet, it was time to part ways, and James offered his services one last time by giving me a ride back up to the trail. We took the same winding road that had brought me to Gatlinburg, and I swear that to this day I have never forgotten the kindness of a man who was not but twelve hours ago a stranger.

The familiar smokey mist still hung in the air, thus giving the mountain range its name, but it had warmed up quite a bit from the days before so hiking was far more pleasant. I don't think I had ever seen mist like I had in the Smokies, for it was incredibly patchy yet nearly everywhere, white and bright, so dense that one couldn't see through it and yet it didn't block out the sun. Whether or not blue skies were visible was only a matter of a few hundred yards. It was a good thing the mist didn't block one's view of the path though, for there were times where it seemed as though one bad step might spell a hiker's doom as the trail would be consistently narrow and incredibly steep sided. I remember passing through an area so completely comprised of boulders that rock hopping through was particularly dangerous, but the unobstructed views were almost to die for.

While traveling through this incredible landscape I encountered a pair of hikers sitting on a log, trying to decide whether or not they wanted to stay at the shelter just down a side trail from where they sat. I don't remember much about the gentleman other then he had short, dark hair and a bright red fleece; the woman on the other hand I don't believe I'll ever forget. She was wearing some sort of colorful plastic skirt, and stood about as high as my shoulders. She was very thin, but strong, with shoulder length blond hair, fair skin, a wide nose, and vibrant green eyes that sparkled like precious stones. Her name was Emerald. I joined in their debate for a little bit--it was far from getting dark, but it would be a stretch to get to the next shelter before the day was out. Having just gotten out of Gatlinburg, I didn't quite feel like stopping early today and decided to go for the farther one, they decided to stay, but I figured I would see them again.

It was far from an easy hike to the next shelter, I really had to push to get there, but made it just before nightfall. It appeared that I wasn't going to be alone staying the night here, there was a group of six men when I arrived, and they had already started a good fire and gotten set up. However, the most notable thing about their presence wasn't the good company, but the fact that they had two camp stoves frying fish, potatoes in the fire, and vegetables as well. Even though there were already six of them, they insisted that I help them eat some of this schmorgasboard, for they had brought way too much for the overnight trip and weren't about to haul any of this back down the mountain. It was pretty obvious they were a little green, so I accepted the request for aid, and I think I ate more than any of them! It was far from a warm night, but the fire helped, and the seven of us spent the evening enjoying the wilderness. Some of the younger ones would step outside and howl to celebrate the lack of civilization--it really is amazing what even twenty four hours in the woods will do for a person.

I was awakened in the middle of the night by a sudden, and unpleasant, urge to vomit. I had at first thought that it may be due to food poisoning, but soon logically deduced rather that this sensation had been brought about by the fact that I had eaten literally pounds of food and neglected to drink a single ounce during the endeavor. I sprung from my bag while pulling on my hoodie and made for the spring just outside. The grass was now crunchy and frost covered, and in my haste I neglected to wear my boots, but the cold had to be endured seeing as I desperately needed water. The spring wasn't hard to find even though I was still without a light, and good thing it was, seeing as I felt like I was about to lose my free dinner. I settled my stomach after dumping over a liter of ice cold spring water into it, and while my feet were burning with frostbite and my innards were still a bit on edge, I must say the stars were particularly lovely that evening.

    Personally, I would have rather hiked into the Smokies three times then hiked out of them once. The way up had been a hard and strenuous one, but the way down was relentlessly downhill, and my knees were absolutely killing me by the end of it! However, I believe it was weather the likes of which I hiked in that day that spawned the first nomads, it was so pleasant to walk in one couldn't help but try and go a little farther just to see what was a few steps ahead. I had the option to stay in the Park one more night at Davenport Gap, but decided instead to go a little farther and set up my tent for the first time in close to a week. This proved to be a good idea, as I found a great spot on a small island surrounded on all sides by a lively little creek and accessible via a downed tree that served as a bridge. To make things better, upon setting up I found that I hadn't lost my light after all, just rolled it up in my tent, still attached to the roof where it had served as a light to write by. Simple mistake, but in a way it felt like I had just acquired a brand new light and wouldn't have to buy one in the next town.

Hiker-ism: Bald

(noun) A bald is a type of mountaintop completely void of trees but nearly always covered in thick grass. First used as grazing grounds for local livestock farmers, balds now offer beautiful views and usually deep, muddy, slick trails.

    One of the great viewpoints in North Carolina is on top of Max Patch bald, also called Mack's Patch depending on how old the person you ask is. The treeless summit provides excellent views of low rolling hills and distant valleys coupled with grand peaks far off in the distance, and is truly not one to be missed. Or so I hear. My experience coming over Max Patch was far from pleasant, and even in hindsight I refuse to say it wasn't that bad, which is quite a statement from an overly devoted optimist. It was the weather in which I crossed that made for such a fowl experience, though it wasn't a blizzard, or a hurricane, but rather fog so thick that it was impossible to see more than ten yards ahead and winds stronger than any I had hiked in before or since. It was one of those winds where one could honestly lean into it and balance upright far past one's center of gravity, resting only on the wind itself!

The trail to Max Patch is well guarded with trees to block the wind so I had no idea what I was getting into when I started the day's hike, it wasn't the best of days but I believe I had seen worse. It was close to midday when I arrived and I remember the exact moment where I knew things were going to get dicey. There is a stair made of timbers and earth leading from a dirt road to the mountain top, and I remember standing at the base of this stair looking up and hardly believing what I was seeing. At the top of the stair, any protection from the elements was completely lost and the wind blew the fog with such force that the difference in weather could actually be seen with naked eye, and it looked like some sort of wind tunnel that aircraft manufacturers use to observe airflow over an new airfoil. "This is going to suck," I said to no one in particular, and made my attempt to pass through the torrent.

It's not very often in life that a man hates to be right, but this was one of those times. As soon as I left the stair the wind and moisture hit me with such force that I nearly lost my balance, clutching my hat to my breast so as to not lose it. I was bundled as best as I could in what I had, but even protected as such the cold, quick mist hit with such force that its icy bane seemed to cut right to the core of me, stinging painfully on any bit of exposed skin. I don't know how far I had to go like this but whatever the distance was it was far too far, for I was unable to see even the posts bearing white blazes to mark the way. I relied heavily on the beaten path, hoping there wasn't a side trail. Eventually the treeline, which meant an end to this frozen hell, became visible through the dense fog, and I raced towards it, thankfully not having far too go.

It seems my fortunes were set to change at this point, for not but a hundred yards into the trees a group of gentlemen had set up camp and had managed to get a good sized fire going despite the occasional gust of potentially extinguishing wind. I asked if I may join them for a minute to warm my bones a bit, and not only did they accept but also offered me a beer! While crossing over the blustery bald I had honestly said that I was going to need a beer after this, my long standing resolution to hard times, but I didn't expect it to actually happen. Ask and you shall receive they say, and I guess it's true at times. Occasionally in life, if there's nothing one can do about a shitty situation, then there's nothing one can do, just press on through it and hope there's something better on the other side--like beer!

It's a wonderful hike into Hot Springs; the mountain path loops along the mountain side, ducking in and out of ravines and crevices as it makes its way gradually downwards. The town itself is visible from a ways off, and is absolutely charming from a distance! The entire thing couldn't be made of more than eight streets in total, but it still boasted a picturesque downtown complete with a small church in the center. In a way it gets frustrating when being able to see a town from so far off, for the trail is long and hard and what little rest one can find is always appreciated. Thus every step with town in sight seems to only cover half the distance of a normal one, but all good things do come with time.

My friend Meagan lives close to the town of Hot Springs, and I had gone months without seeing a familiar face so I dropped her a line and she agreed to come meet me. Megan is a lovely young woman, short and bubbly, bright eyed and bushy tailed with a sort of motherly quality about her. She and I had worked together in Wilmington before she moved to the mountains to start a family. I could hardly contain my excitement upon seeing her, like a long lost memory of pleasant times come back to life, and we spent the afternoon sharing stories from both the trail and the world. Over endless pints of lovely brew Megan filled me in on the latest news from home--I soon found that one of my better friends had passed away and that two others had gotten married, all of which came as quite a shock. There are major events in life that will be missed when one is off traveling, and it is regrettable, but life is not meant to be seen from a stationary viewpoint, and without travel, the greatest lessons in life will never be learned.

It's hard to describe the feeling of one's heart breaking and growing all at the same time, but I realized that I felt such because my friends had become such a part of me that I could no longer be myself without having known them. Everyone that I had ever known has shaped me in some way, making me who I am today, and I can only hope that I have had the same effect on them. Thus, as long as the story of one continues, so does the story of all, and while the names and faces are long lost to history, as long as people interact with people the impact remains and the world will forever be changed from each person who had existed in it.

After parting ways with Megan my original plan was to camp just outside, but I soon found a better option just while walking down the street. A family with a young girl stopped to talk to me, seeing as my appearance at this point virtually screamed 'thru hiker,' and I must say it was indeed a pleasant meeting. It didn't take long before they asked me where I was staying and I told them my plans, the likes of which they decided simply wouldn't do and that I was to spend the evening with them. Any fear of strangers I had was completely gone by this point in my travels, and so I piled into their family car and off we went a short distance to their little mountain home just outside of town. There were three generations living under a single roof, the youngest member being Violet, a very kind and outgoing girl with a heart to help others; Lynda, Violet's mother; Robert, and Violet's grandmother whom we simply called the Boss Lady. They were the very definition of a southern hippie family, spiritual but not religious, kind and giving and expecting nothing in return, and just down right good people. I spent that evening chatting with the Boss Lady about life and what came after it, and we both agreed that it seems there's far too many little things in life that line up far too well for there not to be some sort of guiding hand in it all. However after a fine meal and good nights rest it was time to part ways again, and in hindsight I really can't believe how well it all worked out.

On my way out of town I decided to attend a church service in the morning, though the congregation couldn't have consisted of more than fifteen people including the pastor. I had long wondered how people worshiped in areas of small population, and it proved to be quite an experience. It reminded me more of a bible study then a church service, but I enjoyed my time there, and as soon as we said grace it was time to be back in the woods. Even though I had only been back in town for a day it was good to be roaming the wild--once one becomes accustomed to life away from civilization it's hard, if not completely impossible, to come back from it.

8 NEW FRIENDS AND NEW COUNTRY

Hiker-ism: Privy

(Noun) When hiking, there are two options when it comes to relieving one's self. The more readily available option is to venture slightly off the trail, dig a small hole, and take care of business. The other is usually only available at shelters, and that is a tiny wooden building that contains a toilet seat strategically positioned over a large, above ground pile of poo...stinky.

When I decided to strike out for adventure, I went with the notion that I was going to figure it out as I went along, which I certainly did. However, to anyone thinking about following in my footsteps let me just stress the importance of hand sanitizer! It's hard to believe that such a little thing can make such a difference but trust me, this undoubtedly does! Hand sanitizer was about as far from my list of necessary hiking items as could be when I started my trip, and here I was just shy of a hundred days in the woods before I figured this out. The method by which I happened across such a discovery was a bit unfortunate sadly, for it was here, on the North Carolina/Tennessee border, that I encountered the feared contagion that threatens every long distance hiker: the NORO virus.

NORO virus is a very communicable form of Giardia, a nasty stomach bug that really messes up one's digestive tract. Well, hard to say it messes up one's digestive tract, rather it greases up the sucker and makes it nearly impossible to hold anything in at all. That, paired with a fever and terrible stomach cramps, makes NORO a real bitch to endure, and thanks to the living conditions in shelters on the trail it's also really easy to spread and contract. Most hikers who have good sanitation habits can avoid this nasty stomach flu, but it should be fairly obvious by now that I wasn't one of the lucky ones. In fact, I hadn't even heard of the disease until well after I had suffered it, though I'll never forget what it was like.

The first day that I felt under the weather was by far the worst of it. I felt pretty off and only managed to make it about eight miles before I shut down for the day to rest in a shelter and hopefully sleep it off. I will say that I was glad to have stopped when I did, though I didn't do much sleeping. It seems like just about every hour I was running off to the privy so as to not mess my bag--it would have been a real pain to wash and dry out here in the woods especially seeing as it wasn't all that warm out just yet. While I had hoped that the short day and long night would knock out whatever it was that was bothering me, the reality was that it was going to take more than just a single day's rest to rid myself of this nasty little virus.

We have a saying on the AT: *it's not a matter of if you shit your pants, it's when*--though I'll be honest, it was not this day! Not to say that I wasn't close a few times, though. It's not a common thing for people my age to go hiking anymore sadly, and therefore the majority of my generation will never know the simple joy of using a downed log as a toilet seat in the middle of nowhere, shamelessly laughing at the horrible, yet comical, noises being produced by one's own hind end, taking solace in the fact that there's no one else around for miles to cast judgment on such a terrible excretion of stool and sick. It's the little things in hiking that will either make a person's trip wonderful or awful depending on how one views them, and a bad case of woodland runs is undoubtedly one of them.

It would take quite some time before my case of NORO fully cleared up, but it quickly took a backseat to the other things that were going on in my travels. For example, taking a day off had allowed for Emerald to get quite a ways ahead of me and for Mime and Doc to catch back up with me. Mime and Doc had managed to bring with them a few new faces as well; one was a stout, experienced hiker with short black hair and a goatee to match, whom Mime had named Iron Man due to this man's resemblance to the movie/comic book character Tony Stark, the other was a taller, thin guy with a healthy head of curly blond hair who would be named Extra Mile later down the trail due to a wrong turn. The new duo had been good friends back in the world and in fact had been hiking together many times before, just usually with a lot of camera gear so as to make a documentary. They proved to be good company, and a pair that I always enjoyed seeing.

That being said, these two new faces weren't the only new ones I would get to know--in fact there were three others whom I met at the same time. Three Germans who had watched the same documentary on the AT that I had, which apparently had just recently been translated from English, were out here to try their luck: Milk Monster, his girlfriend Wall-E, and another friend of theirs called Pillow. The Germans spoke English well enough to be good company, but preferred to keep to themselves most of the time. It would seem that my little soiree had allowed for me to spend a bit more time with other people, and I must admit it was a very welcome change. I very much treasure the people whom I met on the AT, for they aren't the type who just sit around and talk about their dreams, but rather full out try and make them a reality. For that reason, and many others, those whom chance to meet out on this backwoods byway across America become friends quickly, and with nearly no exception to the rule.

Whether one starts hiking solo or with other people, it doesn't take long to start teaming up. One such group I encountered was on the first day of spring, at a campsite just outside of Erwin, TN. They were a rather colorful group of individuals, consisting of a tall but fit man named Apple Jacks, a short bearded fellow called Wing Nut, a portly and hairy brewer named Red Beard, the well-read Milk and Beer, and an Alabama native with a fantastic mustache named Cola. The five of them went by Stink-o de Mayo in a clever play off of the renowned Mexican holiday, seeing as there was five of them, they smelled like thru hikers, and they all had a love of Mexican food and margaritas. Hiking with these boys was an interesting endeavor, it was always anything but quiet around them, but they were always good for a laugh. The six of us hiked into Erwin together, a small town in the middle of the mountains that boasted an all you can eat Kentucky Fried Chicken, a few grocery stores, and just over sixty Free Will Baptist churches. I'm not entirely sure what makes a Free Will Baptist different from a regular Baptist, but the only definition I could get from one of the locals was that if someone goes to church on Sunday and doesn't like the color tie the pastor is wearing, they go off and start their own church.

Erwin is also home to the infamous hiker hostel going by the name of Uncle Johnny's, home of the sixty cent Snickers bar, which is about half price compared to everywhere else. When the six of us arrived at this hiker friendly hovel Doc and Mime were already there, along with Cool Story, Crash, Mudder Finger, Italian Stallion, and June Bug, which made for a rather lively gathering on the front porch.

It's something to be marveled at when a bunch of thru hikers get together; there's never a sour face to be found among them, and conversation can range something as simple as the weather to the very meaning of life and travel. I figured that by now I had traveled over one thousand miles by foot, but everyone gathered here had at least gone three hundred without stopping, which is quite a feat in and of itself! We were all experienced hikers by this point, but we had so far yet to go. I know for a fact that the most common word to escape a hikers lips is undoubtedly "food," but a close second at this point has to be "Katahdin." I remember thinking that we could sooner fathom what it would be like to shoot pixy dust out of our nose than to experience the complex surge of emotions the summit of that final mountain would bring, but that doesn't mean it wasn't fun to talk about.

    Uncle Johnny's is run by a short, stout guy who seemed to be in his late fifties, who went by the name Sarge, and if teeth were a form of currency he would have made some dentist very rich. He was one of those guys one either got along with well enough, but not great, or just flat out didn't like, and with no middle ground. He was the type of guy I would expect to see in the saddle of a Harley Davidson motorcycle with a team of like minded individuals, raising awareness for wounded or homeless veterans, and therefore my forearm tattoo which reads "Sometimes good guys don't wear white" struck him well. So much so that he accepted my offer to work for stay, but in hindsight I think he expected a few more of us to stay then actually did. The Stink-o de Mayo clan took off after stuffing themselves at the buffet, Crash and his crew rode into Johnson City fifteen miles away to celebrate Cool Story's birthday, and Mime and Doc decided to get a move on before the evening hit. So it was just me there that night after a day of scrubbing dishes and showers, but Sarge and I both felt I earned my keep, and so I enjoyed a night indoors in Erwin, TN.

    Furthermore, my day of labor had earned me a ride into town to visit the all-you-can-eat buffet at the KFC, which let me just say is a potentially lethal place for a man in my condition at that time. I don't know what that high ranking poultry master Sanders puts in his food ,but I do know that I put away more plates of the stuff then I care to recall. Every ounce of me was turned into a unfulfillable gluttonous vat for the duration the meal, which I'm sure more resembled a shark's feeding frenzy than a civilized consumption of sustenance. If I scared any small children this day I am sincerely sorry, but it had to be done.

    Miles on the trail seem to pass by much quicker after a good night's rest and a full belly, and I hardly noticed the first five miles out of Erwin. In fact, I felt nearly immortal after filling up on delicious chicken. Perhaps chicken is the secret to eternal life known only to the militant powers of Colonel Sanders and General Tso. Come to think of it, have you ever seen Colonel Sanders and General Tso in the same place at the same time? I haven't. It's the same guy! Separated by thousands of years and miles, it's the perfect disguise! This guy is the immortal, and his secret is delicious chicken! Mind. Blown.

While I had been blessed with many new friends over the last few days, some of the finest fellows I would meet didn't become known to me until well after stopping in Erwin. In fact, one such encounter was the product of a serious miscalculation. One of the great shelters on the AT is Over Mountain shelter, close to the city of Rohn Mountain, and it's frequently a spot where AT thru hikers gather for a little fun. I knew for a fact that the Germans had planned to do a little drinking there when they arrived and I had plans to meet them. I was a ways behind according to the trail registers I had been reading, but it wasn't something a really big day worth of hiking wouldn't fix, and so I made sure to be set up early the night before so as to press hard and catch them the next day.

When I awoke in the morning I found it to be raining slightly, but it was the sort of rain that would clear up quickly if given a little time so I decided to sleep in and wait for it to pass instead of sprinting through it. Because of this I ended up short of my goal, staying at Clyde Smith shelter instead, though I believed staying here would allow for an easy hike to Over Mountain shelter the next day. While I was sitting at the shelter gazing over the meadows and trees stretched before it, the rain picked up again but I remember saying aloud, "Everything feels right today," and indeed it did. It was such a simple yet profound statement, one that I don't believe that I had been able to utter in close to three years before then.

As I sat in reverence of my new found peace another hiker came up the side trail seeking shelter from the elements. He was just slightly shorter than I was, and rather hard to judge in age due to a head full of curly blond hair and one of the fuller beards I had seen at this point in the trail. He was built strong, and had become so due to years of rock climbing in Arizona despite being a California native. His laugh was hearty and his smile was kind, and at the time, I had no idea how good of a friend the recent college graduate Chouinard was to become. It was just the two of us at the shelter that night; he was reading the Wheel Of Time series and his accounts of the novels caught my interest, seeing as I've always been a fan of such authors as Tolkien, Rowling, and Lewis. After an evening it soon became apparent that our taste in literature wasn't the only thing we shared, but also many thoughts on life and travel. It was up for debate whether or not he would have enough time to finish the trail however--he had a job waiting for him back in the world, so he was just out to see what he could see before the time came to return. It's a fairly common way for people to see the trail, knocking out sections at a time when life allows, and while I feel it lacks the profound solitude a thru hike has it is certainly more manageable while still providing for a grand, eye opening experience.

We left at different times the next morning, but that had become common for me. I was finding that I didn't hike as fast as other hikers, but managed to travel the same distance in a day because I had grown used to rising with the morning sun and hiking till last light. Chouinard managed to pass by not long after I started and it appeared we were both heading to Over Mountain shelter for the night, so I planned to see him again. That being said, I still had to get there, and I had Roan Mountain standing in my way.

Roan is one of the highest peaks on the trail at well over six thousand feet, and actually boasts the highest shelter on the AT. A fabulous hotel used to stand atop the mountain, and in its heyday would have been an incredible structure. The most famous of the stories shared of the former hotel was that it stood on the TN/NC state line, and while it was legal to drink alcohol in one state at the time it was still illegal in the other. A line supposedly divided the dining room, and a local sheriff stood on one side of the line just waiting for an intoxicated guest to stumble across the room and into jail for the evening.

It was still far from warm out despite being the fourth day of spring, but it was very clear and the view from where the hotel once stood was absolutely breathtaking. However, what I remember most about Roan was not the view but rather the ice, for the trail was simply covered in it! It wasn't just little patches of the stuff either; the dense pine and hemlock forests had sheltered the forest floor allowing for water to collect and freeze upon it, yet the weather had warmed up enough to melt the ice just slightly, making it as slick as could possibly be. I was reminded of a horizontal climbing wall at times, sliding from exposed stick to exposed rock as I went along my way trying to keep my balance. God forbid I had to travel downhill for any length of time--that was simply tragic! I remember one such section had become a virtual frozen water slide and it simply refused to be traveled by anyone on their feet. I tried to go around, but the ground on all sides was equally frozen and would have sent me sliding down the whole ice slick if it wasn't for a very quick, jerking motion of my arm in a direction said arm certainly wasn't accustomed to moving in, at least not at such a speed. I remember my shoulder hurting quite a bit for the rest of the day from this acrobatic blunder, but I needed to keep going and figured it'd just heal up as I went along.

There's a series of balds after Roan which provide stunning views back over the mountain and of the valley below. I enjoyed these balds far more than I did Max Patch, and even paused several times as I crossed them, basking in the quiet beauty of this great planet. While the bald summits hosted spectacular views, my favorite sight of the day had to be that of Over Mountain Shelter itself. The shelter was an old barn that had very little done to it to prepare it for hikers--in fact I would argue that nothing had been done at all! The faded red, two story structure stood overlooking a large valley nestled between two great ridges that seemed to stretch for ages, with a little fire ring situated perfectly at which to gaze upon this pristine patch of nature during the sunset.

Not only had Chouinard made it there, but also Stink-o de Mayo, and several new faces that I had not previously had the pleasure to meet. A Pennsylvania native that had just finished his service to the US Military, named PA System, had decided to set up shop here, as well as four day hikers from Ohio. Most notably though were a pair of brothers with whom I had not become acquainted with until this evening. One was slightly shorter then me, with dark black hair and a full beard, and was known to have a bit of a temper when he started hiking, thus had gotten the name Dozer for violently blowing through obstacles. Thankfully he had mellowed out rather quickly since then, and I found him to be nothing but good company. His brother stood a good head taller than me, but with similar features. He was an electrician back in the world, and when hiking a section of the AT the year before with his lady friend he ended up carrying well over fifty pounds of her gear in addition to his own, hence the name U-Haul. It only makes sense that the Pennsylvania-born brothers were from the city of brotherly love, Philadelphia, and indeed the two were inseparable. Crash's group also made an appearance as well, although the only other person who stayed in the shelter was June Bug, while the others preferred to camp out front. It was a full house that night, but I don't think I would have had it any other way; besides, it was a very cold night and the extra bodies surely helped to keep the place warm.

The warmish room turned out to be more of a blessing than any of us imagined actually. I was the first one up again in the morning and made my way down stairs to take a leak before packing up. I can't say I was fully prepared for the sight that greeted me as I emerged from the shelter. The ground the day before had been completely clear, and the shelter was surrounded by high, dead grass, but this morning well over four inches of snow had accumulated in the area and everything was completely covered in a soft, unbroken, white blanket of snow. I remember rubbing my eyes in disbelief thinking I was still half asleep, but that wasn't the case, and I was indeed seeing what I thought I was. After taking this fine opportunity to pee my name in the snow, I went back upstairs to find some people stirring, just starting to get ready for the day. Apple Jacks asked me how it looked out there, and I remember saying something along the lines of "I feel like we fell through a wardrobe or something man, its freaking Narnia out there." There was an old door in the second floor of the shelter that I believe was used to load hay during the structure's service as a barn, and it was quickly thrown open for many of my fellow hikers to share the same disbelief I had at this morning's discovery. Either way, it was going to do no good to simply look at it, but fortunately we were close to the town of Roan Mountain and one of the nicer hostels stationed along the AT.

I managed to be the first one out of the shelter, and I'm very glad that I was. After I passed Crash, who seemed to be in even greater disbelief than the rest of us as he cleared the snow from his tent, there were absolutely no other signs of humans anywhere! My feet crunched through fresh powder, leaving their own trail as I went along my way in what felt like a new forest--it was an amazing experience! Seeing as the trail was marked with white blazes, the snow covered trees were a little hard to navigate by but I managed, and even drew arrows in the snow as I went where the trail turned in hopes of keeping other hikers on track. At one point I nearly missed a major turn because the trail looked like it was going to follow an old forest road but instead turned sharply right, usually signified by a double blaze. Here I took the opportunity to have a little fun in the snow, and decided to build myself a little snow man. It didn't take long, the snow was wet and held together well, and in next to no time I had built a little waist high snowman, complete with with two sticks for arms pointing the way to the trail. My hat may have become more recognizable to other hikers than even my face at this point, so I placed it on my new snowy friend and snapped a picture before heading out, and it's one of my favorites from the trail.

I did manage to hike with nearly everyone else from the previous night as they caught up, and it turned out to be an awesome day! It was a bit windy, but it was clear, and when crossing Little Hump bald I must have stopped every couple hundred yards to take it all in. Every now and then a tuft of dead, yellow grass would poke through the snow, and the usually blue mountains were now lined with massive snowbanks, visible from miles away. It was hard to tell if it was snowing still or not, seeing as the wind began to vigorously blow the snow around--but in the strangest, most aesthetic way possible, adding even more beauty to this snowy summit. I remember watching a team of hikers ahead of me in the snow, the five of them appearing and disappearing in the distance due to the blowing snow. To me they looked lost out here in the elements, like something out of a bad movie, but that was just my imagination and I was sure I'd see them on the other side.

I'm not exactly sure why but I remember feeling absolutely drained of energy at this point. When trying to pass over the eight hundred feet of prominence on Hump Mountain I could hardly move more than fifty yards at a time without having to rest. It might have been the cold, or the fact that I still wasn't digesting things all that well due to that nasty stomach bug I had picked up, but either way I remember this being one of the hardest mountains I had climbed simply because I was so damn tired! I did finally make it over, and in the next few miles managed to catch back up with some of the hikers who had gone before me as we approached the city of Roan Mountain. At Doll Flats the AT finally breaks away from the NC/TN border, and so I bid goodbye to my home state here, glad to have been back, but with so much more to do before I could stay. It was with a heavy heart I passed the little wooden sign reading "Leaving NC", feeling almost like I had just left home for a second time, but I would be back, and with even more to tell next time.

The weather had a few more surprises in store for us before we reached town. Anyone who has lived in an area that sees snow every year knows that there are two types of snow, and those that haven't should be grateful for their ignorance. There's the light, fluffy, powdery snow that snowboarders dream of, easily moved and fun to play in. Then there is the wet, heavy snow, the sort of snow that practically forms snowballs as it falls, sticking to anything and everything and accumulating in great, weighty masses about a degree away from melting at any moment. It was the latter that began to fall on this fine spring day, and in such quantity that it smothered everything unfortunate enough to catch it with in a matter of moments. This included everything from tree limbs to our limbs, and the normally black jacket I was wearing became bright white, as well as the front of my jeans, back of my pack, top of my hat, and even my beard!

    I was hiking with June Bug and the Stink-o de Mayo boys, and when the ground leveled out we hastened our pace in search of shelter. All seven of us had slipped at some point in the day and Apple Jacks had even managed to get his foot caught up on one tumble in such a way that he wouldn't have been unable to free himself without the help of three others to lift and slide him free. It would be another five feet from there before the ground provided enough friction to stop him completely, and all seven of us were able to get a good laugh out of it before pressing on. We did finally manage to make it to the road to town, and that would be the last time I would see all the Stink-o de Mayo clan together--they were heading into a neighboring town where they had some friends, and I bid them a fond farewell as June Bug and I took off to find a hostel that was supposed to be close by.

    I had already suffered far worse weather and survived, but that didn't mean it was at all pleasant that day and Mountain Harbor Hostel proved to be a God send! I recall arriving at the charming farm home completely covered from head to toe in cold, wet snow to the point where I didn't even want to step inside for fear of bringing at least a solid gallon of water along with me. I did manage to make all arrangements in the foyer before completely thawing out thankfully, and then headed off to the bunk house to dry my boots. The bunk room was more than hospitable--well, at least ninety percent of it was. A small wood stove kept the place nice and warm, and a full kitchen provided a chance to prepare a hot meal for a fraction of the cost of a restaurant. It would appear that I would be in good company again tonight as I was soon joined by the rest of Crash's crew, Chouinard, as well as the brothers Dozer and U-Haul. As everyone entered the old barn that had been converted into a cozy living space they would shake off whatever snow they had collected and place their shoes next to the wood stove in an attempt to dry them, which actually worked quite well! The majority of Crash's group didn't drink, but the rest of us stayed up past dark watching old movies on VHS and sipping a few Yuenglings, which became the unofficial national brew of the AT. It was a good night, and as the weather outside became nearly equivalent to that of a mid winter blizzard , thus we were all incredibly thankful to be spending an evening indoors.

Things certainly did get a little less then friendly weather-wise as the night went on, even indoors. The wind blew so hard that it forced smoke back down chimney from the wood stove, filling the room with smoke and forcing us to extinguish our heater. Dozer and U-Haul, having no other option due to the influx of hikers, spent the night in the ten percent of the bunk room that wasn't as hospitable as the rest, and emerged the next morning rested, but rather cold. All was made right in the morning however, because for twelve dollars a thru hiker can partake of the most amazing breakfast available on the AT! The family at Mountain Harbor Hostel holds nothing back at breakfast, and one would think that this lovely little woman was used to cooking for the Queen of England every morning. Everything a good southern woman should know how to cook was there and then some, serving well over ten items and even providing a full ham! Even the hungriest thru hikers will go away happy from this charming mountain hostel. Or at least that's what I hear, for I decided to save my money for the road ahead and simply ate what I had brought along. Still, I do wish that I would have partook of this smorgasbord of breakfast bliss after seeing photos of it--just one of the downfalls of traveling on a beggar's budget.

I liked the group of people I was traveling with, but gravitated mainly towards the Philly brothers Dozer and U-Haul and California's bastard son Chouinard. They reminded me of myself in many ways: in their mid twenties, out here on their own free will, determined to make it by whatever means necessary! I spent another day tracking the three of them out of Roan Mountain through shin deep snow, completely soaking my boots inside and out as well as the bottom twelve inches of my pants. It didn't really matter though for I had become accustomed to such things; it was still a fine day and the four of us spent a night in the woods, talking about nothing in particular, sharing the brotherhood that was the AT. We all had lives that we had left behind and would eventually have to get back to, they were fun to talk about from time to time, but out here we got the rare opportunity to analyze what we wanted for the future. Sometimes we would talk about what we wanted to do with the rest of our lives, other times we would just focus on what we wanted to do with the rest of the day, and nothing seemed taboo or too far fetched.

The only thing I didn't enjoy about this night's stay was the repercussions of enduring the elements the day before. In the morning my boots, which had been saturated and flexible when I took them off, had frozen solid and proved to be slightly painful to but back on. To make matters worse, my pants had frozen into some variety of arctic bell-bottoms which would have been far from pleasant to put back on in the morning. So I set out wearing ice blocks on my feet and a thick wool kilt, which I honestly found a superior garment in the still present snow, until about midday when things finally warmed up a bit and the snow melted away.

An area I would like to go back and hike in better weather is the gorge surrounding Laurel Falls, for if I was to describe my ideal image of Tennessee this is the area that I would be describing. The trail winds through massive rock formations, at times raising up thirty yards above the path, and along the side of cliffs that drop at a dreadfully alarming rate. A river runs through it all, cutting deeply into the rock as it flows, at times barely leaving a yards width of trail on which to hike. Though the highlight of the area must be the Laurel Falls itself: a massive rock stair leads down to the base of the falls, which cascades over multiple levels of rock into a wide, deep pool that almost begs one to go swimming. While I didn't take the plunge due to the fact that there was still snow clinging to the rocks on the river bank, I did end up getting lost and forging the stream in search of white blazes. It took Dozer, U-Haul, and myself a good twenty minutes of searching around the falls to find our way, but if there's an area to get stuck in I suppose this is one of the better ones, and like I said, I would love to go back someday.

Hiker-ism: Zero Day:

(Noun) While the reason people venture on the AT is to see the entire country on foot, every now and then one has just got to take a break. A zero day is a day in which a hiker travels zero miles, taking in a little well deserved R&R.

Having spent many years in Wilmington, I had grown accustomed to living amongst a large military presence. Camp Lejeune is located an hour northeast of the city and is the largest Marine base on the east coast. Sadly there isn't a lot to do in the city of Jacksonville, where the base is located, that doesn't involve working out or getting a new haircut, and so many of the soldiers come to Wilmington to find a little fun in their time off. Because of this I had a wealth of survival knowledge at my fingertips, which I made good effort to draw from before setting out. I won't say all of its the soundest advice seeing as many of the boys were carrying well over a hundred pounds of equipment, most of which was designed to withstand gunfire as opposed to climbing mountains, but there were indeed a few gems of information to be gained from the troops.

One such bit of advice I decided to put into action on a morning I was having a little trouble getting going. Apparently, what some of the marines would do to fight their body's overwhelming desire to get some rest if ever they were out on late watch, is to take a ration of instant coffee and place it on the inside of their lower lip in a manner such as chewing tobacco. I'm not sure who first thought of the idea, but wow! On the day that I tried this particular trick I was literally running through the woods of eastern Tennessee just waiting for a squirrel or raccoon to look at me wrong so I could exact my vengeance upon the varmint. I must have covered five miles in the time that I would normally do two, throttle wide open as I passed hill, dam, and reservoir alike, all falling in my wake. However the energy surge ended nearly as quickly as it started, for with such haste comes an inability to watch one's step as well as the trail deserves. I still can't recall exactly what happened--all I know is that one moment I was powering along the trail, and the next I was flying through the air completely parallel to the ground like some sort of vagrant Superman in mid flight. Sadly, I didn't posses the otherworldly ability to sustain such flight and came crashing down face first into a loose pile of leaves and earth a solid five feet off the trail.

I laid there for a moment, more in disbelief than pain or anything else, wondering how one bad step could send me so far off course. I had long ago learned to laugh at my shortcomings, and this was no exception as I gathered myself and began to rise from my unexpected resting point. I decided then that the sort of unnatural, super human energy that I had been riding on was best left to those whose lives actually depended on it, and that it had no place on a peaceful hiking trail. Not only that, but I soon realized that I had virtually sprinted past a few scenic views from the top of a lovely reservoir and that I was out here to enjoy the things that I previously had no time for, not just pass them in another all out sprint towards the next day.

So I spent the next few days taking it a little easier, resting often, and really enjoying the changing of the land as I went along my way. The seclusion of north Georgia and the North Carolina Smoky Mountains was begging to give way as I approached the southern border of Virginia. The mountains still rose and fell sharply at times, but compared to what I had traveled they seemed to level out slightly. Endless acres of trees and nature began to be replaced by small, patchwork farms nestled in the mountain valleys while the summits and ridges remained wild and untamed. Many times I would find myself sitting upon a ridge overlooking theses simple homesteads far below, taking time to appreciate the simple living that the people who inhabited such homes must enjoy. I'll admit, I envied them, and still do, to live amongst such beauty everyday, and to enjoy the labors of their own hands as opposed to slaving away for a product many of us never see. It just seems like a wholesome, rewarding sort of living, the like of which I had forgotten about in the hustle of life.

It was on one such ridge just past the Tennessee/Virginia border that I had decided to take a brief rest overlooking the town of Damascus, enjoying the feeling of overcoming yet another state. Every border looks so different yet feels the same; words simply can't describe how amazing it is to pass over one of the imaginary lines that separates one section of the country from another on foot. As I sat propped up against a pine tree (the biting flies had made an appearance that day and they don't care for pine), I spotted a tall, solemn figure coming down the trail. He was a giant of a man, but only in height, standing a solid head over my own but thin, and with a stride that looked casual but was unmatchable in distance. His dark eyes were focused on the road ahead, and with the full beard and head of thick, curly hair he looked almost as if he had grown from the very mountains themselves! I don't think he said a word as he passed me, just smiled a little and nodded as I waved hello, but I was a little worn out and can't say I much felt like talking at the moment, also being very preoccupied with my Snickers bar that I saved for special occasions, such as border crossings. Although the Snickers bar wasn't the only thing I had planned for my recent accomplishment--in the town of Damascus was something that I had been longing to see since leaving Gerogia, a new brewery!

In fact, I had monitored my advancement for the last few days so as to be sure to arrive when the brew house was open, something that only happens on the weekend. I was still very much on a budget, living completely off what I had been gifted or managed to find, but every now and then even the most frugal of men have to let loose a little and enjoy the ride.

There isn't much to the city of Damascus, but they had made quite a name for themselves on the trail by hosting Trail Days, an annual party for AT hikers both past and present, and many on the trail are known to backtrack from as far away as New Jersey via hitch to be a part of it.

It was late March when I arrived, a good month away from the festivities, but Damascus was still overly friendly to the dirty, rugged, and frankly awful smelling people who had decided to attempt a thru hike. I had no trouble getting directions to the brewery, and to be honest had a harder time finding an excuse to break away from the conversation so as to venture to it. It began to rain quite hard as I arrived at the front door of the brew house, and decided that it would be best to take a little time underneath an adjacent overhang to switch into my Beir Lord t-shirt that I kept clean and dry for these special occasions. It's harder then one would think to keep things dry and clean in a backpack, especially when such items tend to settle to the bottom of the pack. After a few too many damp socks, I had found it best to keep my clothes in a large ziplock bag until they were needed, a practice that paid off on this dismal day.

The Damascus Brewery matches the town perfectly, and that is to say there's not much to it. However, they do have everything a true beer enthusiast needs, and that's a large warehouse space with a bar on one wall and some massive brewing equipment on the other. I was pleasantly surprised to find Chouinard, Dozer, and U-Haul there already, along with the guy who had passed me earlier on the trail; his name was Farmer. Turns out that Farmer was a Quebec native, and as a result spoke English as a second language, but that doesn't mean that he didn't speak it fluently. Perhaps it was because of a few pints and a friendly game of darts, but I believe Farmer to be one of the better men that I had met out on the trail, and we all seemed to have a grand time sipping suds at this tiny brewery in the middle of nowhere.

When it became time to leave the brewery I learned that my four companions had already set up at a local hostel called Woodchuck's, and so I decided to follow along to see if there was still room. Fortunately there were still a few beds available, and I must say that it was perhaps the nicest place I stayed on the entire trail! The owner was a previous thru hiker, and this was his first year running a hostel. Come to think of it, I believe the five of us were among some of his first customers. The single family home was slightly off the beaten track, which was hard to do in this little town, but the beds were incredibly soft and Woodchuck had even set up a little honor system shop in his kitchen that was well stocked with the little things that hikers need to track down when they hit town. We spent the rest of that night sipping a few more brews and shooting the shit, and I began to feel as if I'd known these guys all my life.

I didn't really know how amazing this hostel was until the next morning however, but found out in a hurry. Woodchuck had gone out of his way to make his hostel hiker friendly, and in the morning provided a breakfast of toast, doughnuts, and just about every type of cereal imaginable! He had a shelf that nearly spanned from one side of the kitchen to the other, completely loaded with breakfast bliss and all of which was included with a nights stay. We all liked the place so much that we decided to take a day Zero Day here, and enjoy a little well deserved rest. Normally my budget would have knocked me out of this one, but Woodchuck was used to traveling with the occasional underfunded hiker and was willing to let me work for another night's stay. I didn't quite get off free and clear though, as a frozen bag of homemade spaghetti sauce basically screamed to be used.

Dozer and U-Haul were both very used to working in kitchens, in fact Dozer had just left his job at a fine dining restaurant to go hiking, and when the opportunity to use Woodchuck's kitchen arose they jumped at it. I'm not about to say that I was nearly as experienced as the pair of them, but I knew my way around a kitchen having worked in one briefly, and so I took the opportunity to whip up a potato salad my family had come to expect at every gathering we attended. Most of what I needed was there, I just had to buy a little bacon and some potatoes, and after the three of us returned from a local grocery store we laid waste to the kitchen and prepared my favorite meal that I had partaken of on the trail. Dozer whipped up an amazing garden salad while U-Haul secured the noodles and improved on the sauce as I diced and boiled potatoes. For those who have never worked in a commercial kitchen, I feel as though you have missed a very vital lesson in life. Food doesn't just magically appear, it takes just as much work for someone to make it in a restaurant as it does for someone to prepare it at home, and when one has to cook nearly fifty different meals at once it becomes a bit of a hassle to say the least. There's a lot of yelling in a commercial kitchen, both to alert one's coworkers and simply because it gets overwhelming at times, and while the cooking in Damascus was far from stressful we still kept the volume up as the three of us sliced, diced, boiled, and baked various dishes next to each other.

When it was all said and done, there were seven of us sat at the dinner table including Woodchuck and a wayward hiker named Doe-yee, but there was more food to eat then even five active thru hikers could stomach. Between the garden salad, garlic bread, potato salad, and pasta, all of us spent that night full and well rested, thankful for the opportunity to feast. That night we sat about drinking the few beers that had survived the night before and playing card games, and I think it was then that we realized that this was our team. To this day I don't believe that I had met a finer group of men. We weren't well groomed, or well off, our industry wasn't financially profitable or productive, at least not to anyone other than ourselves; nor were we saints, sages, prophets, or holy men, though some would call us sojourners. What we lacked in class we made up in character, unmatched by billionaires, and what we lacked in productivity we made up in passion, drive, and determination. And while we served only ourselves we invited all to come with us to be considered our brothers of the wild, a family of nature and hardship. Indeed these were my brothers, and I still consider them to be- -it's amazing how I set out to find myself and wound up making some of the better friends I had ever known.

9 DEVOTION AND ENDURANCE

Hiker-ism: Shakedown

(verb) I've never been much of a car guy and therefore have seriously neglected many of the vehicles that I have owned in my life. My idea of maintenance is that if something fails and yet the car runs fine, I must not have needed it. So it is with a shakedown; hikers completely tear apart their pack and anything that's not useful is left by the wayside.

If there's anything to be learned by carrying way too much gear for over one thousand miles it's what items are essential, and then what only seems like a good idea at the time of purchase. I had become rather attached to my pack, in fact it almost felt like a second skin to me, but during my rest in Damascus I decided it was a good time for a shakedown. I knew I was carrying more then the average hiker, but until this moment I just figured that I was purposefully prepared for anything. However, upon giving my gear a good hard look, I felt like I had packed to start a colony in central Africa rather then to go for a hike across a fully developed country! For longer then any sane man would I had been toting around extra knifes, twice as many tent stakes than my tent could hold, enough medical supplies to stock a combat medic, insoles that didn't fit my boots, a full reel of fishing line, a massive roll of hemp, and even a five pound sharpening stone! And that's just the half of it. Taking advantage of the hiker box at Woodchuck's, I dropped well over fifteen pounds for other hikers to more than likely ignore in their search for useful gear, and perhaps a few things that could be used at the hostel. By only carrying several lengths of hemp I managed to leave the bulky roll, and by being extremely critical I finally rid myself of the things I continually thought I'd find a use for. I think some hikers take their shakedowns a bit too seriously though, even going as far as to cut every inch of spare strap on their packs, but I felt a little relieved after finally making a solid commitment to using what I had learned out in the wild, not only dropping some gear, but also the pretentious notion that I had any idea what I was doing before I set out.

There were a few items that I didn't want to lose indefinitely, but no longer cared to carry. Thanks to a flat rate shipping box from the local post office I was able to mail my parents a few things, such as the first spiral notebook that I had ever managed to fill front to back with writing, and a large bag of pennies that I had been collecting along the way. Metal coins are possibly the stupidest things a person can carry through the woods; they serve no purpose in a survival sense, and their value is spent before a person even has a chance to use them due to the extra calories it takes to haul them around. All of my silver change I always managed to turn to lightweight paper money via change services in grocery stores, but the pennies I had saved individually and kept them with me. It's hard to explain why, but I do have a reason. It's something that I started doing back in the world--I could never bring myself to spend my pennies unless I had no other currency or credit whatsoever! I sympathize with them, they are so routinely discarded by others, dropped on sidewalks carelessly or in little plastic trays at gas stations. It seems no one has time for the humble penny, often feeling more annoyed and burdened by them then the things are worth, and no one even bothers to pick up one should it fall from a pocket. No one notices or has time for them, but I do. Instead of a worthless chunk of copper-plated nickel I see potential, the most fundamental building block of even the greatest fortunes! Many are beat up, scuffed, scratched, dinged, nicked, run over, or even damaged beyond recognition, but I see their value, and the more damaged one is the more I tend to like it. They make me think of a time when I too was tossed out on the street, hopeless, and forgotten. It wasn't until my friends picked me up and carried me along for a bit that I managed to see my own value again, and now here I was, out exploring the country the way so many others wish they could. So I carry the silent and unnoticed penny, assuring each one that I will someday turn them into something, some adventure, or some purpose that no one else had time to.

When leaving Damascus I ran into Crash's group for the last time; many of them seemed to be running out of steam and not working as well together as they had when I first encountered them. They decided to take the Virginia Creeper Trail instead of the white blazed AT, cutting off many miles of mountains to hike along where an old railroad track once stood. I can't say I approved of the idea--it just seemed to go against the spirit of the trail, losing experiences and days away from hassle of life to quickly cover ground. I suppose everyone gets to hike their own hike, and what feels right to one may not to another, so I wished them well but wasn't terribly bothered to bid them a final adeiu. I began to realize that not all hikers have the same reason for being out here. Some are out in search of conquest, taking every mile seriously, never skipping a single step, even going as far as to backtrack to the exact spot where they stepped off the trail for a resupply before continuing on. Some just want the title, the bragging rights to say that they made it across the country once, almost as if they're seeking some sort of promotion in life to raise them above others which I don't agree with at all. Some are after the experiences that would be had along the way, the story, the little this and thats which don't occur in normal life. And some are out here purely to discover, to explore, to find new things, either in nature or possibly themselves. As for me, I had thought that I had gone for the story, seeing as that's the reason I've had for many of the other decisions in my life, but now I felt like I was staying for the discovery. Also, while it never seemed to be a solid reason to keep going, I'll admit I did really want to earn the title of Thru Hiker.

Seeing as I only ventured on the Creeper Trail where the AT follows it to leave Damascus and to cross over a raging river via a massive, and very impressive, bridge, I can't say that I know exactly where that trail ends. All I know for sure is that if it bypasses the Grayson Highlands in southern Virginia, then whoever takes it is an absolute fool! I had logged ninety nine days of hiking, not counting my off trail excursions or my zero days, when I happened across a parking lot marking the Highland trailhead where I was greeted by a pair of female hikers with a dog out for a day hike. They weren't thru hikers, but were familiar with the AT, and one of the girls, named Sarah, had even done volunteer work on the trail. She greeted me like a thru hiker would though, all smiles and excited to run into someone out on the trail. Sarah boldly bid me welcome to what she considered to be the greatest section of the trail in all of Virginia, which is saying a lot seeing as the state counts for five hundred total miles of the thing. Warmed by such a welcome I thanked her, though if what she said was true it was a shame to arrive at such a spot so soon and with many miles to go before crossing into another state. She tossed me an orange before we parted ways, and again I thanked her, it was a wonderful way to start off what would truly be one of my favorite sections of the entire trip.

I don't believe every hiker experiences the Greyson Highlands like I had the pleasure to, though I would absolutely hope they would. It was the first of April, and due to the harsh winter spring had come late to the area, leaving the grass high and yellow and the trees barren. The ground was void of snow, thankfully, and the weather seemed to finally be warming up though still chilly enough to keep the bugs at bay. It was these pre-spring conditions that made for such a memorable hike, as the familiar wooded path gave way into massive rolling hills of grass with wide open vistas, occasionally spotted by rock formations and stray groves of trees that managed to take root among the highlands. I was completely taken aback by the sheer beauty of this place; the pale, dry grass covered everything and swayed in the breeze, making the rocks stand out boldly like great pillars in a churning sea as its waves broke upon the wooded shore. The clouds hung thin and high, looking almost painted upon bright blue canvas as the sun shone brightly, bleaching them a pure white. It was the sheer contrast of color that took my breath away, but the greatest of all was that this bright and barren meadow stood in front of a backdrop of still, cool, and cobalt blue mountains in the distance.

I moved slowly this day, taking time to observe such a picturesque landscape and breaking frequently at places like Buzzard Rock or other stand-alone rock formations. The trail would wind between the rocks where it could, but was mostly marked by large wooden poles painted at the top with the familiar blotch of white paint that kept us all on track. I remember vividly a small section of trail that captivated me so completely that I don't believe I had ever moved slower in my entire life. Near Thomas Knob shelter a large, barren vista stands completely unobstructed except for a few dead trees, twisted, knotted, and withered with age and decay. The ever present grass blanketed the ridge but in the distance a mountain range stood bold and defined against a clear sky, each peak standing out sharply along a jagged ridge line. The splendor and magnitude of such a view could not be fully described with a thousand written pages, nor could its beauty be captured by the finest of cameras or painted by even the hands of Rafael or

Michelangelo. It was the sort of place that would nearly bring a man to his knees, struck hard and well by such profound majesty, the very image of nature's own soul. I may search the rest of my life and never see such a thing again, though I do hope to someday gaze upon its equal; frankly as far as mountain meadows are concerned, perfection is too weak of a word to describe the Greyson Highlands.

As if the day wasn't good enough, the night became one to remember as well. I hiked as late as the day would let me, though falling short of the shelter I had hoped to reach when I had started the day. Ending up at a large corral called The Scales, which in the past had served as a place for farmers to sell livestock, I set up camp alone for the night, but hoped to catch up with my team in the morning. The sunset was quite lack luster sadly, seeing as the clouds had cleared away and a nearby treeline blocked the horizon, but I didn't feel deprived, having had such incredible views during the day. However, it seems that I was in store for one final sight before putting a cap on the day. After journaling by flashlight and having my evening meal I stepped out of my tent to take a leak, but afterward remained standing in the corral for at least a good ten minutes staring upwards at a brilliant night sky. The moon shined brightly, surrounded by countless stars glowing softly against the night without a single cloud to block them nor a city light for miles to take away from their splendor. I had always taken time to gaze upwards when the opportunity presented itself, and it was only a good stiff breeze that forced me back into my tent as opposed to sleeping uncovered that evening. It's far easier for me to sleep in a vacant field under a star light sky then in the safest of homes or the softest of beds.

Even though I had pushed as far as possible the day before, I knew I would have to be up with first light if I planned to catch up with my team in the morning. Normally, I would have just assumed that I would catch them eventually and not worried so much, but in Damascus we had all decided to meet at Partnership Shelter because it offered a very unique and desirable service--pizza delivery! Food always proves to be a great motivator of man, and it just happens to be doubly so for one burning roughly five thousand calories a day. So when the sun first started to cast its rays upon a new day I was up and packing my gear in haste to get the day going with the knowledge that about thirty miles stood between me and a hot meal. I suppose many would consider this ambitious, if not flat out impossible, but should I make it this day would be my biggest to date, I had trekked many a day averaging twenty miles at this point, so I felt confident. Before the sun even broke the treeline I was awake and fed with only my tent left to break down and pack, but as I emerged from it I encountered a sight I certainly did not expect. The Greyson Highlands are not only renowned for their stunning views, but also frequently traveled in hopes that one will encounter wild highland ponies roaming atop the mountains. I had hoped to see them before leaving the area, but I didn't expect to find one thirty yards from me in the morning grazing in the corral. Even if the Queen of England had been waiting at Partnership Shelter I would have taken the time that I did to marvel at this stout, charming little creature. Its golden mane lay against it soft brown hide and over its eyes, and as I sat looking at this thick yet elegant beast it in turn gazed at me before giving a snort and trotting off to join a pair of other ponies grazing on the opposite side of a split rail fence. It was day one hundred of my travels, and I already felt blessed by it.

My morning haste paid off as I managed to meet back up with the four other members of my team as they were about to depart from the shelter where they had spent the night. It was well known that I would be bringing up the rear seeing as I preferred to hike at a slow and steady pace, and so my comrades asked if they should place an order for me once they arrived at Partnership. It was a fine plan indeed, and so my way was set--no excuses for not making it tonight. While I managed to keep pace for a few miles it wasn't long before I resumed my normal hiking speed and the rest went on ahead, but at least I had made good on my plan to catch them this morning.

It was another beautiful day of hiking; the weather was much the same as the day before, clear and warm, and while the trail didn't provide a view quite like it had the day before the land was still beautiful and pleasant to look at. I remember feeling like I was caught in the middle of an old spaghetti western, a vagrant wandering in the Old West, not looking for trouble but bound to find it. About the only things missing were a covered wagon and a Winchester rifle, but perhaps that's just as well seeing as a gang of bandits also failed to make an appearance. Still, I couldn't help but whistle a few old cowboy songs as I went along my way, passing through wide open spaces and rock mazes alike.

The sun began to set on day one hundred, and I was starting to wonder if I was going to make it to my destination. I wasn't sweating any longer despite being overly warm, for my body was so dehydrated, and furthermore it was impossible to tell how far was left to go. Though when I rounded a corner and began to pass through a grove of surprisingly well groomed trees, I heard someone singing the Rocky theme song and I knew that I had made it. Not only had I arrived after pressing just shy of thirty miles, but there was a pizza and two liter of soda waiting for me! A full band began to play, and an entire team of roller derby girls emerged from the forest to carry me the rest of the way; the president was there to give me the Medal of Honor, and Morgan Freeman swore to dedicate the rest of his life to narrate whatever I was doing. Well, there was a pizza and soda anyway, and I felt like the rest happened, but it's impossible to be sure--either way, it had been a hell of a ride to make it one hundred days in the wilderness. I had made some good friends, I had seen things I never knew existed, I had seen the best in people, and only God knew what else lay ahead.

While it was always interesting to see who would pick up a wayward hiker making an effort to hitch into town, some of the strangest characters I encountered occurred on a day in which I completely failed to find a ride. It was outside the town of Atkins and at a gas station where I had stood for a good hour with my thumb out trying to find a way into town with no luck. Impatient, I opted to resupply at the convenience mart as best as I could, an effort that met with mild success as I was able to find enough supplies to hopefully make it to the next town, though I was forced to resort to things that I had previously counted as inefficient or bulky. The attendant was pleasant though, a quiet, country girl who seemed to be a bit irritated by her job, and she took the time to describe how her boss had just revoked all employee privileges to the soda fountain when I asked her how her day was. The rest of my team had just arrived from a restaurant not far down the street and we all sat outside the store for a moment as I packed up, and that's when things got weird. The five of us were looking as homeless as can be with our big packs and dingy clothes, when a middle aged truck driver showed up and started talking to us. He was about as articulate as a kindergartener, and it's hard to tell if he even passed grade school from the way he conducted himself. Chouinard managed to ignore him, Dozer and U-Haul just sat silently halfway gazing in this guy's direction until U-Haul managed to break away to call his girlfriend, and Farmer just sat completely dumbfounded, unable to make heads or tails of what this guy was saying. Having been a bartender in southern North Carolina I was well versed in the

English dialect that can only be described as Southern Drunkaneise, and while recently unpracticed I was able to hold a brief conversation with this drunken redneck. Apparently, his truck had broken down and he was riding around with his brother trying to earn some money while some repairs were being done and enjoying some cheap brews in the meantime, all of which I really wasn't interested in, but I still managed to be polite. Eventually I was able to dismiss him and Farmer turned to me and asked "You understood that?" still utterly confused by the whole encounter.

I really didn't have time to answer because at that moment an older woman walking out of the store caught her shoe on the pavement and fell hard in front of the gas pumps. We were all in shock having witnessed this, frozen in horror as she laid motionless on the ground. Enter drunk redneck's brother, a gallant, flannel-clad gentleman whose chivalrous nature was only matched by his blood alcohol level, making a grand appearance by rushing to the woman's side and attempted to lift her. It was a fine attempt, but he nearly toppled over himself in the effort, catching himself with his free hand now balanced in some sort of drunken tripod with an elderly woman resting upon his legs. In disbelief, U-Haul had been describing the whole endeavor to his girlfriend whom had managed to retain her wits and yelled at him to go help, which he promptly did, pulling the now two incapacitated pedestrians to their feet, both thankfully no worse for the wear. A young man, dressed in a solid color jogging suit with a white tee shirt underneath and matching bandanna wrapped around his head interjected into the lack of conversation my friends and I were having with a phrase that almost sounded like "Nouw dat shit fooked up,"--what he meant exactly remains unknown. I myself have never tried experimenting with methamphetamine, though I believe this young man had, and most likely within the last thirty minutes, but that didn't stop him from entering the store quietly and removing himself from the odd events unfolding outside. Farmer jested to me "Where's the popcorn?" implying that all of this belonged in some sort of movie, but strangely enough I had just bought a bag to supplement my trail mix and offered him some as the older woman regained her composure and made towards her car. No sooner did Farmer and I start to enjoy our impromptu cinematic snack did the young man re-emerge from the store, violently shoving the door ajar and shouting back inside "Call the law then! And I will get my shoes back, bitch!" before storming off. Seconds after, the previously quiet and pleasant clerk thrust open the door in much the same way the young man had done, now full of fire and brimstone that would make the very depths of hell look cold. "That is slander! And I'm calling the law!" she called after the young man before turning to us and asking if we had just heard the disrespectful remark that he had made. We didn't have to answer, for the drunken redneck that started this whole series of events was more than happy to confirm that he indeed had, and the two of them started ranting about how ignorant some men can be.

The five of us had seen enough, and we slowly made our way around the building and back to the trail, hoping against all hope that we would be able to do so unnoticed. Thankfully it was so, and we hiked silently for about five miles to a nearby campsite before setting up for the night and having a good laugh about it all. I would love to say that I made the whole thing up, but that's not the case; sometimes the strangest things actually happen if one is in the right, or perhaps wrong, spot at the right time.

Hiker-ism: Hiker Trash

(Adj./noun) People start to do strange things when they become accustomed to no one being around to judge them. All the things that our mothers scolded us for doing as children begin to reemerge, from not bothering to wipe mud from our smiling faces to eating things off the ground. Remember when you wanted to eat only ice cream for dinner? That's some hiker trash.

It's shocking how little people will begin to care about their outward appearance after a little time in the wild. It's almost as if each individual feels like the last person on earth, with absolutely no one else around to judge them. Clothes are left unwashed, beards allowed to grow long, deodorant and shampoo long forgotten about, and perhaps the most bazaar changes are with one's eating habits. I swear, hikers must believe they smell so bad that even the germs of the earth are repulsed by the stench and therefore such things refuse to contaminate a hiker's food.

On one occasion, myself and the four other members of my team were sitting on some large rocks besides a river, which in and of itself was a sight to remember. Even though I had come to see mountains, the rivers always managed to hold my attention, cool and clear, rushing over large, smooth stones made to shine after countless years of freshwater polishing. Some rivers would roar as they made their way while others would churn nearly silently, many others fell somewhere in between, but all were in their own way peaceful and soothing to one's soul.

But I digress--sitting on the rocks we all took some time to eat something so as to keep our strength up. The sheer variety of what hikers eat is astounding! Dozer and U-Haul had managed to plan their trip well and frequently ate dehydrated fruits which they had sent out before embarking; I was purely living off hiker boxes and supplies that could be gathered in town but always managed to have some sort of trail mix on hand. Farmer and Chouinard were doing a little bit of both, so it was always interesting to see what they would have-- sometimes it was energy bars, others it was Little Debbie's brownies, and sometimes even something as strange as cream cheese bagels or a solid block of cheese. On this particular occasion, while the rest of us were snacking on something most would consider normal, Chinard managed to produce an entire block of Colby Jack cheese that he had just removed the plastic from and was preparing to slice off a little to enjoy. I had never thought of cheese to be slippery, but perhaps I've just been holding it wrong, because no sooner had my buddy unwrapped his oversized dairy delight did he lose hold of it, sending it into the river. It bobbed slowly by the rest of us until someone was able to fish it out and hand it back to my friend, who looked like someone had just stolen his lunch money. After staring at it for some time, Chouinard grabbed his knife and sliced off a bit as if nothing had happened, and so the legend of Soggy Cheese was born.

Chouinard got a lot of use out of that knife of his, and should have, it was a very nice tool that must have set him back over a hundred dollars. I'd seen him cut everything from pack straps to bagels with that thing, and it served him not only as a cutting tool, but frequently as a eating utensil as well. I had literally seen this man plunge his knife into a jar of peanut butter using it as some sort of serrated spoon, proceeding to lick it clean after producing a massive glob of food. I remember sitting there, watching my friend do this and just feeling like something about the situation wasn't normal, but not in the way one would think. To me, seeing someone completely misuse an expensive piece of gear to preform a menial task had become commonplace, I didn't even bat an eye at the idea, but what struck me as strange, in a brief moment of clarity, was just how NOT strange this all seemed to me! It was now my day to day life to sit for a meal along side a crystal clear river, or rest at five thousand feet to check my guidebook or write a little. I thought about packing up camp like most people think about grabbing their wallet and keys before heading out for the day, my break room was the mountain ridge, and my office the woods. I would set my hat on a walking stick when I got home and the day was done, and settle into my small, self contained living room to unwind before going to bed. All I had was all I needed, and while I would use some of it in the strangest way, to me it was all in a day's work.

Work is the wrong word for it though. While walking through America's National Parks was indeed no walk in the park, the reward was unmeasurable, and far from the stressful daily grind I was used to. While walking over a lonely Virginia bald through a sea of tall grass at sunset, I looked behind me to see what I could see. The sun had become a tiny red dot, burning intensely like the last remaining ember in a fire nestled between distant peaks. The mountains stretched on either side of it making a long and silent valley, painted deep purple in the fading light. Violet, yellow, and blue thunderheads loomed over it all in a stillness that comes before all hell breaks loose in a violent and unyielding storm. The breeze began to whistle past my ear, and I knew it was time to find shelter, but in that moment the world was beautiful, and I wouldn't trade it for the highest position in the largest company. This wasn't work, this was life!

Impulse and whim are the gateway to adventure. My favorite definition of Fate is described as the intersection of opportunity and preparation, and while those who are strictly focused will promptly arrive where they planned, those who jump at life's little opportunities will end up where they are meant to be. So it was near the town of Bland, VA, as my buddies and I passed a paper sign tacked to a tree along side of the trail. On the top of the page was a very formal, English style Coat of Arms, which instantly caught my attention, and the rest was a brief paragraph describing a place near by that was ready and willing to give hikers a place to stay and a hot meal in the morning. All of us had planned to go a bit farther that day, but sometimes one just has to roll with the waves if a good set comes in. We managed to get cell phone service and called the number on the flyer, connecting with a guy who called himself True Brit, a clever hiker adaptation of a old time

Western title, who agreed to come pick us up at the next road.

We didn't have to wait long upon reaching the road, and after a brief conversation about firewood, the real meaning of the word faggot, and Farmer accidentally becoming a little offended in the translation, a black pickup truck stopped and an older gentleman hopped out asking if we were the ones who had called. He was a bit shorter then the rest of us, and quite thin, but just by looking at this guy one could tell that he was not a man to be fucked with. All things considered, the years had been kind to him, though he bore a few lines on his face, and the pistol packing, tough-as-nails, English entrepreneur was certainly one of the finer gentlemen I had encountered in my travels. In true hiker fashion and without much hesitation we all loaded our gear and ourselves into the back of True Brit's truck and took off down the way to Fort Bastion, an off the grid plot of land semi-secretly located a few miles from the trail. There is a password for those who simply come across the property, and while I cant tell you what it is it has to do with alcohol and the current procurement of said liquid.

Fort Bastion, founded and maintained by Nigel Bastion aka True Brit, is little more then a patch of pines with a river running through it, or at least it was when I was there. The frame work for a log cabin was in place as well as a foundation for another, the first meant to house our host and the second to eventually house hikers as they came across the compound. The stream was cool and pure, void of any contaminants, and the pine forests kept the bugs at bay, or they would have had there been any blood suckers fool enough to venture forth in the frequently freezing early spring. The center point, at the time, of the whole complex was a large teepee comprised of a few tarps and lines, big enough for a multitude to sit under and keep warm by a fire burning in the center of this makeshift, yet efficient, shelter.

When we arrived, we found that Milk Monster and Wall-E, two thirds of the German team, had already set up camp and were spending the night, as well as a new couple set up just behind them. I had seen this couple once before, but only briefly, as they were leaving the convenience store at Atkins when the rest of us arrived, but even then it was easy to tell that they were thru hikers. They were a middle-aged British couple, a taller gentleman with glasses and a certain charm about him named Time Out, and his wife who was a phenomenal chocolateir named Crunchy. The pair were dubbed The Brits by the rest of us, and it was the woman's former profession that dictated and decided their trail names as Time Out and Crunchy, which are apparently English candy bars the like of which aren't seen in the States. They were friendly enough folk, and all of us spent time by the fire enjoying an easy day and a chance to meet new people.

    Perhaps the biggest difference between Brits and Americans has to be in the preparation of food, and after a third of a year in the wild without cooking at all I believe I came across extremely primitive to my English host and his two countrymen. While most had at least boiled water to prepare their evening meal, if they hadn't ordered it in, I held strong to true hiker trash standards and had purchased a two pound can of ravioli to chow down during a quick resupply run this day. My steady diet of air temperature chili had raised a few eyebrows, even among my fellow thru hikers, but a young American devouring un-heated ravioli in the presence of a perfectly good fire was simply barbaric to the Brits judging by their expressions. True Brit eventually broke his silent, morbid curiosity and asked if I cared to heat my meal at all, but by then I was already halfway though the can it it just seamed like a waste of time to me. Besides, I didn't want to spoil myself with proper food when I was about to go back on to the trail. Eventually we all got a few laughs out of the whole thing, and if nothing else concluded that it truly is different strokes for different people.

    Amongst the various other things collected earlier in the day were a few packs of beer, which was shared the way thru hikers do, and we all spent an evening celebrating our different walks of life. At one point Farmer and I began to have a conversation in Spanish seeing as we had both picked up a little from Hispanic migrant workers; only on the AT can one find a French speaking Canadian and an English speaking American conversing in Spanish at a British run establishment. While the conversation was in a foreign language to both of us, the origins of our schooling were the same, and that was back home at work. While most of the day is spent exploring new places and meeting new people, thoughts of what truly matters in our life back in the world can occasionally cross a mans mind, and a sense of homesickness can't always be avoided. When hikers get the chance the stories of our good friends back home shine through, each more outlandish then the next. Our friends become legends to us, God-like, all-powerful and extremely foolish at the some time, and every story will arouse a round of laughter followed by the inevitable short sigh that signifies a time past and longed for again. It was in this moment that Farmer looked at the small blaze gently glowing at our feet and said "Fire is universal--it's the same here as at home," and damn it all if he wasn't exactly right. We can't stop time from passing, nor can we keep those we care about around forever, but there is a certain contiguity to life, and while things may vary greatly from moment to moment in some ways there exactly the same. The fire that burns for our old friends is the same as the one kindled for our new friends, and by sharing the stories of those we know we are never without them, nor are they forgotten.

    The great state of Virginia has a reputation among thru hikers. They say that by the time one reaches this five hundred mile stretch of the AT one's legs should be well under them and, comparatively, the limited amount of elevation change in the state should allow one to put in a lot of miles in a single day. It's supposed to be a productive and restful bit of trail, but also very rewarding to those who take the time to look around. The ridges run in long straight stretches parallel to one another, providing not only easier hiking conditions but also splendid views from numerous rocky outcroppings. On one such rocky ridge, I looked across a wooded valley to gaze at the range running along side the one I was traveling and couldn't help but notice a natural phenomenon present there. While the top of the ridge was flat the face of the mountain varied, sometimes reaching across the valley and at others sinking back into the mountainside. The effect of this was that one side of each of theses protrusions received more sunlight then the other and therefore each, in turn, grew entirely different trees. Tall and still barren maple trees dominated the sunny face, easily beating out any others that tried to take root there, while on the sheltered side the slow growing and shade tolerant pines grew thick, radiating with a lush evergreen hue, thriving where others could not. Each species competed with each other, and in the absence of one the other would have gladly taken hold where previously disadvantaged; however, that's just how the world works. Some things are simply better suited for specific conditions, and I believe it is also so with people. If ever one is beaten out by another, perhaps he should try and nurture a different skill, or consider switching locations to a place he is better suited-- it's surprising how even the slightest change in climate can effect things so greatly.

    I was starting to get the hang of reading my guidebook, and was now not only able to identify in advance peaks and valleys that would prove to be challenging but could also make detailed analysis of what services were available in each coming town. One of the greatest examples of this was when I began to draw close to the town of Parisburg, VA, and while the place was hardly two miles wide it boasted an all you can eat Chinese buffet, which may have become my greatest weakness on the trail. In preparation I made sure to hike as far as possible the night before, getting within eight miles of town, and made double sure to be up bright and early so as to get there before lunch prices became dinner prices, a trick long practiced by my budget conscious self. It's strange just how motivated a hiker can be by food--I swear there were times where I would have engaged in a bare knuckle boxing match with a grizzly for the fabled Klondike bar. But my effort paid off, and by about one o'clock I was wandering up to the front door of Lucky Star Chinese buffet, underfed and ready to make up for lost time.

    I stood before the fruitful plains of MSG and noodles, stoic against a backdrop of crudely framed photographs on the Great Wall and off-red wallpaper, ready to go forth conquering and pillaging at will against my defenseless prey. I descended upon the trays of fried rice and meat that resembled chicken like the locust of ancient Egypt, none could stop the onslaught, though I was forced to wait behind a few people in line from time to time. I sacked the lands for all they were worth, piling my spoils high upon generic ceramic plates and laughing at the ravaged pans that fell in my wake, moving ever forward in shameless victory. Not once but four times I laid waste to the buffet, each time as ferocious and merciless as the time before, until my stomach bulged and I could carry no more.

    Although my offense was halted I derived no satisfaction and sat longing for more combat, but without the means to wage further war. It's a strange feeling actually, being so full that one honestly can't consume any more food but still being hungry. My appetite persisted, but I honestly couldn't swallow any more food, I was that full! I had been starving myself for so long that my hunger had become that of a wild beast after a long winter. Picture vultures squabbling with each other over a corpse so large that no single bird could consume the whole thing in a dozen sitting--that was the internal conflict I was currently experiencing. As I sat trying to digest well enough to be able to exist comfortably I couldn't help but want to go get more. It was fascinating and disturbing all at once. I stayed my lunch lust and decided it would be best if I paid up and left before I did any further damage to myself. The entire feast only cost me five fifty, and while I did expect to save a few bucks by making it to lunch I didn't expect it to be so cheap! As luck would have it, Dozer and U-Haul showed up before I left and they informed me that they had just got a room with the other two in our team, the likes of which I was welcome to stay in with them all if I wished. I must say this was most fortunate, because while I had managed to make it to the door there was no way I was making any further progress on the trail today, and I couldn't pass up the chance to let my innards settle in a warm hotel room complete with a TV and a shower.

Only college students and thru hikers would be happy to split a hotel room with two twin beds between five people; no one complained and all took good long showers seeing as there was no possibility of depleting the establishment's hot water supply. Furthermore, they offered complimentary laundry service and even had a hiker box well stocked with energy bars and toiletries, all of which had become a luxury to me. We spent the rest of the night watching whatever full length movies we could find on television and marveling at the fact that Dozer had somehow managed to wear a hole the size of a football in his undershorts--quite a feat for having Smart Wool and only traveling six hundred and thirty miles in it. Farmer and I slept on the floor, using our mats in the fashion we had become accustomed to, but neither of us cared in the slightest seeing as each of us only paid slightly over ten dollars after splitting the cost of the room five ways.

Before leaving Parisburg in the morning I stopped to grab a few things at the local grocery store, grabbing enough supplies to travel for a solid five days. Although there was a slight problem--after it was all said and done I had less then a dollar to my name and another fifteen hundred miles to go, things were bound to get interesting. I had made it a lot farther then I had planned, there was certainly no shame in having to call it quits at this point, but I had been through so much with so little already. I didn't know how I was going to carry on, but I figured I'd find a way and decided not to worry about it. I was pressing forward even if I had to live off snared squirrels and sassafras! I still had five days worth of food stuffs, and I'd be damned before I quit still having the means to travel.

Hiker-ism: Shin Splints

(noun) Now this is a problem. Shin Splints are common among both long distance hikers and people who run way too much. A dull, yet taxing pain in ones lower leg caused by over stressing the tibia and the muscles surrounding it, Shin Splints really take their toll on a full-time hiker.

    I had become an expert in the ways of the hiker box by now, though I won't say that I preferred practicing the art of living off of others' leavings. While I had managed to score some energy bars and dehydrated meals that would normally be out of my price range, most things in a hiker box are left there for a reason. In Hot Springs I had picked up some old, off brand organic chocolate whose main selling point was that it contained probiotics, though was completely void of any flavor a human would desire to taste. I seriously almost vomited trying to choke down those bars; never again, though when it's all there is, one makes due. I think those chocolate bars were the worst thing I had eaten on the trail, but a close second was some organic meal bar that I had snagged in Pearsburg. I don't exactly recall what the thing was made of, but I do remember there were at least three ingredients that people were known to be allergic to and several others that I hadn't considered food until now. According to the packaging, this all-natural, organic, vegan meal bar was supposed to boost one's immune system, and I damn sure hope it did with the way it tasted! There were times where I felt hungry enough to eat the ass off a three day old street pizza and honestly say it ain't bad, but this bar was gross! I tried like hell not to chew the thing longer then I needed to, and though I was far from happy to taste it I was grateful to have it--anything I could do to keep going at this point, I was going to do.

    While quality was severely lacking from my diet, my quality of life was unmeasurable. I would spend everyday walking in untouched beauty and completely free of stress and worry. Sometimes I would set up camp in a spot that would have cost someone millions of dollars to set a home upon, completely free of charge. One night I even crossed a large river via zipline to camp at a gentleman's home alongside the trail. Life was simple, life was good. As I keep saying, such reward is not without it challenges; the terrain, while relatively flat, had become difficult to travel over recently as a large storm had taken out many tree limbs which now blocked the trail. To make things worse, there was a lot of rock hopping in the area which began to take its toll on my knees and ankles. Large sections traversed massive rock faces slightly slanted one way or another, and while they provided great traction walking with one foot lower then the other really wears on you over a long period of time, stressing each leg differently with no way to correct it. While I didn't escape the area unscathed, it was Dozer who really felt the repercussions of the terrain.

Dozer was a hell of a hiker, he was built for it. He stood a little shorter than me which gave him a low center of gravity, but really shortened his stride compared to other hikers. U-Haul, on the other hand, was far taller than me and was able to cover a lot of ground in a single step, and yet the two managed to keep time with one another. What Dozer lacked in stride he made up for in energy, I tried to keep pace with him from time to time but was never able to for very long--hell of an attitude that guy had. However, his intense adaptation had really worn him on the uneven terrain, and he began to fall victim to vicious shin splints. He was in pain, you could see it written on his face as he went along his way. I remember well stopping into Laurel Creek shelter for a rest and to fill my reservoir, and while kneeling at the creekside seeing him limp hardy to the water's edge and plunge his legs into the cold water in an attempt to alleviate the pain. While that never-say-die attitude Dozer had was proving to be a one way ticket to unbearable pain, it was also the thing that kept him from quitting, though him and his brother had decided to shuttle into the next trail town to rest a few days before heading back to the trail. It was the right decision to make, and I knew he'd be back at it after a little rest and relaxation.

Laurel Creek shelter also proved to be a bit of a trail family reunion. Iron Man and Extra Mile were there and they had teamed up with Pillow, who had originally been traveling with the Germans. Mime and Doc were set up as well, accompanied by Tree Beard and Margarita as they prepared their evening meal alongside Time Out and Crunchy. It was great to see so many faces I knew all in one spot, and Crunchy had somehow managed to track down some fine Belgian chocolate which she passed around to much delight. It was one of the finer moments in the woods, sharing a meal with so many fine folk. Time Out instructed me that I was not to eat cold ravioli again, even if he was forced to cook it himself, but fortunately for him I had found a dehydrated meal back in town so his services weren't required. Chouinard and Farmer had gone on ahead and I soon set off to try and meet them, meaning that I didn't spend the rest of the evening with everyone, but whether it was a night or simply an hour, the time that I spent with these good people really shaped my experience on the trail and I will be forever grateful for it.

Of all the things that set me back perhaps the two most troublesome were the occasional lack of water and running out of daylight with miles still to go. Some people, like Moxie and Ibex, didn't mind hiking at night at all, but I wasn't one of them. Now granted I had to do what I had to do at times, and even without a proper light I was able to get away with a hike at dusk when I needed to, but there's some places that are just flat out dangerous to travel without the light of day. I had heard about a great place called four pines hostel where hikers could stay for a donation or a little labor if they needed, and the owner was made out to be a great fellow. I had intended to make it there one day, but a few sharp inclines and lack of daylight seamed to make that an impossibility by natural means, so I began to mentally prepare for a lengthy night hike over a rock formation called the Dragons Tooth.

With still an hour or so of daylight, I encountered a pair of SOBO hikers setting up just off the trail and shy of the rock formation by about two miles, and having come to love chatting with everyone out on the Trail I found the time to talk to them a bit. I never really had much trouble making friends back in the world, though I would tend to be a bit quiet until I was talked to, but out here the long periods of solitude made crossing paths with another human being a blessing and I full well cherished every chance to chat for a moment if the other party felt inclined. The male/female team had just made it over the Dragon's Tooth and seemed to be more than ready to find a place to rest, though they shared my enthusiasm for conversation. They were about my age and went by the names Sockless and Blaze, a fine pair out exploring the nation. I told them of my plans to make it to Four Pines by pressing through the night, and they instantly became shocked and concerned by the idea, having just crossed the Dragon's Tooth themselves. They seemed to be pretty experienced hikers, so their word of caution struck me hard, and I had to ask why they were so opposed. It was hard to get a straight answer out of the pair, the words just didn't seem to line up properly, but the general consensus was that crossing the Tooth in the dark was about as wise as wearing cement swim fins.

I had come to terms with the fact that no matter how smart I think I am at the time, in hindsight I nearly always consider myself a fool and thus wasn't in haste to add another mark to that record, so I decided to camp with these two for the night. If nothing else, they had just gathered way to much food during their last resupply, and they practically insisted I take some. If my current financial situation wasn't enough to encourage taking on a little extra weight, the fact that they had Tang certainly did. I had thought the powered orange drink mix was put out of production along with my favorite cartoons sometime in my early childhood, and therefore relished the chance to try it again. Tang hadn't changed too much, it still didn't taste like oranges which NASA had promised, but the artificial semi-sweet drink brought me back to the only other time in my life where things had been as simple as they were out here in the woods.

In the morning, I made note to inform my camp mates of some of the finer places to stop farther south and then bid them adieu before I continued north towards the Dragon's Tooth to see what all the fuss was about. The approach to the summit was simple enough, which left me a little disappointed, but if nothing else it was well worth waiting for daylight just to see the rock formation! A pair of jagged rock pillars rose violently from the earth nearly ten times the size of a man, and truly resembled fangs that once belonging to a massive, bloodthirsty beast. I ran into Chouinard here while gazing at the rocks, which he set about to climb, having gained most of his outdoor experience in such a way. People all see the world differently, and to me these stones were nothing but a geological oddity well worth the effort to see, but to Chouinard they were a playground and a challenge only fully appreciated once one stood atop. I don't believe either of us were wrong on our appreciation of nature--instead I find it rather inspiring to get a glimpse into another's perspective of things.

While I had yet to find a reason it was supposed to be wise to put off tackling this section of trail till morning, the descent reviled that the warning I had received the night before was well founded--this was truly one of the more bazaar and frankly dangerous segments I had ever traveled upon! There were times on the AT where the way had been cleared and marked so well that even a brain damaged mule could follow it, while other times the trail nearly vanished, forcing hikers to just wing it and hope they were going the right way. The path down the Dragon's Tooth, however, looked like it should have been blocked off to prevent people from falling down the damn thing! Walking on narrow ridges was nothing new to me, but there were times where one was forced to navigate a rock ledge no wider than five inches, hugging the rock and trying not to fall a good fifteen feet onto the nearest landing. It was time consuming, carefully traversing the rock faces, trying not to lose my balance while carrying over fifty pounds, but I actually loved hiking here. It was challenging and required a lot of focus, but it's something one doesn't get the chance to do everyday, which is the stuff my fondest memories are made of.

After navigating the Dragon's Tooth, I did in fact stop a Four Pines hostel to see if it truly earned the reputation other hikers had given it. From the outside it's nothing special, just a three stall garage behind a small home nestled between a few farms with similar residences. The familiar sight of lawn chairs and cornhole boards helped to ensure that this was indeed a hostel, as well as a massive wooden sign baring the AT symbol stuck in the front yard. When I arrived, there was a young man sitting in one of the chairs outside. He was about as lean as a chap could be, I would doubt he weighed more then a hundred twenty pounds soaking wet with his shoes on, and while he was comparatively well-shaven, a thick blond mustache sat boldly upon his lip and he had shoulder length blond hair to match it. Perhaps the thing that was most eye catching about his fellow was not his hair or stature but rather the pair of tiny shorts he was wearing, barely covering enough to keep him publicly decent and yet somehow fitting loosely. He went by Prefontaine, taking his name from an Olympic long distance runner who competed in the 1970s, and this hiker perfectly fit the profile of the time period. Inside was another gentleman who had sadly fallen a bit under the weather in the previous days. His beard was so thick, dark, and curly that it would hide his mouth when he wasn't speaking, and with a laid back, easy going attitude he went by the name Cool Breeze. The pair of them had been hiking together for some time, and were waiting at the hostel to meet up with Perfontaine's parents who lived relatively close to the area, but until then I enjoyed talking with the lads.

While I had heard great things about John, the owner, the real reason I had made a point to stop into Four Pines was the legendary hiker box that seemingly got larger every time someone talked about it. Those who had seen this infamous box of leavings described it as the Holy Grail of hiker supplies, a virtual black hole of foodstuffs packed so densely that a man could live his entire life and then some off it's contents, rumored to be the final resting place of the Arc of the Covenant and inhabited by the last of the American Nymphs. Upon seeing it myself, the stories weren't far off--this thing was huge! John and his lady friend had taken it upon themselves to go around to local food stores and cart off whatever the stores could no longer sell, dumping a mismatch of goods into large totes for hungry hikers to pick through. From chicken salad to raisins they had it all, and even had filled an entire tote with enough juice boxes to quench the thirst of the entire county's elementary schools. My pack was pretty well loaded up, but I jumped at the chance to gather what I could, and even managed to whip up a quick meal using what I could find with a few farm fresh eggs John had provided for those who cared to cook in the hostel's kitchen. But perhaps the greatest find was the wonderful baked goods the lady of the house, Donna, provided to hungry passerbys--absolutely scrumptious! I felt bad not being able to leave much for John, though I did wash all the dishes and straighten up a bit after filling my pack, hoping it'd be enough until I was able to repay him someday in the future when my finances were more in order. When Prefontaine's folks arrived I bid everyone a fond farewell, but not before packing in a few baked goods the thru hiker's mother had brought along and simultaneously feeling slightly overwhelmed by the willingness of people to help those who had decided to travel.

Hiker-ism: Cowboy Camping

(Verb) Picture a bunch of young cowboys out on the range at night gathered around a campfire, strumming a guitar, whittling, spitting, winding down after a long day out on the range. Do you see them with tents? Hell no you don't! Cowboy camping is sleeping out under the stars with nothing more then a sleeping bag and moonlight to cover you.

While the Greyson Highlands were undoubtedly still my favorite hiking location in Virginia, a close second would have to be area around McAfee Knob, and I believe I'm in good company when I say that. McAfee Knob is a destination hiking spot in Virginia, frequented by day hikers or those out for a weekend, but it was easy to see why. Upon reaching the main trail to the summit, the ground appeared well worn and graded due to the multitude of foot traffic, which made for easy hiking. While I did encounter many people

I didn't get much of a chance to talk to them, for many were out hiking for the day with their family; the young were too busy running about examining everything and the older folk tended to be red in the face and out of breath. I wondered how I must have looked when I started hiking--I knew it was over a week before I felt like I was starting to get the swing of things, but had I really struggled nearly this much?

Whether or not I struggled when starting, today's hike was seemingly stressless, allowing for many chances to take in the scenery. The view from the summit was certainly one to behold! When the trees break they reveal a path onto a large smooth rock ledge overlooking a wooded valley spotted with farms and homesteads. It was a clear day and there seemed to be no limit to my sight, gazing over endless rolling hills and meadows. I imagine the first man who glanced upon this land must have been so awe-stricken that he could will himself to go no farther and thus settled here below--can't say I blame him, because for a moment I thought about it myself. I encountered a couple of day hiking, hippie types setting up hammocks and taking in the view. Indeed the winter had finally broken, and who could help but enjoy such a pleasant day in nature?

I had seen many barren summits along the way, but this one was different. The rock was extremely flat and level and dropped off sharply at its end. Also, large cracks appeared on its surface, dropping a good ten feet or more and big enough to swallow a man should he slip, but they were well worth leaping over to get the full effect of the view. The most renowned spot on this great mountain allows for one to hang their feet off the edge of a large flat rock that juts a solid ten feet over the side of a cliff, and it's a famed spot for hikers to have their photo taken. Farther down the trail, many of the larger cracks can be accessed as a sort of natural maze, which could have easily hidden a forgotten settlement or mythical creature, but if nothing else were fun to look at and wonder what could be there.

It wasn't just McAfee Knob that made hiking about this area so beautiful and unique, but also the miles after it. I couldn't help but look back at the Knob every so often as the mountain stood alone and stoic over the neighboring valley, glowing red in the last light of the day. I had hoped to make it to the shelter in Lamberts Meadow, but the rising moon was beginning to signal that my desired location may be a bit beyond reach and so I found a nice clear spot on the ridge to set up. It had been dry and warm for the last few days, and the lack of clouds ensured that the night sky was bound to be one to remember, and so I decided to cowboy camp, having never done it before. The full moon began to shine as it rose above the trees and I made to lay beneath it, so bright that I didn't have to use a flashlight to journal, its light falling softly on the mountain behind and the trail ahead. It was too perfect a night to let slide so easily, and so I rose again to look about, taking in the stars and gazing with ease over all that I had seen that day. The thought of hiking more miles in such a pleasant scene crossed my mind, but instead I decided it best to be at rest and relax for a little while, simply being still and happy.

It's strange, but I never felt alone at moments like this; though I may be miles from the nearest person, I felt embraced by the Earth herself, sitting close as she showed her softer side. She was just like a woman at the end of a long day, her hair let down with none to impress other than those she dearly trusted, glowing with a simple beauty usually masked during the day. The little things she thinks nothing of in her nightly routine a man can't help but smile at, his heart touched by the simple, human side of his lover. The earth was my lover, and while quiet and reserved she was always there for me, she showed me things I had only dreamed of, and she never ceased to amaze me.

.

Shirtless, I washed my face and arms in the stream in Lambert s Meadow, splashing water on my back in a manner that was both refreshing and shocking, though my biggest surprise came when I went to wash my under arms. The only thing I had seen this color in recent memory had been perched on the rim of a shot of tequila; several of the hairs in my pits had undoubtedly become lime green, coated with what appeared to be moss or mildew. If it got any worse, I'm pretty sure the Whos down in Whoville would bar me from their village lest I attempt to steal Christmas. I was repulsed, I was disgusted, but mostly, I was amazed that such a thing could happen! With no other option I laughed at my misfortune, washing as best as I could in the stream and noting that it was indeed time for a proper shower.

I met back up with Dozer, U-Haul, and Farmer in Daleville, and they kindly let me sleep on the floor of their hotel room for the night at no cost.

Having found a good place to stay, I was still in want of food for the night and had almost reserved myself to dealing with it and going to bed, when I remembered an old, yet unsavory, trick a friend had taught me. He was an interesting fellow, and had made it around the country several times by hitching and hopping trains, occasionally taking a bus should he find the means, and had managed to do so without ever spending a cent! I'm not about to go into full detail as to how he managed such a feat but one of the more resourceful tips he could give was regarding pizza parlors. Apparently, pizza parlors rarely keep their pies overnight to be served the next day; honestly I'm not sure if its legal for them to do so, and as a result whatever is unpurchased at the end of a day is simply thrown away with the rest of the garbage. If a hobo times it right, he can snag a nearly fresh pizza, still warm in the box tossed out just after closing time--and there just so happened to be a pizza parlor in town.

Like a modern day urban hunter I sat out back on a hill, camouflaged by some tall grass and waiting for my prey to arrive. The night air was warm and the street lights provided good visibility, and it was just a matter of time before my target arrived. I didn't have to wait long when I got my chance; a young doe appeared, fatted with her bounty, carrying several boxes, and unaware of my presence. She stopped and dropped them in dumpster out back before heading back to safety, closing the door behind her, blissfully unaware of my intention. This was my shot! Like a sniper on a calm day I took aim and fired without hesitation, diving headlong over the rim of the steel vessel and finding my prey perched safely on a bag of dry trash, just waiting to be taken. I suppose I could have brought the spoils back to my clan but I figured this victory was best enjoyed alone, seeing as the rest may not find my means satisfying to their liking. So on yonder hill where I had waited and shot down my target I also enjoyed its spoils, depositing the skin and entrails back in the dumpster where I had gathered it. No harm no foul, right?

It took a little effort, but I was able to restore the proper color to my underarms after a good long shower, and so I slept that night well fed and in good company, even if the method had been a little unorthodox. In the morning my companions rested far longer than I did, seeing as Dozer and his brother were going nowhere quickly in his condition, so I decided to take advantage of the continental breakfast the hotel offered. I suppose if they had gone to dine I would not have, but since they decided to pass it up it would have been wasteful not to go in their stead. While it was a little forgettable as a meal it served me well, and so it was back to the trail, rested, fed, and clean for the first time in far too long. This happened be the last time I would see the Philly brothers on the trail, though I had hoped it wasn't at the time. Dozer decided to take an entire week to rest his shins, thus putting the pair of them far behind myself--its a shame to have left them, but I was blessed to have ever met them and still count them among the best people I had ever known in life.

Life is full arbitrary dates that people assign meaning to. A year doesn't technically start on January first, Christmas would be just as merry if it were on June third, and people in America would get just as drunk on Saint Patrick's day if it came around at Halloween time. A year is no shorter or longer no matter what moment you decide to mark it from. However, one annual event that I do believe keeping special is one's own birthday. Everyday in one's life should be one to remember, and on birthdays we get a chance to look back at how far we've come in a years time, how we have changed and what we have been blessed with. I just so happened to celebrate my birthday this year in the middle of nowhere, wandering along the AT in central VA on the fifteenth of April. I suppose it could have been like any other day, but this one was mine and so I wanted to commemorate in the best way I could think of: by hiking in my birthday suite! Out of courtesy for any families I may cross I didn't go full monty sadly, but I felt as though a good hike in my underwear would suffice, and so I set out to make it so.

It was far from a pleasant day however; the days before had been beautiful, but on the morning of April fifteen the sky was dark and a light drizzle made getting out of my sleeping bag seem like the last thing I wanted to do at the time. I was undeterred in my pursuit of underclad hiking, for this was my day and I refused to let a little weather stop my celebration of it! Dressed only in a pair of boots, my ever-present utility belt, sweet hat, and undershorts, I set out on the trail, laughing a little and happy to be able to go about things my own way out here.

Little did I know that mother nature was either in no way happy with my current life choices or in the mood to play a bit of a joke on me, but if nothing else she had at least taken the time to get me something for my birthday. Perhaps I should have taken the dreary start as a warning, but I didn't, and things got far more interesting from there. The rain started to fall heavier, little bit by little bit but quite noticeably, and intensifying with every passing minute. Before long the little I was wearing was soaked through, but this was my day dammit, so I continued on, a barrel short of looking like I had just lost a bad game of poker. Well if I was going to be stubborn apparently so was nature, and the rain soon turned to sleet as the temperature suddenly dropped. Ever onward I marched. The sleet turned to a wet, heavy snow and began to coat my naked legs and chest, but it was bearable provided I kept my heart rate up and my blood flowing. It started to snow sideways in a stiff wind! Mother nature was out to make this a day to be reckoned with--I just laughed. Of course it would be on the day that I struck out grossly under prepared that winter would make its last stand, but rather then abandon my plans I rose to the challenge! This was the start of my twenty sixth year on this planet. The age of twenty six was going to be my time to stride forth into life, to progress where I had otherwise failed, and come what may I was moving forward my way! The snow turned to an icy rain, which was worse, seeing as it stung every bit of exposed flesh it happened across, and I currently had a surplus of that. Was I insane? Had I finally lost it? Gone off the deep end? Crazy as a loon? Fit for the nut house? Here I was in terrible weather, striding through the woods in next to nothing, boldly laughing at my misfortune, and actually enjoying it!?!

Actually, I felt more together than I had for a very long time; for while I always wished to celebrate my birthday the last few years I had actually come to lament it. I'll never forget the day my life changed forever, no matter how long I live, or how hard I try. April thirteen twenty eleven, undoubtedly, unequivocally, hands down, without question, the worst day of my life. What was said on this day is a blur, a bad dream I can't believe was real, and I guess it doesn't really matter in the end, but what is forever burned into my memory is this: standing on the sidewalk outside of my apartment watching a car and trailer pull away with my fiance and son, not even a year old, both bound for California without me. It had been coming for a month or so; she had already kicked me out and changed the locks, rendering me homeless, short of work, broken beyond measure, but despite already being at an all time low this day hit me with no less weight. I had tried to talk it out with her, to fix things, to be present, but it was as if my heart had attached itself to my tongue the day she cast me out and they both became twisted, confused, and useless, so there was no reconciliation. I had always believed that a man could do all that he set his mind to, that nothing was too great, but even after I invested everything I had into trying to be a husband and a father I came up short, and my whole life shattered underneath the wheels of a westbound car and trailer. There isn't a word for the feeling that overtook me, either not enough men haven't felt it or they had all been rendered equally speechless, closest I can come is just plain broken. I didn't cry, I didn't scream, didn't feel like it. I wasn't mad, wasn't sad, wasn't irate or suicidal, just utterly empty and completely inconsolable. So, silently, feeling nothing, staring straight ahead, I went to a bar, grabbed a beer, and spent the better part of three years drinking it. I had never really gotten over it, some days were better then others, occasionally I found a reason to smile, but every year this time in April I would wake up staring straight ahead, hardly able to do anything other than drink. But not this year!

This year I was not going to fail, fall short, give in, break down, or even settle for less then I desired! I had spent enough time trying to find the answer, to fix things and make it all go away, but no longer. In the wind rain and snow I realized that some things are never going to be alright, somethings don't have an answer, that the storm will not let up, that life will not just give one a break, and that time will not stop for a man to catch his breath. However, life will go on, time will continue before you, and it's up to us to weather what may, in pursuit of happiness and better days. Things between me and my son were never going to be perfect, or even really fixed from the damage that had been done, that storm will forever rage and what was supposed to be there is gone. I had tried to find a way to be with my boy but I had no means to relocate, and even if I did his mother is as fickle as a spring breeze, going wherever, whenever she pleased, literally from South America to East Asia as soon as the opportunities presented themselves, my son in tow. My son was getting to do the things that I had always dreamed of, he was well taken care of, and experiencing things at an age that will shape him into the most worldly, loving, unprejudiced being that ever lived, and I was so glad to know it. However, one thing will always bother me. I know one day my son is going to ask me "Why weren't you there, Dad? What were you doing?" and the fear of that question has always been devastating. I will never be the father I wanted to be, but I can do something: I can be the man I want my son to someday be. While I will never have a good answer for my son, I can be a pillar of strength in an unyielding storm, I can withstand the mightiest of blows and not be moved, I can live a good life so that when my answer fails, my example can lead my son in the lessons I was unable to teach him. It is a harsh reality, but it is our reality, and rather than sit crippled by the past I will endure for a better future.

As nature raged against my naked body, alone in the wilderness, my laughter was not of madness but triumph! Bring what you may life! Have at me world! Take your best shot! Here I am, and I am broken no longer! Like the trail blazed before me my path was made clear; I was reborn.

I managed to hike over half the day in this far from pleasant weather, clad as I had begun it, before the day began to clear up. As it did, I decided that my point had been made and so I suited up properly after spending about thirty minutes in a shelter, wrapped in my sleeping bag to warm up. The half-naked hike wasn't the only way I ended up celebrating my new year; the shelter I stayed at that night had a few gifts of its own. When I arrived, Farmer had begun to make a fire--quite a feat seeing as all the surrounding lumber was well saturated--and Perfontaine and Cool Breeze had managed to catch up with us and were also setting up. Someone had left a plastic container with oatmeal and a few bars that were free for the taking, which I did, as well as a couple packs of Ramen noodles. Farmer was feeling particularly generous this evening and offered me his camp stove to cook some noodles for my birthday, and a hot meal on a cold day in the woods is far better then any cake I have ever had! Except for maybe a red velvet cake I had one year--but that's a different story. Warming my bones and drying my coat by the now raging fire I couldn't help but smile. Things were no different from the day before, but I felt different; for the first time in years a smile hit my face on my birthday.

10 DON'T FORGET TO REMEMBER

It's impossible to not change while traveling. New experiences and massive amounts of time to reflect have a profound effect on a person, so much so that it becomes noticeable even in the midst of it all. For me, one of the biggest indicators was the change in how I would journal at night. In the beginning I would slap something down just because I felt like it was something I should be doing, my handwriting was sloppy at best, and I would write major things that happened in just a line or two. Now, I was marking specific details, such as daily miles and minor thoughts. The entries became longer, far more legible, reflecting not only on what I had done but also on what I had thought. I have never really felt out of place in the woods, even as a child, but now I truly felt as if I was assimilating back into the wild, like it was home to me.

What is home anyway? I have heard it said that it takes more than a house to make a home, and I agree, but I have also heard people describe things as large as a city to be home, or something as small as a lover's embrace. I have come to believe that home is more than a place, more then just a word even, home is a feeling brought about by something that brings great comfort. Also, who says that each individual is limited to a single home? I have many: the bar on Front Street, the city of Wilmington, the state of North Carolina, and now the woods of North America themselves.

Virginia was a marvelous state to hike in! The trail near the road to Glasgow in particular was a real treat. The James River cuts a wide path through the mountains, providing exquisite views from the overlooking peaks. It's picturesque really; a train rolls alongside the river and the peaks look painted against the sky, they're so perfect! Also, the footbridge crossing the James is the longest foot bridge on the trail, and it is quite a sight to behold. I remember that when crossing this bridge I came across a ragged looking young man walking the opposite direction, and that his appearance screamed thru hiker. As we drew near to each other I pointed to him and said, "SOBO?"

"Yep. NOBO?"

"Yep."

And as we passed each other we high fived, thus ending our

interaction. It seems silly to have left it so short, but it was something I had hoped would happen. Sometimes it's the little things that make a day memorable.

I did meet another Northbound hiker around this area as well, a fellow in his late forties named Gary who seemed to be rebelling against the whole trail name thing, but a few of us decided to call him Gung Ho anyway, due to the fact that he was very early to rise and didn't stop short, ever. Other than 'Hello' he never really said much; nice enough guy, but liked to keep to himself. However we did enjoy the summit of Big Rocky Row together after a steep climb, well worth the effort, and lovely enough that one doesn't need words to find it beautiful.

In the valleys spring was coming into bloom, though the higher elevations still remained barren. The trees began to bud and sprout new growth, little wild flowers seemingly sprouted overnight, and stalks and sprouts began to push their way up through the earth. Many of the trees bore flowers of white and fushia, birds began to sing again, and the whole world seemed to be rubbing the sleep from its eyes after a long winter's slumber. It had been a long time coming, the winter of 2013 had proven to be particularly rough, and these first signs of spring were reminiscent of an old friend coming to visit again. The days grew longer, the nights warmer, and while I had truly loved the silence and solitude of winter, the signs of spring were more than welcome in my eyes.

When immersed in such rugged, beautiful country, it's no wonder why whomever had gazed upon it would want to blaze a trail so as to share it with the whole world. There is a peace that being so far from everything brings, unlocking long dormant portions of the mind, inspiring art and poetry, ideas and intellect. Truly, if ever there was a way to decipher the mystery of life the answer lies not in books or study, but rather observation and discovery. It is my desire that everyone would get the chance to see the world as it is, untouched by man, and it is the same desire had by others that brought about the one thing I had been most conflicted about along my whole journey.

The Blue Ridge Parkway is a graded, paved road stretching hundreds miles through the mountains, overlooking many of its most scenic locations, providing even those who have lost the ability to walk a chance to see the natural wonders of America. As a young, strong, healthy man this is my dilemma. While I realize the usefulness of this road, it's quite a hindrance to my isolation, from modern convenience and hassle. Like a great man-made scar the road blazes through what is otherwise nature's own to keep, and as the foot path winds through the mountains hikers are interrupted by passing motorcars and irreversible damage to the land. Man's desire to see the wild has robbed him of the very wild he had meant to observe! While I was far from happy to encounter the Blue Ridge Parkway, I had to remind myself that the old, the young, the disabled, out of shape, and people entangled in a web of modern obligations were just as much a man as myself and had just as much a right to experience the profound simplicity of nature. Perhaps even more so, for I remember the first days I spent wandering and the relief they had brought; I have seen the smiles on day hikers and heard stories at night around campfires that weekend warriors would share, completely captivated by the things I had started to take for granted. I truly believe the BRP does more good than harm, but I still don't like it, and am entirely opposed to similar roads being constructed through the other natural wonders of North America.

I spent most of these days hiking alongside of Prefontaine, Cool Breeze, and Farmer, encountering them several times each a day. As usual I was unable to keep their pace, but by taking shorter breaks and starting bright and early I managed to keep our daily miles roughly the same--and we were covering many in a day. There was a time that Cool Breeze and I were trying to meet our comrades at Matts Creek Shelter, and by some miscalculation ended up hiking at a brisk jog trying to reach the shelter before the night fully set in. With effort and by straining our eyes in the last bit of the day's light, we managed to make it and set up. I had planned to sleep in the shelter but it was already full and one of the hikers there had fallen ill, making it a less than desirable option for the night, and so tenting it was. Everyone there was friendly however, especially a young lad by the name of Mad Hatter, who was most eager to tell of the day's adventures and how he had spent the previous evening with Moxie and Ibex, whom I always seemed to be about a half day behind.

It's interesting how the little things can hang one up as he travels, most notably supplies. I had become the undisputed master of rationing, but even the strictest diet will eventually consume all of one's provisions, and so I was forced to stop into Buena Vista, pronounced Be-YEW-na Vista by the locals. The hitch into this fine city is perhaps the hardest on the entire trail, seeing as the AT lays close to ten miles east of town and the city only boasts six thousand people. When I arrived at the road to town Farmer had already been standing there for close to an hour, and he was no closer to his destination then when he had started. The pair of us stood there for roughly another hour before Gary joined us, and the three of us tried to look as presentable and friendly as possible. We removed our hats, moved our hair out of our faces, and myself storing all but my smallest knife in my pack we stood there hoping that some kind soul wouldn't be overly offended by our outward appearance. There are worse things than standing alongside the road in good company, and eventually we started to make excuses for those who passed us by, saying they must have an appointment or be in haste to deliver some antidote to the now deathly ill President or something. Perhaps they had a soccer game to get to which is why a solo person driving a minivan wouldn't stop for a few hikers, or perhaps there were several ninjas in the back holding them hostage while remaining unseen. Whatever the reason, Gary eventually called the hostel in town for a ride, but as soon as the shuttle appeared a van pulled up and offered us a ride. I had hoped to work for stay at the hostel, or at least raid the hiker box, but in case that fell through I would have felt guilty taking the shuttle in and so Gary went to the hostel and Farmer and I accepted the hitch.

    I halfway wish I had gone with Gary, for the fellow we chose to ride with was kind enough but had obviously grown up in the mountains and was very used to driving on the winding roads. Farmer had hopped in the front seat of the van, I didn't mind seeing as he had helped me out along the way, but that proved to be the only other seat in the van--so I had to try and find something to hold on to while sitting on the floor in the back. Perhaps it was because I hadn't ridden in a car in quite some time, but this guy seemed to be driving as if he was training for the motor speedway or something as he raced down the mountain. It became a challenge to to maintain my place on the floor as we sped left and right around corners, hoping that at very least I wouldn't slam into one of the windows, breaking either it or myself. I will say the ten miles went rather quickly, though not quickly enough for the discomfort, and while my nerves were a bit rattled by the endeavor I still managed to thank the driver upon arriving safely in town. Perhaps I was just thanking him for the chance to step out of the vehicle--that remains unknown. Even though my ride was over, Farmer needed to get back to Daleville to pick up a parcel that he hadn't been able to earlier, so he continued on as far as the driver was willing to take him before continuing to hitch back to where he needed to be, a brave sole...

While the night in town had been a fine rest, the night I spent back on the trail the night after was certainly far more memorable. It was the evening before Easter and the three of us had decided to spend it, fittingly, at The Priest shelter in northern VA. The shelter was like any other, apart from a strange rock formation standing on the trail near the blue blazes to the shelter, but what made the night memorable was the views from the nearby ridge. As a thru hiker I consider myself a connoisseur of sunsets and star light, a man who has sampled the finest of light and drank deeply from the grandest illumination. The sunset on Easter Eve over the Priest overlook I believe to be the the purest and most astounding of any I have ever partaken of! The valley was lovely to begin with, a deep cavern lined on all sides by steep mountains with several streaks of exposed rock highlighting the wooded walls, but it was all made even more marvelous in the evening light. There is no science of prisms or climate that will ever be able to fully explain such majesty! As the sun sank below the low lying clouds they turned vibrant, regal shades of purple and violet, stunningly contrasted on all sides by a golden orange with streaks of red. Every inch of the sky was bathed in this glorious layering of light and dark, and as the sun sank over the valley the last rays of the day seemed to shine upon my very soul, warming my heart so profoundly that it prompted the whispering of an honest 'thank you' for such a marvelous sight. To this day I have not seen this evening's equal, though I don't intend to stop looking, and even if I am to spend the rest of my days searching for such a sight again I would not consider my life wasted.

It seems that the Priest Summit will ever be determined to astound whomever managed to wander over it. Even in plain morning light the views are ones to be remembered, and the three thousand foot descent off the mountain is a force to be reckoned with. While it was absolute murder on my knees, I really enjoyed walking off the Priest; the trail follows a mountain stream, crossing it several times as the water falls playfully over rocks and collects in crystal clear pools. The mountains were fully striding into spring time, covering the forest floor with wildflowers of every hue--tiger lilies, and daisies, azaleas and dandelions, flowering dogwoods and sumac--every flower, root, and weed rejoicing in the new year. According to the guidebook, The Priest is the last peak where a thru hiker is above four thousand feet until the state of Vermont, but Three Ridges on the other side of the descent falls only sixteen feet short of the title.

While I did greatly prefer the three thousand foot accent as opposed to its descending counterpart, such a climb was far from easy and required a great deal of energy to summit. Virginia had provided some amazing meadows as well as incredible balds, but Three Ridges proved to be a unique and memorable blend of the two. It's a very rocky climb with lots of open views of the surrounding valleys, and a rock formation called Chimney Rock is an excellent playground for any climbing enthusiast. Though my favorite part of the peak is on the north side, a place called Hanging Rock Overlook, boasting such an incredible view that if there was a water source close by there is no question that it's where I would have set up for the night. Sadly my need for water after the climb surpassed my desire for a fine evening view and I had to make my way to the next shelter, but this three thousand foot valley is without question a place that should be on every hiker's wishlist.

Hiker-ism: Trail Town

(Noun) Pretty self explanatory. A trail town is a small city either directly on or easily reached from the trail. The inhabitants of these burrows are well aware of the AT and those who hike it, many of the shops, and especially restaurants, have specials geared towards long distance hikers.

Everywhere is different. Hell, take a brain damaged mule from the Grand Canyon and drop it somewhere in west Michigan and even that poor bastard will be able to see such a simple truth. While this simple truth is widely known, it seems to often be forgotten in man's futile effort to find some sort of greater meaning to life and the universe. Instead of searching for some sort of grand continuity, I say celebrate the differences! Each trail town was so different, it was always exciting to hike in and sample the local flavor, and while they all were thru hiker friendly some were certainly more excited than others about the coming of myself and my vagrant kin. There has been a long standing debate between thru hikers as to which of these blessed havens is the most hiker friendly, and I don't believe a winner will ever officially be declared. However, if I were to cast my vote, after much deliberation, I believe it would be for the city of Waynesboro, VA.

To be fair, a big part of my decision is based on the fact that the people of the city have independently organized to shuttle hikers into town. There's a Welcome Center nearly directly on the AT, marking the south end of Shenandoah National Park, where thru hikers may call for a shuttle off a long list of numbers provided there. If that wasn't a fine enough welcome, the attendant at the Welcome Center gifted me a fair sized bag containing some hiking essentials and a Bible courtesy of the local church. While I was grateful for the gift, if the church continues to spread the good word in this method I would suggest that they supply the smallest, most travel friendly Bible they can find. The full sized text is a bit hard, and rather undesirable, to carry due to its weight and bulk, but carry it I did until I found a proper place to deposit it for other hikers.

Not only was the list of shuttles convenient, but the drivers were prompt and eager to assist. I hardly had to wait ten minuets until my ride arrived, and before he dropped me off in town he offered to give me a driven tour of the city so I would know where everything was. Waynesboro was big enough that walking around the entire city could be a little cumbersome, so the tour greatly helped, and eventually the ride came to a close as I was dropped off in a park near the YMCA. Most cities are greatly opposed to people camping in public areas, just trust me on this one, but one thing that made this city so unique is that the citizens had taken it upon themselves to designate an area were such an activity was not only appropriate, but also encouraged! Thru hikers, and apparently fellows who were having some trouble with their old lady, were welcome to set up and stay for a night, or two, in a quiet, safe place complete with a port-o-john, gazebo, and a nearby YMCA that offered free showers to those who asked! Wait, there's more! Two blocks away from the park was a public library just bursting with books waiting to be read by weary travelers. Waynesboro was proving to be a little slice of hiking heaven.

I had been hiking alone for a few days before hitting town, but at the park I ran into Prefontaine and Cool Breeze, which was a welcome turn of events. As we were catching up an older gentleman came walking up to the gazebo where we were seated and proceeded to sit and rest among us. If there's one thing being alone in the woods will teach a person it's the value of company, and so it wasn't long before this gentleman was included in our conversation. His exact age was hard to pin down, but it was no secret that he had seen many years on this good planet. He was slightly hunched over, thin, and with only a few wispy hairs sticking out from under his hat, but I'll never forget meeting my friend Leaim, one of the kinder souls I have ever encountered. The four of us spent a good time chatting before Leaim offered us a ride to a different part of the city to visit a fast food restaurant, and while I was still broke, Prefontaine offered to pick me up a sandwich so off we went. This venture was rather uneventful, but during our meal Leiam insisted that he be able to take us out to dinner later. While the three of us felt that he had already done more than enough he stood firm in his offer and it truly felt rude to refuse. Our host dropped us back off at the park with instructions that we were to meet back with him later, to which we all agreed and set about to kill a little time before dinner.

Prefontaine and Cool Breeze went to supply, but I needed to do a little fund collecting first, so we parted ways for the time being, them to spend and me to beg. At this time however some bad weather began to roll in, starting with a light rain and gradually intensifying, rendering the streets empty and therefore void of fine folks to spare a dollar. It was for the best I believe; the city was already being so kind and I felt guilty asking for more, and so I went to the library to wait out the storm.

While seated, warm and dry, in the basement of the library, reading a tomb of Tolkien's unfinished tales, I decided to do something I hadn't done in years, that being to just randomly call my mother. When I first moved away from home I used to call every Sunday, just to chat and keep posted on recent events, but when things fell apart in my life I stopped. I'll admit I was very embarrassed by how horribly I had failed at starting a family, and the immense shame I felt had kept me from contacting anyone directly related to me. I felt like I had let them all down seeing how there had never been a divorce in my family, let alone a child born out of wedlock. However, I felt that if I was truly going to start moving forward again this would be a grand place to begin, so I took my phone off airplane mode, breaking radio silence for the first time in months. While for many it's no big deal to ring home, I was nervous, on edge, and as the phone rang I was tempted to hang up before the call could be answered. I mean, how do you even start a conversation like this after years of painfully awkward communication that had been reserved only for holidays and always preceded by a decent amount of drinking to calm the nerves? Still, the sound of a familiar "Hello" meant that the conversation had started, and it was best to not overthink it and just talk, so I did.

I responded with a sheepish "Hi Mom," very uncertain how this conversation would turn out, but thankfully she was overjoyed to hear from me! Before setting out I had told my mother that I planned to walk across America, and that I wouldn't be using my phone along the way, but that was months ago. Since then, I had just been lost in the woods, and in hindsight I can hardly imagine her relief in finding that I was still alive. She had been supportive of my idea to go, though I could tell she was a little worried--it's not easy to hear that someone you love is just going to drop off the face of the earth for a year or so. I can hardly remember what else we talked about, but talk we did for about an hour, mostly about what I had been doing, though I did find out that my cousin was getting married in August which was something worth trying to make. I wanted to apologize for being so distant, but couldn't find the words, so I just continued on about the places I had seen and the folks I was encountering. I'll admit I may have just been too caught up in the enjoyment of telling the tail to switch into a depressing conversation, but either way it was just nice to hear from someone from back in the world.

Like any concerned mother, she had asked how I was getting by, if I had enough and what not. I just told her that I didn't know how I was going to make it but I was going to and doing fine, though I changed my tune a bit upon finding out that I had a sizable tax return waiting at home. I had completely forgotten about my annual obligation to Uncle Sam, but fortunately my father hadn't, and I had the foresight before leaving to switch my mailing address to my parents place. It seemed like a wonderful turn of events, but it didn't take long to realize that there was no way for me to sign the check from acrsoss the eastern time zone, thus rendering the thing useless unless I shipped on home which wasn't happening any time soon. My family has never been rich, but thanks to my father teaching high school financial planning he had been able to take his family from a trailer to owning an expensive building on Main Street, and the two of them were doing quite alright at the moment. Realizing that there was no way to legally deposit my return, my Mother offered to deposit a personal check in the amount that I would receive into my account and wait for me to return to reimburse them with my actual tax return.

All I can say is one, thank God for many nation wide branches of Bank of America, and two, I really didn't see that coming. I had been digging scraps out of dumpsters and public boxes for so long that even twenty dollars seemed like a small fortune, and this would be enough to complete the rest of my travels! It's hard to say if my voice wasn't shaking when I said "Yeah, that would really help actually" to her offer, but I certainly was, and a giant weight instantly fell off my shoulders. Anyone that knows me well understands that I don't ask for help, I will accept it if it's offered, but I would rather sleep on a park bench in winter then ask to bum a couch for a night. The whole trip had forced me to shed my pride and become humble, to be grateful for the kindness of strangers, but I believe I would have starved if I had no other choice but to ask help from people I knew while on the road. It doesn't seem like much to some, taking a loan from one's own parents, but I had literally chosen homelessness over asking for their help before. I knew I could make it on my own, I had proved it time and time again, but damn it all if it's not nice to have some help now and then! There's a reason pride is one of the seven deadly sins, and I was learning how to do away with it.

We eventually said our farewells, leaving the conversation with my father running off to a local branch of Bank of America, check in hand, to try and get some cash to me by the morning. I can't really tell if I liked the feeling I was experiencing having had that conversation. I was indeed glad to have reestablished contact with my mother, and happy that it looked like I would now have the funds to complete the trip, but I was still getting used to asking for help. I was relieved and disappointed all at once; I don't know if I would have been able to accept the gift if I hadn't previously earned that amount by my own merits, but I knew it was a good thing that I had done so I just tried to build off of that notion.

The rain had stopped and indeed Leaim held up his offer, arriving on time to pick up the three of us for dinner and driving over to the local Chinese buffet. The three of us who had been stuck in the wilderness for the last too long ate enough to put a lesser business under, while simultaneously enjoying stories of our gracious host's past. He had led an interesting life, working for the forest service, and greatly desired for there to be an arboretum in the city for the young folk to learn from and the old to enjoy. It was a grand idea and I hope the city picks up on it, it would help us hikers as well being able to identify the usefulness of the things we spend so much time around. The time seemed to pass to quickly, and when it came time to leave our new friend insisted that he pick up the check. I think I would have protested if I had been in higher standings, but that wouldn't be until tomorrow at best and thus accepted his kind offer before parting ways.

Back at the park I met with some familiar faces. Farmer and Chouinard had caught up again and along with them came Tree Beard and Margarita! I don't know if I was happier to see them or the case of beer that they had brought along, but either way it was a grand reunion as we spent the rest of the evening sipping brews and laughing in the park, rejoicing like gypsies under a star lit sky.

There was an outfitter on the way out of town that I decided to visit for a moment; most of the people I had spent the night with were going to hang out there for a little bit and ask about the aquablazing program the outfitter offered. Aquablazing is apparently the process of renting of a canoe for about a week so as to drift down the Shenandoah River to Harpers Ferry, roughly one hundred trail miles away, and I must admit that it looked like a good time. Farmer, Chouinard, Tree Beard and Margarita eventually decided to undertake the adventure, though Farmer stated that afterward he would return to Waynesboro in true purest fashion to hike the blazed trail back north, a noble effort if ever I had seen one. That was Farmer though, he never said anything that wasn't worth taking the time to say, and he also never did anything that wasn't worth doing right. I hope to see the guy again someday, though I've lost contact with him after seeing him there in Waynesboro. I heard about him further down the trail and had really hoped to see him again, but it was not to be so. Still, Farmer had proven himself a great friend, and if nothing else I ever wish him all the best.

Now I'll be honest, I was about seventeen hundred miles into my travels, and had been out in the elements for a hundred and twenty days. Therefore, my body was about as fit as it had ever been and well used to the strain of hiking, so Shenandoah National Park in the northern part of Virginia may not have been as easy as I remember it. The low rolling mountains and well worn and marked trails made for easy hiking while still offering great valley views, but to be honest I couldn't wait to get past Shenandoah and be done with it. My biggest problem with the area wasn't that hiking here wasn't a challenge, or that the landscape wasn't beautiful, because it was, but the problem was the over-accessibility of the area. It felt like the entire National Park had been turned into a sort of rustic Disney World, with many parking lots, pavement, large drive in campgrounds, over-worn trails, and even souvenir stands called waysides. After exerting so much effort to climb mountains and see the unsettled parts of the east it bothered me that anyone could just drive along the Blue Ridge Parkway and stop for a moment on a summit that took me hours to reach. It's not that I didn't want people to see these wonderful things, but I could tell that those who simply drove up usually lacked appreciation for what they were seeing.

    I'll never forget the moment that confirmed my suspicions about whether or not people out here were taking in the full grandeur of the nature they were here to witness. I was walking along this magnificent ridge overlooking a grand valley in the middle of the day, the noon day sun shining brightly in a cloudless sky, illuminating the budding trees that had changed from their winter gray to a lush red as they made to grow new leaves. It was warm with a slight breeze, quiet and seemingly far removed from the rest of life, the sort of thing that stops a hiker in their tracks for a moment just to smile and give silent thanks for such simple perfection. It had become common to pass day hikers upon entering Shenandoah, and it was indeed easy to tell them from long distance hikers--they had very little or way too much gear, cheap shoes, and if nothing else I could smell laundry detergent and shampoo on them from at least a good ten feet away. So it was on the ridge as I passed a family group who had apparently just walked up from a nearby parking area, seeing as there wasn't a speck of dirt on them. I smiled as I passed, glad that they had taken the time to see the mountains, but there was one middle aged man amongst them that really caught my attention. He was wearing a nice red and white checkered button down shirt that was perfectly tucked into a pair of white slacks, with a pair of dress shoes and a receding hair line to complete the ensemble, standing on the trail. What caught my eye was not how he was dressed, but rather what he was doing. He had his back turned to the vista, paying it no mind, frowning with his head buried in a smart phone and his hand swiping across its screen. It wasn't just a quick check either; from the moment I saw him until I passed his demeanor never changed, obviously so caught up in something that he couldn't even spare a moment to be present in one of the most spectacular places in the free world! As I passed I said to him "There's a great view to your right you know," to which he looked up briefly and gave me the sort of smile a man wears when he's trying to sell you something you don't need, before resuming his apparently unpleasant business. He was so caught up in sending a message the he didn't catch the message that I was sending him, and it was truly disheartening.

If one goes through life always saying "I just gotta..." you'll never have time to say "I'm just gonna." So many are so caught up with things like "I just gotta take this call quick," or "I just gotta balance these accounts first." Take my preoccupied passerby for example: he stood there about as far away from the office as a man could be in this country, and said "I just gotta send this message quick," robbing himself from having an actual in-life experience! One thing always leads to another, it's never a single "I just gotta," starving the soul of the simplicity of things like "I'm just gonna go for a walk around the block," "I'm just gonna relax for a bit and read a book,",or even saying "I'm just gonna live and love life today"! I'm all for seeing new things, having a small adventure in the middle of a busy life, but for the love of God if you're going to be out there in life then live, damn it all! Don't just stare at a phone or leave one's mind ensnared in the daily grind, breath fresh air, think simple thoughts, live. It's because a simple drive to the top of a mountain to make a phone call is completely lacking in reward and accomplishment that I am opposed to the idea, and I just hope that those who do take the small amount of time to drive into the Shenandoahs at least take a good, long look at them.

Hiker-ism: Bear Bag

(noun) Bears are big, like, really big, and therefore are really hungry all the time! The only thing coming between a bear and a hiker's sack full of delicious snacks is usually the hiker himself, who becomes suddenly less attentive while sleeping. By hanging all food stuffs and other scented items high, hikers not only get to keep their food safe, but also their sleeping limbs.

I honestly didn't have any problems with bears during my hike, which is pretty much everyone's experience. That doesn't mean that I never came across them though; in fact, one of my first encounters was in Shenandoah. As I was walking along, halfway lost in my own thoughts, my eye caught some movement over to my left. I turned to look and not more than thirty yards from me, a huge black bear was walking the opposite direction. This thing was massive! Even on all four paws this thing must have been standing chest high on me, moving slowly with heavy, powerful steps and so close to me that I could see the grizzled hair on its back. It was an unnerving encounter to say the least, and all I managed to do was flinch, pull a stupid face and say "W'sup bear?" as I kept moving.

"W'sup snack?" he replied, and we both continued our separate ways.

At night on the AT, I had gotten used to hanging my food to avoid bear encounters, usually using hemp and a tree limb, but Shenandoah presented a new option. The shelters had large metal poles with a series of hooks on top of them with which to hang bear bags from. It was almost a sort of bad carnival game trying to hang bags on this oversized coat rack--one would have to use a large metal pole that must have weighed close to forty pounds without a bag on it, and attempt to raise the desired items while balancing the pole straight up and snagging them on one of the hooks. While it's always a good idea to hang food and such, the day's encounter had reminded me of its importance so I played this deranged sideshow sport instead of my normal method, thus hoisting my supplies high in the air. I'm a bigger guy, so it wasn't terribly troubling for me, but many of the people I hiked with stated that they had spent a good twenty minutes trying to snare a spare hook, missing left and right wildly while trying to not drop their bag.

I slept easier that night, having stowed everything from food to toothpaste out of reach of any would be provision predators, but as Murphy's law would have it, I didn't escape the night completely unscathed. While bears were an obvious threat, mice were by far the bigger problem, and there's very little that can be done about the little bastards. I awoke in the morning to a nasty surprise, having forgot that some sunflower seeds that I had received in Buena Vista had remained in the front pocket of my pack the night previous, and thus some tiny terrorist had chewed a hole the size of a golf ball to get to them. There were seeds everywhere! And while I was upset about losing the snack the real damage was done to my pack--there's no fixing a hole that size easily. Not a good start to a day, and the fact that I had taken so much care to hang my supplies the night before added insult to the injury. I decided to just continue on with my day, rose from my sleeping bag and grabbed my boot, turning it upside down and rapping the bottom to knock loose any rocks I had picked up the previous day or any unwelcome insects that had decided to inhabit it in the night. A shower of sunflower seeds poured forth from my footwear, and after a brief moment of confusion I realized that the same mouse who had chewed my pack had made a good store of my food in my boot before claiming both for its own that night. Just when I thought it couldn't have been any worse, I looked back at my pack to realize that it was on the right side of my sleeping bag, and in some sort of tragic comedy my boots were on the left. This crumb snatching, disrespectful, pint sized, vandalizing, piece of work fucking field mouse had not only robbed me of my food and defiled my boot, but spent the entire night doing so by running directly over my legs!! I was irate! Livid! Blind with rage! Not to mention just plain pissed off, and for a solid thirty seconds I strung together a series of swears that would have struck a seasoned sailor as obsessive. In a small act of revenge I swept the seed out of the shelter and far out into the woods in front of the shelter in hopes that the birds would get them before the dirty burglar, though I found the act not nearly satisfying enough.

Although, my vindictive sweeping spree did give me a chance to cool down a bit, and before it was done I started to laugh at the whole endeavor. Every part of it, from finding my pack pilfered to the hate-fueled cleaning, was just so ridiculous that it became funny nearly as quickly as it became infuriating. Even with the greatest planning and preparation things can go horribly wrong, and tragedy can strike even the most cautious of people. While I didn't relish the idea of undoubtedly hiking in an indiscernible amount of mouse pee, it was nice to be reminded that it's impossible to control everything. Bad things can happen even with no real fault of one's own, and in the end all that can really be done is sweep up the mess and move forward.

I managed to push through Shenandoah in only four days by putting in over twenty five miles a day, which was no small feat for my usually slower hiking style. Along the way I passed countless families, several elderly women, a deer that just didn't give a fuck anymore about people staring at it, a luxury resort, the entire People's Republic of China, breathtaking scenery, and enough side trails to keep a hiker busy for over a year. Also, after about a month of relentless pursuit, I managed to catch up with Moxie and Ibex! I hardly recognized them actually, the last time I had seen them they had both been covered head to toe in shiny new winter gear and now were clad in the usual thru hiker rags and about a quarter inch of dust. It was great to know they were in the area, and I looked forward to hiking with them in the coming states.

11 NEW SOULS

Sometimes out on the trail I had to wonder if things were named by a lonely teenager who was obsessed with internet jokes, or it may just be that I have a sense of humor like a lonely teenage boy obsessed with internet jokes and notice the aforementioned humor in some names. For example, Manassas Shelter is right next to Dicks Dome, which caused me to snicker a bit, and therefore I couldn't help but stop in at Snickers Gap just north of the pornographically named shelters. There is a restaurant and an antique shop at the Gap, and absolutely nothing else, so being conscious of money I made for the antique store to try and grab a soda or something. When I arrived it had been raining all day, so I was pretty well soaked through, and really looking forward to being dry for a bit while I planned the rest of the day. The shop was small and quaint, the exterior boards had aged to gray with a few charming pieces of folk art hung upon them. The drive displayed a few more artistic bird feeders and metal sculptures near a flower filled garden, giving the whole place a sort of storybook charm that invited its visitors to take it easy for a moment. To my dismay the shop was closed for the day, though it did have a nice, dry, covered porch with a few chairs and other antiques scattered about which seemed to be a fine place to rest for a bit and reevaluate my guidebook.

As I sat and munched on a snack cake, a woman came out of the little house past the garden and called over to me before pulling up her hood and walking over. She was a rather small woman, but only in stature, and while she was getting along in years she possessed the sort of southern class that made her glow with an lovely and youthful essence. I have forgotten her name sadly, though remember it was one of the classic, southern, two part first names like Mary Ann or Betty Lou, and seeing as it appeared as though she was coming to shoo me from her home like a pesky stray cat I didn't think to ask for her name at first. I smiled and acted polite, like any young man who grew up below the Mason Dixon line, and while she at first indeed seemed a little irritated to find me lounging about her little shop her demeanor suddenly changed after a few words and she invited me into her home for a hot drink if I cared for one.

On a day like today, to be warm and dry was really about the only thing I could think of, and so the idea of a quick warm up seemed too good to be true, and this I gladly accepted! Her home was just as charming as the rest of the property, small and made of felled logs with a multitude of old gadgets and gizmos hanging about in her kitchen where we sat to talk. She spoke kindly, though with great prominence, it was apparent that she lived a simple life, but if she had told me she belonged to an ancient line of royalty I would have believed her. She soon not only put the kettle on to boil but also produced a plate of dried fruit, fine cheese, and crackers for us to dine upon on this dreary mountain day. The stories that we shared seemed to fascinate each other, mine of the things that I had crafted back in the world and hers of her dearly departed husband and grown children, all of whom had come of age here in this lovely hillside hollow. So was the day that I sat down for tea with the Mountain Queen, indeed it was a lovely chi she provided, and after my bones were warmed and my rain coat had dried by the fire it was time to be going again. To this day, I don't believe that I had found another place quite as charming as the little shop in Snickers Gap.

The last gift that the Five Hundred Mile State had to offer was a grand psychological boost, and that came via one very significant mile mark. The AT travels through an entertaining section known as the Roller Coaster, which consists of over ten small summits and valleys appearing in short succession just before the West Virginia border. Embracing a moment of trail insanity I would throw up my arms and scream as I passed over a peak and began to rocket down the mountain side, acting as if my boots were bound and rolling on a metal track. While it was a blast to rejoice in one of the simple pleasures of life, a small, painted fence slat resting on a tree alongside a small river inspired a phenomenal sense of satisfaction. Green numbers outlined in a vibrant purple mark the one thousand mile mark for northbound thru hikers, and while I figured I was a good eighteen hundred miles into my personal travels to actually see a number with four digits was unbelievably satisfying! I paused for a moment before the sign to try and take it all in, but felt I couldn't until the mark had been passed, and so by placing my feet together and hopping forward with one great leap I earned my thousand mile status. Suddenly filled with immense joy and good cheer I began to laugh uncontrollably, raising my voice to the heavens to mark my accomplishment. My heart grew lighter than ever and in turn so did my pack and my feet fell softly yet strong as they danced along the way; this day was mine forever, the woods were my only witness though were also the only one I needed, and every drop of rain that fell danced with me along the forest floor. It was now impossible to tell if my feet simply left their marks along the trail, or if with every step the trail left its mark on me.

After meeting back up with Moxie and Ibex a few days before, they asked me exactly what was in my pack, seeing as I carried so much on the outside of it--and for the first time I actually stopped to think, what exactly WAS in my pack? When I started out I had been carrying so much food that there was little room for anything else apart from a change of clothes and a journal, but I was a far more savvy hiker now and couldn't believe that I had not thought to repack until this point. Many days, when my food stores become low my pack would lie nearly flat against my back, with the straps pulled tight and my tent and bag flopping haphazardly on the exterior. This was just plain stupid! I took a moment to reposition my kilt into a large stretchy pocket on the outside of my pack, seeing as it took up the bulk of my carrying space, and found that I could now easily fit not only my tent inside my pack but also, with a little effort, my bag as well. My cooking pot remained on the outside of my pack seeing as it was metal and hung nicely on a carabiner, as well as my shovel and hatchet, which I knew was foolish to carry but refused to give up, and now my food stuffs also fit inside with a little repositioning. It was a wonder that I had never thought to do this before, especially after the shakedown in Damascus, and while I had come to love my ragged appearance this was far more practical, seeing as I could now make efficient use of my rain cover, having it now ecompass all that I owned.

It was rather fortuitous that I came across such an epiphany when I did, for Virginia seemed to lament the imminent moment of our parting, crying heartily for a solid three days. Either that, or the good Lord found my body odor too pungent and offensive for even the noses of wild animals to tolerate and sent forth a good long shower in an attempt to cleanse me. My feet became waterlogged as my boots were completely saturated, old trails became new rivers and water poured from the underbrush to flow in the footpath which offered the least amount of resistance. It is rumored that April showers bring May flowers, and if that's so it was bound to be a colorful spring! Furthermore, I could no longer tell if my hat was serving to keep the rain out of my eyes or simply keeping my head wet as it draped over my ears in a manner that forced me to wear it further back on my brow in order to see from underneath it. There was no fire to be had at night, neither was there a piece of wood nearly dry enough to start one, though my last night in Virginia I happened across the Blackburn AT Center which offered four walls and a wood stove to dry myself by. I spent the night there with a couple who went by the names Satoci and Snacks, and while I didn't get the chance to know them well they proved to be good company for the few days I encountered them.

Virginia was truly an amazing state to hike through--challenging, rugged, and beautiful. It was the last stand of the South, a gateway to the North, home to a multitude of wonderful people, and in every way a blessing to have experienced.

Hiker-ism: Mail Drop

(Noun) This is how smart people hike long distance. By planning ahead, hikers can send supplies to themselves by leaving them to be in the care of a postmaster or a hostel owner and pick up the package when they arrive. Works great! Unless one hits town on a holiday or a Sunday, when the post office is closed.

The rain continued for half a day as I crossed into West Virginia, the shortest of the segments of the AT and barely holding four miles of the trail, unless one would count the other sixteen miles spent skirting its border in Virginia. Though I associate West Virginia with the landscape of northern Virginia more than Virginia itself. Every few miles a small and run-down stone wall would appear, signifying a boundary that existed back when the country was new and no one knew just how big the thing was. The mountains had become low rolling hills, occasionally presenting a challenging spike but for the most part pleasantly rising and falling around small farms and cities. Even the vegetation seemed to be stunted; the trees grew shorter, the waxy rhododendron replaced with low green ferns, and while it was still wild the woods seemed far more quaint and settled. That's not to say anything was lost or missing from them, only that they had their own personality with jagged rocks and wide streams. They seemed to beg to be discovered, like a fair young woman playfully peeking from behind trees and running ahead, staying just out of reach but inviting one to follow.

Where the Shenandoah River meets the Potomac is the town of Harpers Ferry, named for the ferryman who set up along the banks of the Potomac, shuttling people across long before a bridge had even been thought to be put there. The narrow streets, built in a time where people traveled mainly by foot and occasionally by horse, had been widened as best they could to accommodate automobiles while still leaving the historic buildings untouched. Still, many small alleys remained intact, winding between the streets like a brick labyrinth. The whole place did feel a bit like a maze, seeing as the town had been built on a hillside with nearly every storefront at a different elevation, and some of the older shops even had a few stairs inside of them adding to the old world feel.

While the shops and museums were fun to venture through, the main attraction for thru hikers in Harpers Ferry is of course the Appalachian Trail Conservancy Headquarters, located about a mile from the historic downtown. The ATC HQ is about as close to the middle of the trail as civilization allows, and is a celebrated stop by nearly all thru hikers. While the place is a wealth of information about the trail ahead, the main reason many stop here is to have their picture taken by the staff and added to that years scrapbook as well as to discover how many thru hikers had come through earlier in the season. Thanks to my massive head start I believe I was hiker number thirty four, meaning I had gained about twenty spots from Mountain Crossing in GA, which was rather encouraging I must say.

 As luck would have it, I happened across the ATC HQ at the same time as some of my old friends. Margarita and Tree Beard had just arrived from their aquatic adventure, and they were enjoying the chance to be warm and dry for the first time in close to a week. According to them, rowing down a river doesn't keep one nearly as warm as hiking, and in the heavy rain avoiding hypothermia became a real concern for the four of them. Other than that, it sounded like a blast! They had even managed to find some high quality, backwoods grain alcohol to sip on along the way, which may or may not have caused Farmer to pass out and almost drown on several occasions. While Margarita and Treebeard had traveled with Chouinard and Farmer, neither the latter of my two companions were present at the time; Farmer was traveling back to Waynesboro with the outfitter who had kindly retrieved the vessels in which they had traveled with, and Chouniard was spending the evening in Washington DC. The nation's capital was just a short, and inexpensive, ride away on a commuter train and is an easy day trip for thru hikers, so much so that its hard to pass up. Realizing that I had all the time in the world I decided that I too should go see the Capital while I was here, for it would never again be so easy to get to and would be foolish to pass up, in my opinion. All I had to do was find a place in the area to spend the night and in the morning take the train, explore for a day, and then catch another back in the evening before continuing on again.

 As I discussed my plans with Tree Beard and Margarita they informed me that they would be staying at Tea Leaves Hostel in town, though it may be booked up for the night, but by now I had acquired quite a knack for figuring these things out. One of the fellows that was working at the Conservancy must have overheard, for not long after he came by to talk with us. He was a shorter fellow, his beard and hair pure white with age and many lines had formed on his face from countless smiles. He spoke softly in a way that would make one think he didn't say much unless he had something worth saying, and it was easy to tell that he had found great peace in life and that his worries were few. He had a trail name that meant Grandfather Lion in a foreign tongue, and it wasn't long before he asked where I planned to stay for the evening. I said that I hadn't figured that out yet, which I had found to be a great open ended response, and he told me that if I wished I could stay with him for the evening. Everything seemed to be falling into place for ol' Gizmo today--not only had I hatched a plan to go sightseeing but also found a warm bed and even managed to get a little taste of home from the only mail drop I received on the trail.

Before I set out I had never even heard of a mail drop, and as I walked I really had no desire, or funds, to set up my resupply points. However, when I had contacted my Mother earlier she had wondered if she would be able to send me anything for my birthday from the family, and while I hate to admit it I really needed a new pair of boots. My decision to buy Danner Brand boots had indeed proved to be a great one; I had eighteen hundred miles on this one pair of boots, while many of those I hiked along side of were already on their third or fourth pair of shoes. What brand I was going to trust my feet to for the rest of the trip was not up for debate, I loved these boots, though regrettably it was nearly impossible to find a replacement pair out on the trial. I had been able to accept kindness from strangers without hesitation but I still struggled with receiving it from family members. However, this time my need outweighed my pride, which had been beaten to a normal measure, and I was able to ask for a new pair of boots. I knew of a place near where my folks lived that carried Danner Brand and that they had a six inch hiking-style boot that I thought would be perfect for the remaining miles. While that style was a bit lighter than the one I was wearing now, I believed the worst was behind me and that it was now better to save a few ounces then to be able to trudge thru eight inches of water. The ATC HQ offered the perfect place to pick up a parcel and so I had my little care package sent there, which I received with a great deal of excitement and gratitude to accept the help of those I knew best.

When the Conservancy closed down for the day, I went off with Grandfather Lion to his place a short distance away with my package under my arm and a smile on my face. It's truly a blessing to be picked up by Trail Angel, and not something that should be expected by thru hikers though it tends to happen to all of us at some point. Furthermore, there's nothing like watching your skin instantly change colors as one washes off a well earned dust tan in a hot shower. My host needed to run off for a moment to handle some affairs, leaving me completely unattended to wash up and make myself at home. It's wild how natural this all seemed to both of us; I had just met the fellow an hour ago and now here I was in his home with his blessing to use whatever I could find, a privilege I refused to abuse, and simply took the opportunity to cleanse my clothes and self.

  The reason he had been so confident in leaving a strange hiker in his home soon became apparent upon his return, as he opened a fine bottle of red wine and poured into a pair of glasses. He had been a thru hiker himself once not too long ago, and his wandering had not started nor ended with that adventure. I listened with eager ears as he told of his travels to mount Kilimanjaro and Japan, he had wandered near and far after leaving a successful restaurant in California, and with every word of his stories he left me further enticed. While I knew I had never met this man before there was something that seemed very familiar about him, like I had seen him before but could not for the life of me recall when or where. It wasn't until he further described his experience on the AT that I figured it out. In the documentary that I had seen years ago, the same one that let me know of the existence of this grand trail, Grandfather Lion had been one of the featured hikers! If it had not been for this man I would not have been hiking this trail. I was absolutely stunned! It was the equivalent of meeting the biggest star in the world to me, this man had helped to inspire me to undertake the single greatest, life-changing venture ever personally embarked upon and now here I was in his home sipping wine with the guy, unbelievable! I began to attempt to describe this to him but I couldn't find the words, that and I'm not sure he would have wanted to hear it if I had. To him, the trail was just a part of his own journey through life, and for it he needed no praise or recognition, and that is part of what makes the trail so astounding. While many of us undertake this feat together it is all retested individually, the rewards and battles and triumphs of one may not apply to another, and so while we all walk the same path it is also uniquely our own. I had spent that night in the pride of Grandfather Lion, and when I departed in the morning I did so not as apprentice and master, nor mentor and student, but rather simply as comrades and friends.

  I did indeed travel to Washington D.C. in the morning, and spent a day admiring the great monuments and learning at the museums. I mailed a few more things home, and as luck would have it met up with Chouinard! However, this wonderful chance meeting concluded with a rather sad departure, as Chouinard told me he was indeed heading home after spending months on the trail and this was to be the last time we met. He had decided that his job here was done, that he had proved his worth and it was time to head home for a job that wouldn't wait much longer for him. He wouldn't have had enough time to reach Maine because of this, and decided it was better to wander elsewhere before his leave was over, and while I was unhappy to hear it I understood; one thousand mountain miles is quite an accomplishment in and of itself, after all. We took a quick photograph together within this concrete jungle, and it has ever been my pleasure to recall the fond memories made with this fine hiker.

Harpers Ferry presents a rare opportunity to thru hikers seeing as it borders on three different states. West Virginia is still the shortest of the states on the AT, but a close second is Maryland, which contains less than forty miles of trail. Because of this, many hikers attempt what is called The Four State Challenge, which is to try and venture from Virginia to Pennsylvania in just a day while passing through West Virginia and the whole of Maryland. Some skip starting in Virginia and simply try the Maryland challenge, which is of course to pass through Maryland in a day-- which seemed to be too grand of an idea for me to pass up. I had rationed a fair amount of food for the day and planned to keep my energy high throughout its duration knowing that the last few miles were bound to be the worst, but that didn't present to be my main problem this day.

In my haste to lighten my pack the day before I had unknowingly made by far my worst mistake on the entire AT, and that was to send my old boots home, leaving me only with my new footwear. It doesn't seem like a big deal when it's just an idea, but when put into practice it's reality is extremely painful! New shoes resist forming to a person's feet for a few days, which is a good thing in the long run seeing as they won't wear out as fast because of this, but during those first few days they will rub parts of a hiker's foot absolutely raw! I didn't foresee it being a problem. I was wrong. Before I even made it ten miles into the state of Maryland my feet were screaming in pain, and every step made it slightly worse. I remember literally shouting at full volume in a mix of pain and rage as this stupid, superficial, and ever present irritation plagued my body, made worse by the fact that I had no other option but to endure it and press forward. I tried many things over the course of the day to relieve myself of this problem--I put three socks on each foot, I taped gauze pads to the inflamed areas, I tried walking with the damn boots untied for a bit, but nothing worked. At one point I stood in an ice cold mountain stream with my feet fully submerged in knee deep water to hopefully loosen up the leather on my new boots. While the frigid water felt amazing on my poor pedal appendages, the quality of my new boots became apparent as my shins became unwilling to bear the icy current while my feet had just started to find relief. The pain got to the point where I dreaded the next step, which was made all the worse because all I had wanted for the last few months was just to see what the next step would bring. It is hard to think of anything worse than fearing to do what you love. Needless to say, I will NEVER hit a trail with unbroken boots again.

At one point on that fateful day I decided to abandon my hopes of seeing Pennsylvania before the evening, and removed my shoes to nap upon a large, smooth rock that had been warmed by the sun. As I rested Moxie came hiking along the trail and must have found the sight quite odd, for she stopped to talk a little while. I told her of my plight, and that I would be calling it a day sooner than later before inquiring where it was that she and Ibex had laid their sights for the evening. We examined our guidebooks together looking for a shelter that would suit our needs, when we happened across a place that appeared to be almost hidden amongst the rest. Shelters, towns, and campsites are usually written in a bold text in the guide book, but tucked between several bland landmarks is the Annapolis Rocks campsite which seemed to be within reach, even for my battered bones. Keeping pace with someone wasn't going to be an option for me today, so I just said I would aim for there and that perhaps I'd see them at the Rocks before I returned to my rest, trying to forget the feeling of blisters and raw flesh. The mountains of Maryland are none too challenging thankfully, though there are still several ups and downs worth noting, and in an effort that can only be described as a masochistic rage I managed to make it to the Rocks in the last light of the day and in a lot of pain.

It's hard to say that it was worth it at the time, but in hindsight Annapolis Rocks is one of my favorite spots at which I camped. The side trail takes one along an astounding overlook gazing over a small city in a valley far below, large rocks suddenly drop a good hundred feet straight down and help keep the view free of trees, allowing for hikers to gaze upon distant mountains as the sun sank behind them. I sat there for sometime with

Moxie and Ibex taking it all in, finding a little peace in the day's chaos, and I was glad that I put in the effort. While I dreaded putting my boots back on in the morning, I enjoyed the evening, taking in the sights and filling my reservoir from an impressive spring present at the campground, its flow clearer and stronger than any other I had seen that day. Even in the worst of times, if one cares to look for it there is always something to rejoice in.

Mountains rise and fall, seas roll with the tides, the deserts shift with the wind, the trees grow different everywhere from Florida to Alaska, each place having its own unique feel and the people that inhabit all the spaces in between are much the same. While every place has something that makes it different, I have never felt such a sudden change in social dynamics as when I crossed the fateful Mason Dixon line. I've long been a southern boy, and my heart belongs to Dixie always, and this was the first time that I had ever seen the actual line that divides the south from the north. It's funny just how literal this thing is; when it was drawn it was supposed to be a straight east to west line marking ten miles south of the southernmost home in Pennsylvania, and now this infamous divider between the Rebels and the Yankees marks Maryland's northern border. There's a train track that runs along the line where I crossed it as well as a small wooden sign. I stood on the southern end of this little plank of wood, looking from the tracks, I promised myself that this was not going to be permanent as I took the last few steps into Pennsylvania.

Thru hikers have a nickname for the first state north of Dixie, Rocksylvania, because the whole thing is rumored to be nothing but a mess of boulders piled on top of each other. Folks in the south made it out to seem as if one crosses into a barren, treeless Mordor, scuttling over rock and stone in a waterless wasteland void of anything but ticks and rattlesnakes. It would appear that they exaggerated a little, for I found the woods of Pennsylvania to be lush and full, rejuvenated with the coming of spring just as all the mountain paths before it. It may have been because of the extremely harsh winter but I had no trouble finding fresh water, and the tales of the rocks were also a bit far fetched, or so I thought. I had been preparing for miles and miles of major boulders and having to rock hop for days across the state, and while there were large rock formations here and there it was the little rocks that proved to be a problem. After over a thousand miles of hard packed dirt with the occasional root being the main form of pedal support, one's body gets used to carrying itself in a certain way. Myself, I had gotten used to leading with my heel and rocking my weight over the ball of my foot before springing lightly off my toes to propel myself forward, but that suddenly had to change. A nearly infinite amount of fist sized rocks spotted the trail, half buried in the earth, and positioned sparsely enough that there was indeed dirt between them all but nowhere was there a spot big enough to place one's foot. This leaves hikers with two options: one, half step on the dirt between rocks and flex at the ankle to travel over and between the stones in the same manner that a snake unhinges its jaw, or two, step with the center of one's foot balancing on each rock carefully moving from one to the other. I chose the latter, taking strides of uneven length to move cautiously along the trail, though moving in such a way didn't seem to slow me down at all.

However, while things seemed to be better than I had expected them to be there was one other major issue to consider. My boots were still unbroken, meaning my feet were beat to shit before I crossed into Pennsylvania, and stepping from rock to rock on the arch of my foot was absolute murder! This inconvenient rock balancing act seams to destroy everyone's feet, but went double for me, and I seriously became faint at times from my feet being in so much pain! Still, the journey went on, and I wasn't about to let some superficial pain stop me from continuing the adventure, especially after I had come so far.

Perhaps the greatest thing to note about southern Pennsylvania is the crossing at the AT Midpoint. It's hard to believe that it took me well over one hundred days in the woods to come only halfway, but then again I did start in Florida. Regardless, the AT Midpoint is a monumental milestone for thru hikers and comes with its own special challenge. Hikers that reach Pine Grove Furnace State Park are presented with a rather strange but coveted food challenge, and that is to attempt to eat an entire half gallon of ice cream in one sitting! While nearly everyone tries this infamous binge not all succeed, but I felt as though I could have done it twice by now having starved myself for so damn long. Regrettably, I had been making excellent time through the mountains, and therefore arrived before the store that offers the gluttonous free-for-all was fully open for the season, and thus was unable to try the official challenge. However that's no reason not to still make an attempt! I had arrived at this point with Moxie and Ibex, who were also up for slamming a near ungodly amount of frozen delight, and we set off to a nearby town in search of massive tubs of frozen bliss to initiate our own challenge.

After a short hitch we landed at a drug store on the outskirts of town, and while the drug store didn't have half gallon containers of ice cream, we were each able to come out with a half gallon in total after some quick math, or at least Moxie and Ibex did. After a price analysis I discovered it was going to be far cheaper to purchase slightly more than a half gallon, and opted for the greater challenge in order to save a few bucks. It wasn't terribly cold out, but windy, and as the three of us sat on the curb downing spoon after spoon of frigged bliss we all started to get a bit of a chill. I look back and try and imagine just how odd we all must have looked, dressed in dirt, sitting on a curb outside with several electronic devices plugged into an exterior outlet, fully immersed in an act of gluttony that could possibly send even the Pope to hell, and gave absolutely no fucks about the whole matter! To top it off, I'm sure we must have smelled like rabid beasts but had long lost the ability to notice; still, I wouldn't have changed a thing about it all.

Before we had finished our challenge, or at least before I had, seeing as Moxie and Ibex weren't able to accomplish the task in a single sitting, a woman in an SUV stopped in the parking lot and called out to us. It's hard to tell what she had thought of us all at first, a dingy dude and two equally unbathed babes sitting on a drug store curb, but part of me believes she found us homeless. Still, she had the kindness to ask where we were spending the evening, prompting my tried and true "Haven't figured that out yet" response. I think she put two and two together at this point and realized that we were out hiking the AT, and she told us to hang tight for a moment while she ran home and asked her husband if he was up for housing a few adventurers. Ice cream and a warm place to stay? Sounds like heaven if you ask me, and so we decided to stick around for a bit to see is she came back. It wasn't long until she did indeed return and said that if we wished we could come and spend the night with them, though her husband wasn't terribly fond of company.

I could tell that my companions were a little hesitant, but by this point my faith in humanity had been completely restored and I didn't think twice about taking this kind woman up on her offer. Our hostess was a shorter but strongly built woman, her hair was maybe an eighth of an inch long, which is to say nearly shaved, and she was absolutely covered in tattoos. I typically love people that look like this, though I know many people find them intimidating, but I think that anyone who is willing to display their life story on their skin has very little to hide and can always be trusted. Hell, anyone with multiple tattoos obviously values their own beliefs over public opinion, they won't lie to you, but they may also tell you something you don't want to hear, which is why I think people have a tenancy to avoid them. I myself am rather illustrated, having well over a dozen separate pieces of my own at this point and the intention to keep collecting, so the sight of a colorful new friend was indeed a welcome one. As it turns out, our new friend Elly had just won her battle with breast cancer, which explained her haircut, and she was quite the traveler herself having been in the military and stationed in Germany for over four years with her husband. The four of us were soon loaded up and on our way, all of us glad to get to know each other.

Elly's husband Jerry actually turned out to be quite a fine fellow himself, for a man that typically doesn't care for new friends. He was a giant of a man, being a little heavy set but undoubtedly strong as an ox, with a full graying beard and a bit of a devil-may-care attitude, a fine complement to the eccentric ball of energy that Elly was. In fact, Jerry was actually a very pleasant person once I got him talking about his time overseas and the beer that he had enjoyed there; however the other three housemates were a little harder to win over. They had three pit bulls, all short and stocky, and while I don't want to sound ungrateful the dogs were more than a little spoiled, having nearly complete run of the place. They were good dogs though, even in spite of the fact that I never managed to fully gain their trust, and while they were eager to jump and bark at you I really enjoyed playing with them for a bit. There is no finer companion a man can find than a dog, for they are loyal, adventurous, protective, and if nothing else always ecstatic to see you, which can always turn a bad day into a not so bad day in less then a second.

We were given a spot in the basement to set up, which housed a multitude of boxes and a single futon, and at this point in our venture this was utopia! Not only did a warm, dry basement embrace our trail worn bodies for the evening, but it came with a hot shower, which we all were in great need of! I showered second, after Ibex, and remember sitting with her and Jerry chatting a bit when we were joined by Moxie. She was brushing her long, freshly washed hair and I couldn't help but notice that she was actually quite beautiful. Out in the woods were all so covered in dirt and sweat it's hard to tell if the girls are even girls at times, and furthermore being so caught up in the excitement of new discovery and the physical demands of hiking people just simply become people regardless of gender, race, or anything else. Now that I had a chance to rest I began to see the simple charm this woman possessed. She was fair of skin and soft spoken, fit and built to travel with a lovely shy smile and quiet eyes that sparkled when she laughed. I got the impression that either no one had ever taken the time to tell her just how lovely she really is or that she was simply exhausted by the trail, which is a shame because I believe she had turned far more heads than had been made clear to her. It crossed my mind to possibly be the first to tell her, but for some reason I didn't, and that may be my only regret of the entire trip.

I had rolled out my mattress on the floor to sleep that night, being a gentleman and letting the girls take the bed, and I awoke refreshed in the morning to find proper breakfast and hot coffee waiting for us all. I was finding at this point that it was undoubtedly the people met along the way that makes traveling great, not just new discovery. People can be good natured and caring at heart, and sometimes all they need is the opportunity to show it. Elly soon gave us all a ride back to the trail where the four of us took a quick picture and set off again to the forest. I keep the memory of that night close to my heart and reflect upon it on days that aren't going so great, and it has never failed to bring a smile to my face. It's true when they say that the greatest of blessings can not be measured, for they are matters of the heart and soul, and it's days like this that have filled both these vessels so well that it is now impossible for them to be rendered dry. I am blessed indeed.

Now fully in the thralls of spring, the forest had found its voice again. The pure and unbroken silence had now given way to a melody of small birds, all playfully bounding from limb to limb as they sang. The frozen creeks now babbled lively, and the spring sun was fully shining; it all cast such a feeling upon the earth that all things must rejoice in it, myself included. A smile was never absent from my lips as I made my way and the entire world seemed to greet me as a friend. As I came to a broad stream crossing the trail I noticed that there was a well constructed bridge stretching over the water as well as a large fallen tree which would serve the same purpose. Being filled to the brim with the majesty of nature I thought it such a pity to not partake further of her bounty, thus I said batsass to the works of man and made to cross upon the fallen trunk of this barkless tree. I bounded merrily upon yonder natural crossing, my arms held aloft to balance and my feet falling quickly across this lovely log, humming softly as I went. That's when my foot slipped, and I landed directly on my balls.

It's been awhile since I had taken a good shot to the genitals, and time had not lessened its sting let me just say! Also, as if my own body weight wasn't enough to cause a nearly sterilizing blow to my bits this fall was made all the worse by the approximate forty pounds strapped to my back. As I sat straddling this log in a mix of pain and shock, the same slimy coating that had caused my foot to slip now refused to keep my body in place and I began to slide to the side, unable to maintain my unpleasant position. I had two options, either slide off and fall completely sideways into the water below, or launch myself from my pelvic roust and land on my feet--I opted for the latter. As my foot landed in the stream below I found out quickly that this was not a sandy, high elevation spring but rather a muddy and slow moving mire, thus sinking up to my knee in decomposing leaves and muck. A second step, of similar material, allowed me to leap onto dry land and collapse in a mixture of embarrassment and pain as my male-exclusive injury took full effect. Not one of my finer moments. I managed to not vomit, though I really felt like I needed to, and after a few moments on my hands and knees I was able to stand again, though still very uncomfortable, and resume my hike. This lovely spring day could go to hell for all I cared as I carried on, half walking, half waddling down the trail.

Sometimes while traveling one comes to a spot that is just so amazing it stops a man in his tracks. Some places are so awe inspiring and beautiful that they demand all of one's attention, leaving room for nothing else as one stands mystified by the sheer awesome power of what is being witnessed. Duncannon, PA is not one of those places, in fact quite the opposite, but it had the same effect on me anyway.

Picture, if you will, the last pirate stronghold in the Caribbean. A dirty, dangerous, whore-ridden, booze-fueled free-for-all where anything goes and the rum flows like water on the shore. Now take that place, move it to landlocked Pennsylvania, add a police force, and bring it back into roughly the 1970s and you have Duncannon. This place is essentially a dive bar turned into a city; the streets are narrow and dirty, the buildings have fallen into disrepair, and yet somehow, this grimy little town felt like home to me. There's not much here, just a laundromat, a gas station, the only strip club that lays directly on the trail, an ice cream parlor, and an absolutely wonderful hotel called The Doyle.

    The Doyle needs to be on every thru hiker's "To Visit" list--without question this place embodies the spirit of vagabonds and wanderers, serving cheep booze, greasy food, and offering very affordable rooms for the night. The kind couple that runs the joint are a pair of travelers themselves, having made it across the country in their younger years, and while they may not come running when you walk into the bar they are indeed glad to see you. As I sat there chowing down on a glorious deep fried creation called a chuck wagon burger with a massive side of fresh cut fries, another thru hiker entered and sat alongside of me. I had not seen him before but knew he must be in it for the long haul--he just had that look. He was thin, dark skinned, dusty, had two long black braids of hair draped over his shoulders and went by the name Cloud Walker. We shared a few pints and plates together while swapping stories; he had earlier finished the Pacific Crest Trail, which runs from Mexico to Canada along the west coast of America and had hopes of completing the Continental Divide Trail, which cuts through the heart of the Rockies, thus earning the title of Triple Crown in a single year! I'd like to think he made it because he was flying down the AT, having started in late April and catching up to little old me who had hit the trail a good forty days before then.

    Neither of us stayed at The Doyle that night sadly, though I have fond memories of the place, and we went off to camp on a nearby ridge after crossing the mighty Susquehanna River. I consider this to be my first major river crossing, though the guidebook would say otherwise. The bridge spanning this body of water was simply massive! It took us a good ten minutes to hike across the damn thing, but it was well worth it to set up high above the town of Duncannon and see her lights shimmering off the mighty river. I was reminded of the day not so long ago that I sat on the unfinished building in Wilmington and watched her lights dance upon the Cape Fear, it seemed like a lifetime ago. I began to realize how much I had grown in less than a year, how doing less gave me so much more. There were still many miles to go, and I was thankful for the chance to learn more about myself, but I also began to feel my time for heading home was drawing near, and when it came time to travel back, I would be ready for it.

As I approached ever closer to New England, the trail took more and more turns through meadows and farmland. I really don't like hiking in meadows actually, and that is because the treeless fields make it impossible to tell exactly how big said field is and at what angle it presents. Many times I would get tired while hiking through meadows, partially because I was walking on an incline most of the time but was unable see it, thus pressing father per stretch then I would in a forest, and also because of the abundance of pollen being thrown into the air by flowering plants. I'm not allergic to pollen, or anything else for that matter, but the stuff builds up in one's throat and lungs making it hard to breath at times. Being punished by beauty is a real son of a bitch... or a marriage.

I remember walking through one such field as a farmer was tilling it to plant his crops, turning acres of wildflowers and buckwheat into clean rows of soft brown earth ready to house what he would sow. The trail was not to be plowed however, and a good ten foot wide stripe of beaten grass split this farmer's field in two, marked by large wooden posts baring white blazes. As I approached the end of his field the farmer hopped out of his tractor and came to greet me, saying that he had never actually met someone who was thru hiking the trail before. I touched briefly on how wonderful my experience had been, but soon transitioned into thanking this man for his labor; without farms, none of us eat, a fact often forgotten by higher society. Farmers never get the thanks they deserve sadly, and I feel as though every man, woman, and child in America should buy a local farmer either a gallon of diesel fuel or a few packets of seed--just think how much cheaper it would be to produce food if everyone gave just a little to those producing it! I digress.

As we talked, he told me a tale of the trail that took me a little by surprise as it was not like any other I had heard while traveling. Apparently the State, in order to preserve the trail, had forcefully purchased it from the farmers, giving them no say in the matter. Then, they turned around and let the farmers work the earth near the trail, apart from the aforementioned stripe, but would charge the farmers a fee for using state land. Not only did the State snatch this land at a price far below what housing developers would pay, but by charging the farmers to use the land necessary to grow a profitable crop, the state in no time at all will make more money than what they bought it for, and from those whom they essentially stole it from! The AT is life changing, it indeed needs to be protected, but how in God's name is this right?! In short, it's not, and I'm enraged by such blatant exploitation of the working class! I feel that if the State were to truly look out for the trail, they should make the fact that it runs through someone's family farm a blessing and not a curse. To make this justified idea a reality, I feel as though the State should refund the difference in price paid for the land versus amount earned from it, and then allow the farmers to work this land for free provided they help to maintain the trail as they already are forced to be doing at present. These are the demands I lay down upon the nation that has sworn to represent me, and I will not be satisfied until they are met.

Sometimes people make what is right and what's wrong far too complicated, and it's just childish. It's as if men have forgotten how to be men, especially in political society, all trying to play King of the Hill with one another, insisting that they stand atop the mound and thus that they are right and no one else is allowed to be. It's as if no one has had a father that cared enough to smack them across the ass if they were being a pretentious little shit, bullying other kids on the playground, now they're fully of age and these overgrown children think stepping on others is the only way to go. Out here in the woods I was doing a lot of what some would call 'Man Shit,' that is to say, doing things that portray the essence of manliness from society point of view. Things like building a fire with flint and steel, wrestling a bear, or not shaving for months on end would fall into this category, but the idea of 'Man Shit' got me thinking on what it is to really be a man. I realize that I don't get to ensure that my son is growing up to be proper gentlemen, which still causes me no end of grief, so I figured that for his sake, and perhaps my own, I should try my best to make a short list of what it really is to be a man. I came up with the following.

One: A man has the ability to think rationally and then make a decision, not the other way around. Boys are whimsical, spiteful, and quick to judge, while a man will try to see the argument from all angles before directing his energy into one. That's not to say that a man won't make mistakes; we are all regrettably human and thus quite fallible, and thus a man must always be ready to take responsibility for his actions, or the lack thereof, and seek to make amends if necessary. On the other side of the coin, should a man do something worthy of praise, he should accept it not boastfully or in higher standings than those around him, but rather graciously and gratefully before moving on to the next endeavor. I'm not saying that all men have to be leaders, but they should choose carefully who they follow.

Two: Integrity. If a man gives his word that should be the end of the conversation, for he should have established a reputation, through his actions, of being honest and trustworthy. I'm not sure where I heard it first, but I believe with my entire being that if one gives their word, then they had best intend to get it back, for there is no more important thing to be had.

Three: The ability to turn ambition into action. Some have so much ambition that they couldn't possibly do all that they desire in a hundred lifetimes, while others have the drive to do nothing more than pay their bills and watch movies. Neither of these paths are wrong, provided that one takes action towards making it a reality. Boys do a lot of talking; they let their imaginations run wild and it's not a bad thing, but I have seen too many wasted lives of those who did nothing more than dream or hope when all they had to do was act! Sometimes it's not easy, being a man usually isn't, but I myself had thrown away many years of my life drinking and waiting for something better to come along like a foolish frat boy. Whatever it is that one wants in life, it is up to the individual to go get it.

Four: Emotionally mature. It is a common misconception that men have to be straight faced and hearty always, completely void of emotion and caring. I have come to find that that it is indeed important for a man to be in touch with his emotions, and unafraid to let them show more often than not. It's OK to be afraid, or depressed, or in love, or hurt, or enraged, or ecstatic, or happy, or anything else, we are human and we feel damn it all!! However, a man will never allow his emotions to get in the way of what has to be done, and he will not make decisions based solely on how he feels. Take time to comfort, console, or celebrate one's self and those around, but do not allow it to stop one from moving forward, for life is short and there is always something that needs to be done.

Five: Responsibility. This is where life gets tricky, and sometimes it's hard to know what the best course of action is when a man is obligated to be responsible. When a man is responsible, sometimes he has to do things that he knows to be wrong in order to make things right. If a man and his family are hungry they must eat, and if they have no money to pay they must steal or poach. A man should try with all his might to do what is best for all, ever trying to find the best course of action, but in the event that he must do something wrong he should find no pleasure in it. It's hard to justify war, or killing, or destruction, but sometimes these things must happen, though anyone who is made happy by them I do not consider to be a man. Don't run from one's responsibilities, take what will come from your actions, always try and do the best that can be done, but ultimately do what must be done.

There is most certainly more that can be added to this list, but I had put a good deal of effort into simplifying it as best as I could, trying to cover the broad categories, not every little situation. It may not be a flawless system but I feel that anyone who follows these guidelines to the best of their ability has earned the right to be considered a man. While I have not always met my own expectations, especially in years past, I try to live up to them now, leading by example, and I hope that come the day my son is presented with this list, he will do the same.

I had taken to calling Pennsylvania the Preposition State simply because so many of the decisions I had to make hinged on this article of speech. Do I walk OVER these rocks to avoid those other rocks or do I walk AROUND those rocks to avoid these ones? Do I go UNDER this boulder or OVER it? Do I go THROUGH this shit and get it over or do I try and squeeze BETWEEN this shit? Sometimes it was nothing more than a trail filled with rocks when I had to make several of these decisions, other times it was wooded boulder fields! At times, hikers have to pass through what was called a 'rock maze', which I actually thought were a blast. I'm fairly certain that these were made purely for sport, and that the easiest path through the area would have bypassed these formations, but where's the fun in that? These mazes would require a little climb here and a small drop there, tight squeezes and wild left and right turns. Pennsylvania was really keeping me on my toes, literally, but I personally found it fun.

All my labors weren't for nothing--many of the views were simply incredible! It's hard to explain how I felt while traveling here. It's almost as if I felt a part of the woods and distinctly different from them at the same time. I felt like a well received visitor, simply passing through, but that my host begged me to stay as long as I could. There was a sort of intimacy between myself and nature now, almost as if I walked alongside of the wild instead of merely through it, dearest friends who had long run out of things to say yet still valued each other's company. I recall sitting on many rocky vistas overlooking the rolling hills below and feeling very at peace; one in particular that I certainly enjoyed was called the Pinnacle. It's a little off the beaten path but I strongly suggest that whomever comes across it take the time to glance a quick look, it's simply marvelous! Rumor has it, that the Pinnacle is the first place one can gaze upon New Jersey, but I can't say for sure. It wasn't only at the mountain vistas that I would take time to rest a little and simply be for a moment but also the rivers and springs, which were clearer than any others I can recall. One night I made camp alongside a stray stream and let the lively water sing me to sleep. There's nothing else like it. Truly the mountains had forged a home in my heart.

12 JOEL

Hiker-ism: Hike-o-path

(noun) Ever seen a bad horror movie about some crazy dude who thinks it perfectly normal to

just, I don't know, stab people repeatedly? Psychopaths! Well now visualize someone who has

that same sort of twisted obsession but only about hiking. Hike-o-paths! All thru hikers have

crossed the line a time or two, but some people never come back over.

    I spent my last night in Pennsylvania at a free hostel beneath a church in the Delaware Water Gap (DWG). This charming little city sits along the banks of the Delaware river, and serves as the only feasible crossing point for AT walkers. I wasn't the only person to be crossing the Delaware river bright and early this morning, in fact I was in rather good company. I had spent the night before with a few hike-o-paths, one named Grover who pushed twenty five miles between four thirty am and eleven am to get to the DWG in the middle of a horrific rainstorm. Another was Swiper, who had been a companion of Cloud Walker for a fair amount of time, and despite our simultaneous departure, he was across the Delaware in half the time it took me and I had not seen nor heard of him since. I thought that putting in twenty five miles in an entire day was pushing it, but some of these hikers were doubling that regularly, it was just insane! It's just a matter of hiking your own hike I suppose; they were fulfilled by challenging themselves with big miles and hearty inclines, I was fulfilled by the opportunity to slow down a little and gaze upon the little things in life. Neither of us were wrong, and that's the beauty of it. There is no wrong way to be happy with yourself.

    I remember being in grade school and learning about the American Revolution, and how George Washington had crossed the Delaware River in the middle of the night to assault British forces. At the time I really wasn't that impressed to be honest--guy crossed a river, on a boat, big freaking deal--but now that I could see the bloody thing the nocturnal, winter crossing was nothing short of a miracle! The Delaware River is big, really big, massive, immense! This thing is like a moving lake! What kind of lunatic just looks at a water feature like this and says "Know what, fuck it. I'm rowing across this thing with a army, let's see what happens," which I'm pretty sure is an accurate historical quote from America's first President. I can't even begin to tell how long it took me to cross the thing on foot while having a very nice highway bridge spanning the treacherous gap, all I know for sure is that there is no other place from here to the Jersey shore where the AT could have accomplished this crossing.

Upon crossing the Delaware River I landed in New Jersey, the Garden State. Nearly everything I had ever heard about Jersey made it sound like the armpit of America, fondly referred to as the GARBAGE State, populated entirely by juiced up douche bags and where every publicly accepted way of greeting someone would elsewhere be classified as sexual harassment. That being said I was incredibly surprised when I crossed the Delaware River, and in a good way, this place was gorgeous! Not a sleazy bar or filthy shore in sight, but rather majestic rolling hills painted green and boundless vistas peering over large plots of forest with only a few power lines to break up the endless sea of trees. Large rock formations and small ponds really made for a hike to remember. To be completely honest, I found this to be one of the more beautiful states along the trail, and I can only hope that more people take the time to hike here.

However, like anything else there were some drawbacks, such as I believe the state had made an honest attempt to kill me. In one day of hiking in Jersey I had seen more snakes than on the rest of the trail combined, and the deer ticks were alive and well here. There's really nothing good to be said about the mother fucking, blood sucking, disease ridden, nature tanks that are deer ticks, for if one doesn't remove them quickly they will bury their head into one's skin making disposal of them rather difficult. Furthermore, they are well known to transmit Lyme Disease. Also, when hiking through the Garden State one will know a good quarter mile in advance if they're coming up on another group of hikers, The Jersey accent is piercing! Though they were all really quite friendly.

While the natural beauty here was phenomenal, what truly stands out in my opinion were the man made structures along the trail. For example, there's an impressive, white stone tower on top of Highpoint, which is by no coincidence the highest point in the state. The tower can be seen from miles away and a short hike down a side trail will bring one to its base, I know because I accidentally hiked this way. I had not meant to stand alongside this marvel of man, but am glad I did, though trying to find my way back to the trail proved to be a real pain in the ass. While Highpoint was incredible, what I found to be absolutely stunning is what I like to call 'The Great Wall of Jersey,' which is close to a mile of boardwalk traversing a large swamp area near Glenwood. The amount of man hours that went into the construction this crazy thing must be too many for one man to count; a seemingly endless amount of posts driven into the mud support the causeway as it twists and turns over ground that I was grateful to not have to step in. Furthermore, a large suspension bridge crosses Pochuck Creek in the middle of this quagmire madness, the construction of which would have been a marvel on solid ground and nothing short of awe inspiring here. Truly the people of the Garden State take great pride in its natural beauty.

One of my more memorable food binges occurred alongside a crystal clear spring near Wawayanda Mountain where the water poured from one large stone pool to the next, a truly ideal spot for camping. I had just resupplied in Vernon, and couldn't help but notice that things in the north were beginning to get far more expensive, thus I passed on the opportunity to fill my stomach in town. That doesn't mean I left empty handed however, as I had purchased a pack of hotdogs to consume later in the evening, and what more perfect place to cook them then alongside this serene little spring! It didn't take long to gather the wood for a campfire, even less time to get a blaze going, and a small whittled branch made for a perfect cooking utensil. I sat merrily on a fallen log cooking frank after frank, filling my stomach as the sun began to sink--at least that's how it went for the first half a pack or so. I had no good way to store an open pack of hotdogs, and if I let them be they were bound to spoil or attract hungry pests and predators. Thus, I had no choice but to finish the entire pack in one sitting, which is not as easy as it sounds. Over the course of an hour I must have consumed more sodium than a single human being should have access to, let alone ingest! I began to find it difficult to keep eating; I was still hungry but my body just seemed repulsed by whatever these things that I was attempting to jam into my system were made of, seemingly unwilling to tolerate anymore of this reckless disregard for my arteries. Consuming the last four may have been the most difficult thing I had done on the trail, and I felt utterly gross from the inside out, but I refused to let them go to waste. Eventually I did make it through the entire pack, but barely, and I decided to sit outside near the fire well after dark just in case my body decided to send it all back up the way it came. I don't think I've even been able to think of hotdogs after that moment without feeling slightly sick on my stomach, really should have at least bought some buns to eat these slimy little bastards with!

Before I knew it New Jersey had come and gone, having only spent five days there before crossing into New York, but I think of it fondly. New York wasted no time in making its presence known, as the trail became significantly more difficult. When I think of New York, I of course think of the city, America's great front door to the world, bright lights and Broadway, Time Square, sky scrapers and nightlife, good old NYC. That being said, the city barely covers a tiny corner of the state and the rest is glorious, untouched wilderness, including the Adirondack mountains. There is more wild to be explored in the state of New York then can be seen in a decade of constant travel as a nearly endless series of trails wind through some of the most rugged and beautiful places on the east coast.

Sadly the AT doesn't summit some of the state's greatest peaks, seeing as it runs fairly close to the coast, but this segment still proved to be challenging in itself. What the mountains lacked in grandeur the trail made up for in difficulty by sending hikers thru a virtual adult jungle gym of rock formations! I remember well my introduction to the rock scrambles of New York because of a very odd guidebook entry very close to the southern border. Most of the reliable landmarks in the guidebook are shelters or summits with the occasional, unmistakeable vista, but I'll never forget seeing the word 'ladder' proudly posted on AWOL's pages. Thinking it would just be a rock formation, or perhaps a few pieces of rebar buried into the rock as I had seen a few times before, it managed to catch my attention without really standing out, until I arrived at a literal aluminum ladder in the middle of the trail! There may have been a more obvious way around this area, but I'm glad the trail went the way it did, climbing through wide, deep cracks in the rock and over mounds of boulders. The area where the ladder was would have been impossible to pass in this foreign object's absence, propped up against a formidable rock wall three times the size of a man, and I was certainly grateful for it being there. Though all I could think of is how much effort it must have taken for some poor volunteer to haul out a freaking ladder over rock and root, between tree and boulder, into the middle of nowhere just for some hiker to pass a single rock wall! It's moments like this that really make one realize just how much passion people have for one of America's great trails.

Another stoney passage that could have been easily avoided, but thankfully wasn't, is a massive rock known simply as 'The Lemon Squeezer.' Practically a small mountain in and of itself, this mound protrudes vertically out of the surrounding area with only one useable passage over it. As I stood at the entrance of the passage I soon realized that this was going to be harder for me than earlier anticipated, for it ran through a large crack in the rock too thin for a man to pass without turning sideways, and I was still carrying a lot of gear! The walls of this great crevice rose sharply on both sides, meaning one has to hoist their pack directly overhead and shuffle sideways for quite a distance before being able to resume a normal hiking position. So hoist my gear I did, and with great effort I might add, as I made to work my way through the Lemon Squeezer. This was exhausting! To hold my pack with fully extended arms over my head was a formidable chore as I made my way, but I made it before long, tossing my gear from my shoulders as soon as it cleared the walls. The victory was short lived, for immediately after the crack there is a ten foot high rock wall boldly blazed as well, indicating that one has to somehow scale it too. With my pack back upon my person in a normal fashion I somehow managed to be mightier than the wall, but climbing with a hearty weight pulling one backwards is not easy at all! Still, when I look back on it all it's the things like this that really made the hike amazing. Just as in life, the greatest rewards always come after the biggest challenges.

I think one of the main reasons the trail is made to traverse such difficult terrain is because of its proximity to New York City, at one point passing within thirty five miles of the metropolis. It's only a theory, but I suspect that nature enthusiasts venture out in search of a little wilderness instead of constantly surviving in the jungle that is NYC, and thus need as much outdoor challenge they can find in the little reprieve they can muster. There are a few points on the trail where one can actually see the skyscrapers of the city while standing on lonely, barren mountains, which brought me an immense sense of accomplishment. I had walked from the city of Fort Lauderdale, Florida to New York City! How cool is that?! While I still had quite a ways to go, looking at a set, measurable landmark was a huge boost to my confidence, it was a concept that people could grasp easily, and I thought it one to be reckoned with. It was a massive personal victory, and the pride I felt from it was not short lived as I continued to wear the smile brought about from it.

While it's not instantly thought about, one of the reasons that NYC had grown to such size is due to its location along the Hudson River, which in years past had allowed for supplies to flow in and out of the city with ease. The Hudson is another massive obstacle for hikers to traverse, though much like the Delaware crossing it had been made easy due to a massive bridge in Fort Montgomery. While the city is home to the river crossing it also has a slightly larger significance to hikers, as it boasts the official lowest elevation on the entire AT. In what's known as the Trailside Zoo, hikers pass by animal exhibits, educational plaques, and a wonderful statue of Walt Whitman, one of America's finest poets and a man of great significance to any nature lover or wandering soul. Though I truly enjoyed passing by some of the words of Whitman carved forever in stone, I found the whole experience of passing through this zoo to be rather depressing. I had never really been a fan of zoological gardens and the like, for I have never seen an animal in one that appeared happy. In my wandering I had seen many of God's fine creatures, from bears to squirrels, otters to deer, opossums and rabbits alike, all of which would bound playfully or at least move freely about their environment. Here the creatures sat fatted and lazy, mangy and disheveled, as if they had lost all will for life though they were undoubtedly fed well. Just as men were not meant for cages neither were any other of the world's animal population, and just as no joy will be found in prison, or office, neither does it exist in a zoo.

The lowest point of the trail is just outside the bear exhibit, and I find it to be the lowest in multiple ways. I remember watching the pair of brown bears wander about in captivity, and found it terribly depressing. Such proud creatures in the wild reduced to a life on display, exploited and confined though committing no crime, pacing about inside the walls whose perimeter would take me no more than a minute to walk around. I felt bad for them, and a bit ashamed of my own kind for treating these magnificent creatures in such a way. With as much technology as we have, people should dismantle these establishments and should they wish to see the creatures of the wild in motion one should simply look up a video of such--I'm quite sure it's no different. While I also realize that these places rehabilitate injured animals or aid those that are disabled in some way I believe it would honestly be better to let nature takes its course with these unlucky creatures, though I also believe that man must take great care in not producing situations that cause such unfortunate circumstances. The existence between man and animal needs to be not one of master and slave, but of equals as we all share this earth. Make no mistake, some of these creatures would gladly harvest a human for food should it come to that, so man should feel no shame in doing the same provided it's for that reason--that's just the natural order of things. Livestock should be allowed to wander about his farmers grounds, treated kindly until it's time for slaughter, not shoved into metal cages and nearly force fed to in turn feed us. In short, we are equal to all other life on this planet, from field mouse to moose, and while I feel no shame in harvesting these creatures from time to time they should not be imprisoned for the sake of our gluttony, or worse, entertainment.

Another instance of imprisonment came about as I crossed the Hudson over a massive bridge leaving Fort Montgomery, though quite of a different kind. Spaced out along the way were little gray boxes, highly visible when walking, all of which contained telephones that connected directly to the suicide prevention hotline. It was a grim reminder of life back in the world, and the stress that frequently coincides with it. Some people feel so imprisoned in life by so many things, that the only way they can see out is just to end it all. I'll admit, I had thought about it myself when things were at their worst, but am so glad I made it through, for I would have missed everything that had happened on this journey. If one is willing to leave everything so suddenly and permanently with zero regard for what they leave behind, why not just grab a backpack and go? To live as if one had just died and set forth on his own rebirth! If one truly wants everything to end then why not do so with a grand new beginning, for while I have not yet experienced death myself I have not known anyone whom had been able to come back from it. Before breaking one's prison with his demise he should attempt to break the bars with rebirth, as I for one honestly feel as though I had not truly lived until I started to travel.

While the rocks and hills of New York were gorgeous, one of the better moments came from a beauty of quite a different kind. A place that every thru hiker should visit along their way is the Graymoor Spiritual Life Center near Fort Montgomery, where the humble friars invite one to sleep in what is little more than a shelter placed upon their grounds. I didn't get a chance to meet any of the men who chose to live and worship in this place, but it's not for charity or kindness that I recommend one stay the night here. The arrangements for hikers aren't great, there's a hose, solar shower, and a covered area with a few picnic tables that serve as beds, and it all kept me dry for a night, but it's the morning that made the stay worth while. Some places hikers stay offer a hot breakfast in the morning, others send you on your way with a warm embrace and well wishes, but here the friars offer simply the gift of music to start one's day. I awoke just after dawn, per usual, but not just to the first rays of the morning sun but also a melody of bells chiming in the distance. The clock tower isn't visible from where I slept, but every thirty minutes it would chime out the time followed by a short hymn that carried softly and sweetly to my ears. I had grown to love the songbirds playful singing in the morning and the melody of a soft breeze across my ear, but the bells of New York sounded ever beautiful in harmony with my morning coir, and provided one of my favorite mornings of my travels. I stayed in my sleepingbag longer than usual waiting for the next round of chimes and packed up slowly to further enjoy it, and while I never met the men who live at the center I thank them greatly for the simple hospitality they offer so freely.

And speaking of hospitality, New Yorkers know how to make a freaking sandwich! I had heard legends of the New York delis and the awe-inspiring creations they compile, but until now have yet to witness it. I took a quick detour to Mountain Top Deli on my last day in the state, for I would have felt wrong leaving without seeing if the legends were true, and blissfully found that what I've heard holds full weight--that sandwich was amazing! Now granted, I was essentially starving and thus everything tastes better, but I'm pretty sure that had little to do with my diagnosis. Just to be sure however, I feel in the future I may have to go back to NYC and conduct a proper survey.

If nothing else I must say that traveling in the northeast is incredibly rewarding simply because of the number of state lines that are crossed in short succession! New York seamed to pass in a day and Connecticut stayed half as long, though I do remember it being distinctly different. It's amazing how much can change in a short distance, for while New York had been rocky and rugged, Connecticut's trail followed the rivers. There were large flat sections near broad and fast streams, and I could frequently be found resting at their side.

By now spring had taken full hold and was sprinting headlong into summer, and I was surrounded by the nearly unbroken green of plant life feasting and fattening in preparation for the winter. With the pending summer came the heat of the season, which I found to be far preferable at the moment to the many months of cold that I had already endured, but it also had me sweating on a consistent basis which I was not used to. I had always loved water; in fact at one time I had thought it impossible for me to live any farther then a thirty minute drive from a major body of water simply because the thought of doing so was thoroughly depressing. These rivers made me smile, and brought me back to days I would spend surfing or on the beach back home, so much so that I couldn't help but go far a quick swim now and then. As far as many are concerned, myself included, the only way to go swimming on the AT is as God intended, which is another way of saying buck naked, and let me just say it's astounding! The rivers were still cool and crisp despite being so large, and it would take my breath away as I plunged into them, but in the most delightful manner. I would always bring my head above water laughing, watching the dust wash from my skin in small grey streams running down my shoulders, some dirtier than others, and I would spend quite a bit of time trying to work my fingers through the course, matted mess that I liked to call my hair. After each dip I would let the sun dry me before putting my clothes back on and resuming the hike, my clothes still smelling of dirty hiker and myself of dirty river, but happy nonetheless. Sitting naked in the rivers of Connecticut and dried by the sun's rays along the banks will always be a fond memory of mine, being back in nature as man was intended and loving every moment of it

Hiker-ism: Flip Flop

(Verb/Noun) The act of starting the AT somewhere in the middle and then proceeding to hike to one end before traveling back to either where you started, or the other end to hike the remainder. Usually done if one misses the annual window to reach Katahdin before Baxter State Park closes or to optimize seasonal conditions.

    The towns of Connecticut are ones to remember as well, as they have managed to maintain their old world charm, the very essence of urban New England if you ask me. One such town is Kent, which is hardly a hiker town and really more of a place for the wealthy to venture out and sip wine, but it's still charming nonetheless. What makes this town stick out in my mind however is not anything within the city limits, but rather who I met walking back to the trail as I ventured in. I'll say again that a thru hiker can be spotted a mile off, they just have a look about them, and the pair that I encountered here were no exception. There was a woman about my age and an older gentleman, both heavily laden and unfamiliar to my eyes. Hark, new friends! The fellow was well built, stocky, and a fair bit taller than me with graying hair and a stern look about him, who went by the name Paco. The girl, on the other hand, couldn't have been any more different. She was thin and a fair bit shorter then me, with curly hair pulled back into dreadlocks, wore glasses, and may have literally been bouncing off the walls with endless energy if there had been walls to bounce from, she called herself Goat Gurrl. The pair of them were rocking a flip-flop starting at the DWG and were heading north to Katahdin before heading back to the Jersey border to hike south to Springer. I can't recall if I had seen another long distance hiker since losing Moxie and Ibex in Pennsylvania, so the idea of hiking near a pair was a welcome change of pace. While I knew it would take me a little bit to catch back up with them after I stopped in town, this was far from the last time we met.

    While Kent was a fair city to visit one of my favorites along the entire trail was yet to come, that being the tiny town of Falls Village. The reason why is simple, and that is the Toymaker's Cafe, a hiker-friendly haven run by a fine English couple who were more than happy to allow people to camp behind the shop. It's a good business model really, to allow a bunch of half starved eating machines to spend the evening behind a breakfast house and incite them in the morning with the smell of fresh coffee and waffles--worked on me at least. Little did I know of the day that was in store.

    I had slept well the night before, and it was a little cool out so I was able to wrap up in my bag nicely, which always induces a pleasant slumber. Come the morning I felt as though I owed it to the fine folks of the Toymaker's Cafe to at least grab a cup of coffee, but I had also heard their waffles were amazing from a post in a trail register that some southbound section hiker had written back at one of the shelters along the way. Not wanting to miss out, I decided to stick around for a proper breakfast, and what a breakfast it was! First off, their waffles are so massive they cover an entire plate; second, they have some incredible and unique serving styles including the thru hiker friendly fluffer-nutter waffle, which means lots of peanut butter and marshmallow cream. Unable to contain my curiosity I ordered one of the aforementioned delicacies, which was piled so high with peanut butter and the rest that it should have been logged in AWOL's guidebook as a food challenge! After that masterpiece and four cups of coffee I felt like I could suplex a freight train, and I hit the trail running for what was to be by far one of the best days on the trail.

    In case you're wondering, there is indeed a waterfall near Falls Village, and yes it's worth seeing. A short hike into the woods will reveal a small falls, which I had thought were going to be the main attraction, however not but a few hundred yards farther there's a massive falls that is unlike any other in the AT! It's awe inspiring, broad and exposed, and in all honesty I could have spent an entire day just goofing off around the falls, but I'm glad I kept going. The sun was shining, it was warm but not to hot, a light breeze, and the trail wound through sticky pine groves which kept the bugs at bay--it was perfect. The views just kept coming, from an amazing meadow view gazing onto evergreen peaks to the rocky summit of the Lions Head, this day just kept getting better. Though the greatest mountain view I had come across this day was on Bear Mountain, which is the highest peak in Connecticut, though it wasn't just the summit that held an amazing view. Bear Mountain marks roughly fifteen hundred AT miles, which meant twenty three hundred for my motivated ass, what an accomplishment! As I stood atop the summit overlooking it all I felt fulfilled, I was actually proud of myself just for being myself and no other reason. I felt satisfied with who I was, whole, that there was nothing I could not do. With under seven hundred miles left to travel I was so close and yet so far from my final destination, but I was ready for it to come now. While still being miles from Katahdin I felt as if I had done what I set out to do, but that it wasn't OK to leave this unfinished, not after being so close. My body had grown strong and my soul had followed suit, not only was I unbroken, I was made better then ever before.

While the final steps in Connecticut were phenomenal it was my first steps into Massachusetts that stole the show. It had already been a day beyond measure but as I entered the commonwealth I did so in Sage's Ravine, which is one of the most enchanting places I had ever seen! The trees grow thick here, and are covered in a damp, dense moss, the light is well blocked making it appear to be twilight even in the middle of the day and a quick, clear, and playful river runs through it all. In fact, the ravine is made by the river which had cut deeply into the surrounding rock for countless centuries, pooling here and there with small falls in between. It's the pools themselves that make the ravine so surreal, as they had been in place long enough to carve into the stone walls, undercutting the rock into shelves and snake-like channels. Roots and limbs grew covered in algae in many of the pools, making them look very old and dark; if ever a nectar for eternal life or infinite wisdom poured forth from the earth herself it would have been in this place. I will return to this place someday if the good Lord grants me the time to do so, for every cool, damp breath here brought me peace, and the sounds of the river would sooth even the most savage beast--a place well worth remembering.

This perfect day ended alongside a half a mile long exposed ridgeline overlooking the whole of Massachusetts. As the sun dropped low over the lush green hills of New England I fully understood what hiking was all about. There is no destination out here, every step has the chance to surprise and fulfill; there is no greater purpose to it all, it's meaning is locked inside itself, it is there in each moment to be reflected on for the rest of one's life. It's the simplest unsolvable riddle that ever was, nonsense that makes perfect seance to those with no sense, a chance to stop and progress at the same time. I had become so connected with the world that I could hardly tell where I ended and it began, and while my years on earth are few I will have been here in this moment for eternity. Hiking is the most profound nothing that ever was, a simple trip that becomes an epic legend, but as far as I was concerned, I was just out for a walk.

What I distinctly remember about Massachusetts is just how far one could see when at a great height. The mountains flowed like a rolling sea, with a seemingly endless number of ridges coming one after the next. There were no jagged peaks like the Blue Ridge mountains had, just calm and faintly changing slopes farther than my mind could comprehend. Much of the wildlife had become more active in recent weeks, and they made their presence known, from playful woodchucks to stoic deer. I had even begun to encounter porcupine for the first time in my life. I came across one such beast near Upper Goose Pond Lake as he got caught up with me in a bit of a game of keep away. The trail was clear but with walls of shrubs and stone surrounding it, here I happened upon a ground-wandering porcupine that sat in the middle of my path. Thankfully he wasn't in the mood to stand his ground or it would have been me who was severely inconvenienced, but rather he seemed to be startled by my coming and made to run ahead to avoid saying hello. Though as I said before there was nowhere to run but further up the trail, and so as I advanced along my way I would encounter him again and again, always with the same result as he would make a quick shuffle only to soon be startled again by my arrival. I don't know exactly how long the game went on, but when the path opened up again my playmate took full advantage and scuttled off not to be seen again; still I thanked him for the game and wandered on merrily for the rest of the day.

I didn't go much farther that day however, and am very glad I didn't, for I had heard a rumor that there was a cabin on this lake that served as a shelter but operated more like a free hostel with the potential for a hot breakfast. I had decided that it would be in my best interest to take the half a mile side trail to the cabin at Upper Goose Pond Lake, and at its end I found a most glorious sight. There stood a two story cabin painted fire engine red, making it stand out boldly against the vibrant green woods of New England, and it truly was more of a hostel than anything else. There was a fire place in a fully enclosed common room with bunks upstairs, a kitchen in the back, two privies that even normal people would have considered to be clean, and a small dock jutting out into the lake which lay before the entire compound. There was a full time caretaker on sight, a kind older fellow who went by the name Wanderer--an appropriate name indeed, for his very presence seemed to radiate adventure long traveled and his eyes shone soft and calm, imprinted upon by countless views of nature's vast and infinite beauty. With a smile he greeted me, also asking if I was to stay the evening, and while there were still a few useable hours in this day I decided to enjoy them here instead of pressing farther.

    The cabin at Upper Goose Pond Lake is the sort of place a man could sit for a week and feel as though he's only been there an hour, a paradise in the middle of nowhere. I spent most of the day chatting with Wanderer, enjoying a pipe of tobacco as I did so, when later in the day we were joined by another, a young woman so lovely that as she approached I half wondered if I was simply daydreaming or if I had happened upon one of the woodland nymphs of lore long renowned for their beauty. Either the serenity of the lake had thrown me into a full out hallucination so realistic that I still haven't fully snapped from it or I actually met this beautiful young lady--which is which I'll never know, however this potential product of imagination had decided to stay the night as well and went by the name Flash. She was a section hiker from New Jersey out here for a week or so to help stay in shape in between triathlons, and she seemed to be fully enthralled by the stories that Wanderer and I continued to exchange. It's amazing how complete strangers can become good friends before they're even properly introduced out here in the woods.

    The cabin even had real mattresses, or at least a plastic covered block of foam which I had come to call a real mattress, and I slept amazing that night, waking with the dawn. I decided to go greet the sun that morning and made my way to the lake to await its arrival in the cool, damp, mountain air. The lake was still and smooth as glass, its water crystal clear and reflecting the golden yellows and soft red hue of the dawn. The nightingale and owls had gone to rest for the day and the morning songbirds had not yet awoken, even the very insects seemed to rest at this hour, and not even a breath of wind dared break the stillness. I breathed deeply of nature's bounty, letting it flow into my lungs in a most cleansing and filling manner as dew began to collect in my beard while I stood upon the dock mirroring the stillness of the morning. I began to laugh, but not the sort of outburst that comes from a fine jest or pleasant surprise, hardly audible even in this serenity. It was the sort of full, hearty laugh that comes from absolute peace, and finds its roots not in impulse but rather deep in a man's soul.

    The rumors of breakfast proved to be true, and after I returned from the lake Wanderer had made a pot of fresh coffee and was working on frying up some hot cakes. There's nothing like a hot breakfast to start a day off right. I sat with Flash for a bit beside the fireplace talking about our hikes and whatnot, and she was indeed quite pleasant company even though I was still rather intimidated by her beauty. After breakfast the three of us stood on the front porch of the cabin, loaded and preparing to move out though I remember having the strongest urge to stay. Wanderer assured me that the best was yet to come, having walked the trail himself, but he first couldn't help but remark at the fact that I still carried a multitude of gear on the outside of my pack by saying that I resembled a modern day vagabond. Personally I think this may have been one of the nicest things anyone had ever said to me in my entire life. Flash figured she would be hiking a bit slower than me but let me know the next shelter she was staying at and asked me to write her a note in the register there if I felt like it. And so the three of us parted ways just as quickly as we had become acquainted, but I for one still smile when I think of them.

Hiker-ism: Carin

(noun) The piling of stones to serve as trail markers date back to ancient Scotland, but have found a new home in the woods of America and serve as a way to mark a trail when no other method is available. Sometimes people make small cairns of their own to signify their passing through an area, or to remember to those who travel with them.

Progress had been easy to make for far too long; the land rose and fell here and there but due to the proximity to the eastern seaboard there hadn't been a good mountain in quite some time. That changed next to instantly as I reached the great state of Vermont which thus proceeded to kick my ass! It was as if someone had just changed the difficulty setting on a video game from easy to expert and didn't tell me, but I had missed putting a lot of effort into a day and was glad for the chance to work again. I started to notice a change in the vegetation again, this time being the abundance of hemlock pines which I had come to know to thrive in the higher elevations of North Carolina and Tennessee. I also began to happen upon signs of moose which I had never encountered before, and wondered how that would play out in the future seeing as bull moose are rumored to be extremely aggressive during their mating season. I hadn't realized how tame the woods had become the closer in proximity to NYC they were, but now every step seemed to send me farther into unsettled wilderness.

It's here that the AT becomes one with another long distance hiking trail, which actually pre-dates it by several year--that being the Vermont Long Trail, which apparently runs all the way to Canada from what I hear. The origins of both trails can actually be found here in Vermont as well, as they were thought of atop Stratton Mountain, which seems to have a knack for inspiring people. While the trails were thought up from the top of a pine, those who wish to see the awe-inspiring view from the top of this peak no longer have to be so adventurous seeing as a fire tower had since been erected, providing a more stunning view than had ever been possible before. Even after viewing thousands of miles of trail I was still floored by the view here in the Green Mountains of Vermont.

In fact, the entire state seemed to ooze inspiration from every rock and root, tree and valley, and the dense hemlock forests are littered with small cairns crafted by those who have ventured here. The trees grow tall but with little underbrush, allowing one to see through the forests for a good ways while still being totally immersed in nature. While the Green Mountain Range was proving to be incredibly beautiful I couldn't help but laugh at the sighting of Kid Gore Shelter, and while the name came about by compiling the last names of two nature enthusiasts the place still sounded like the most black metal spot on the planet! I decided to make this my home for a night, half expecting the shelter to be covered in metal spikes and Norwegian death metal band logos, but I was sadly let down to find it much like the others I had stayed visited. I can't say I was terribly surprised to find it this way however, though I must say it was one of the more peaceful and lovely roofs that I ever had the chance to sleep under. It was a simple three sided shelter with a bunk built at each end and a makeshift table in the middle, but the view one could witness by laying here and looking forward was that of a far stretching valley with several peaks lining the sides. In the evening hours every summit was illuminated with a different color from the setting sun, and a small spring ran close by to lull one to sleep. It was the sort of place that nearly every folk-style, acid-induced lovesong of the sixties could have been written at, and I'm pretty sure that if one strained their vision enough they could see the Von Trapp family fleeing from Nazi Austria over one of the distant mountains.

I had found much time to think while wandering the wilderness and had gotten quite good at it, which I'm sure my mother will be glad to hear seeing as it was never one of my strong suits as an adolescent. I would let my imagination wander freely, occasionally solving one of life's great mysteries for sport only to forget it moments later, retained in the blank space of memory to be called upon should the conversation stir it. Memory is a strange and fickle thing, and in addition so is a man's entire ability to comprehend and reason, blending fact and legend to create gods and monsters, leaving reality a distant second to perception. I played a game with myself one day where I tried to stretch the ability of my mind to comprehend the known universe, testing just how much one can truly comprehend about his own existence. Rather than ponder the vast stretches of the galaxy, or even the globe, I started with something small and easily visualized in my mind, a simple sphere of no particular color and small enough to fit in the palm of my hand. The image was easy to conjure as I had seen such a thing in reality, I was even able to examine and manipulate it in thought, entirely sure of its existence. I then envisioned two like spheres sitting next to each other, and was able to do so with the same ease as before. My game began to get more complex as I mentally added spheres, first three, then a two by two matrix to make four, three by three to make nine, and so forth still with great ease. It's when I started to get to the larger numbers reaching in excess of a hundred, or a ten by ten matrix, that my mind began to strain, and I envisioned a parlor table being covered with my spheres to help bring about the image. While I could see ten on each side the middle appeared muddled in my vision, and to pick one item up individually became difficult against the multitude. Such things soon became impossible as I stretched into odd sized matrices such as thirteen on a side or twenty two, and while I full well knew such a sight could be easily brought into reality I lost the ability to bring it about mentally.

It's possible others could stretch this game as far as a hundred on a side or perhaps a little more, but I myself could not comprehend so few of these spheres to not even entirely cover the floor of a small room. In conclusion I reasoned that human comprehension is extremely finite, lacking in the ability to fully grasp all that which is not but ten feet from him, let alone a mile or a light year. I became dumbfounded in my own inability to understand that which I knew to exist--the oceans I had surfed, the roads I had wandered, even the forests that lay before my very eyes were far too vast to comprehend! If a man cannot even begin to understand what he knows to be real, or even that what he can at present moment see, how is he ever to understand the eternal?! What arrogance possesses him to say he knows the will of God, or that he knows in all certainty there to be none, when he can not even bring to his mind all the items on his grocery list? I reasoned that I may travel a lifetime in these mountains and not be able to see them all, that I could wander a millenia and leave things untouched, and that the greatest and most profound aspects of life would ever allude me. However, I feel there is great worth in seeing all that I can, to experience all that I'm able, and to take from it all the lessons I may. While it is all greatly beyond me to understand even what lay around my person, it is still good to venture over every peak I'm able--I simply have to decide what mountains I wish to climb.

    I had lost much of my desire for the conveniences of modern life, and had not only learned to live without them, but also preferred to. Electricity, temperature controlled air, and clean water on demand were simply mind blowing whenever I ventured into town and had the chance to experience them, but I certainly didn't miss them when out in the forest. In fact, about the only thing I missed apart from frequently sitting down for a good beer with good friends was having access to enough food to satisfy my constant hunger at all times, which made every resupply day exciting. The trail towns weren't hurting for a fine selection of cheap places to eat but certain things were next to impossible to find, namely a good burrito. Ah the burrito, possibly the finest American bastardization of another country traditional fair, flour tortilla wrapped around a delicious assortment of meats, cheeses, rice, beans, sour cream, various vegetables and spices, and should I feel sassy a fine helping of creamy green guacamole. As a surfer, this simple, delectable dish frequently stood as my only source of nutrition for weeks at a time during the summer, and how I wished to savor its flavor once more.

    After nearly twenty five hundred miles of absolutely beautiful, but sadly burrito-less, scenery I finally got my chance to break the fast in the middle of Vermont's Green Mountains. To fully describe my absolute need for a burrito please let me lay out the following scenario. Imagine being lost in the desert for days, the sun beating down hot and heavy on one's shoulders while pressing on across miles of burning sand. The water containers have long since been rendered dry with no chance to refill them as the heat relentlessly pulls every last bit of moisture from one's body. Down to your last drops you resort to crawling, no longer possessing the strength to stand, thoroughly dehydrated and too thirsty to think, moments away from giving in and letting death sooth one's thirst. Then suddenly, you see it. An oasis just ahead! Too weary to care if it's only a marriage or not you pull yourself from the sand, rising to your feet in an all out final sprint towards this final hope for survival, completely exhausted and yet invigorated. Absolutely insane from heat you erupt in an uncontrollable, cackling laughter reserved for lunatics and mad scientists upon reaching the shore of the cool, clear dessert pool. Not slowing for a second to greet it, fully clothed and without hesitation, you dive headlong into this angelic harbor, plunging beneath its surface in a wave blissful, life restoring refreshment and drink deeply of it. Springing upright with a roar of triumph and joy, strength fully restored you then look over to find a well dressed bar man standing besides you who promptly cracks open a brew before passing it over with a smile where you then spend the rest of your day drinking fine ale until the evening. That, my friends, is how I felt about Cilantro's Burrito Joint in Manchester Center Vermont.

Perhaps it was because of my long extended burrito drought, but I must say that this was one of the best burritos I had ever eaten! The ingredients were locally sourced and fresh, the quality was impeccable, and even by thru hiker standards it was a hearty serving size. As I sat close to tears on a park bench outside the place my joy was only slightly disrupted by the fact that I wouldn't be able to eat here again anytime soon, but even so I was beyond grateful to have found this place. Like I keep saying, it's the little things that really make life wonderful.

Hiker-ism: Work for Stay

(verb/noun) Pure bliss for hikers on a budget! Occasionally, a kind hearted hostel owner will exchange a night's stay for a few hours of work instead of money. Now that I think about it, all hostel stays are work for stays, seeing as people work for money, but that's besides the point...

If there is one thing I could change about the human condition it is the misfortune that I am only able to see the world through my own eyes. The planet is packed to the brim with an eclectic blend of people, each one an island unto themselves, what wonders I could learn if I could only experience life as they do! The perception of normal is unique to each individual, and what seems wild and radical to one is a standard occurrence to another. While I lack the ability to fully know the world as another dose I am able to live amongst those who are different from me, and hopefully be open minded enough to learn something from each encounter with the bazaar.

Undoubtedly the most profound immersion into another's way of life came about in the small city of Rutland VT when I stayed with the people of the Yellow Deli and Hostel. To be honest, I had completely overlooked it in my guide book and it was only when I met a day hiker who had just come from there that I even considered stopping in. He had told me that they were a strange sort of people, but nearly always accepted work for stay offers so instead of stopping short of town for the night and making my way in to resupply in the morning I pushed hard to try and make it to the hostel before night fall. After I insured a pair of young ladies at the trailhead that I wouldn't kill them they offered me a ride to town as the sun sank low in the sky, and I arrived at the Yellow Deli in the last of the day's light, wondering if I had arrived too late to work for my keep. When I entered the building I had to check to be sure that I had actually left the woods, the architecture was astounding! The walls are adorned with massive murals, the lighting is low and soft, several structures made of reclaimed wood fill every available space utilizing beams and barrels making it feels as though I just walked into a gypsy camp instead of a deli. Everything in the place was built strong and sturdy by hand, though I don't think there was a straightly cut board in the place, it was the work of many master carpenters crafting costume works of art to fit this incredibly unique, and frankly beautiful, space. The people were just as unique as the the space, and never before have I met such giving people. They belonged to the Twelve Tribes of Israel, a religious based group of individuals who live communally in several locations across the planet with great focus on selflessness, charity, and hard work. The first person I met here was Reuben, who greeted me kindly as I entered even though I was dressed in rags and smelled to high heaven while asking if I could stay at the hostel tonight. He seemed to genuinely be happy that I had asked and promptly showed me upstairs to the bunk room where he then asked if I wished to pay for the night or work in the morning. I was used to nearly having to beg for the opportunity to work for stay and the fact that it was freely offered really took me aback for a moment, but only a moment for I graciously accepted the opportunity. I'll never forget his response, he simply said 'that's encouraging' and invited me downstairs after I settled in for some 'hospitality'. Having grown up in America I full well knew 'hospitality' to mean 'chance to buy shit from us', which would completely negate the entire reason I wished to stay here, but I was the only person there that night and so I decided to head back into the deli to at least try and figure what this place was all about.

    I was still awe stricken by the atmosphere of the place, though strangely felt right at home, and after taking a seat at the incredibly well crafted bar I was soon greeted by others from the deli. I remember meeting a fine young man named Onyx, and another named Drock, before being greeted again by Ruben whom had brought along a lovely fresh vegetable sandwich, garden salad, and baked potato and placed the plate before me. It appeared I had made a grand mistake by appearing in the deli and would now be paying the price, literally, but before I could could even offer a half hearted 'thank you' Ruben said simply "On the house" before walking off. If the woodwork, murals, and folk music weren't enough to completely take me aback the kindness here sure did! They served me like a host would an old friend whose arrival had been long awaited, and without being prompted, I'd never seen such a thing from a business before. If I wasn't intrigued by the place before I certainly was now, and was certainly looking forward to the morning where I would have the chance to work alongside these people, hopefully gaining some insight into their community. Before I turned in for the night I was asked if I wanted to join them in the morning when they gathered as a community, which was to be proceeded by breakfast, and while I loved the idea of a hot meal just the chance for me to get to understand these people a little more would have been enough for me to accept the offer.

    I woke close to dawn, per usual, quite earlier than required to meet up with a man named Aish who was to take me over to the community when things were close to getting underway. He was a friendly, stout fellow with a full beard and long hair pulled back into a ponytail, which seemed to be the preferred style among the men here, and we chatted a bit in the morning hours. He had made a pot of ma'te, some sort of Argentine green tea, which next to instantly became my new favorite morning beverage seeing as it was packed with antioxidants, provided a natural boost of energy without a pending crash, and had about half the caffeine as a cup of coffee, not to mention had a lovely, earthy flavor. Invigorated, the two of us made to walk a few block to meet up with the rest of the community, I had met only a handful of them the night before and was curious as to how many of them there were. We came to a good sized, farm style home a few blocks from the deli and I began to notice not only

a fair amount of people scattered about the place, but also a several children playing outside in the early morning hours. We gathered in the living room of the house, close to thirty people in all, and all at once they started to greet each other and myself in a very endearing and cheerful manner. It appeared to be some sort of church service that they performed every morning though I had never really seen anything like it. They gathered in a large circle until one person, seemingly at random, would start singing a song of praise and the rest would join in shortly thereafter. I remember the songs being catchy, upbeat, and cheerful, and while they were singing some would gather together in the center of the room and dance in a manner I had never seen before, arms linked in a small circle stepping in time, and while the steps must have been choreographed the dance looked very loose and free. Some had instruments, others clapped along, I just stood back and smiled, it was a sight to behold its equal I had never witnessed before. After a few songs they would stand silently until someone began to speak about various blessings in their life, or how a bible verse or spiritual analogy had helped them through the day. While one person spoke all the others would stand silently and listen, never interjecting or talking over each other, always showing respect and acceptance of another's opinion. From there a sort of communal devotion began, with one of the older fellows leading it and the rest sitting back, taking notes or simply listening. When this had concluded all members of the community raised their hands and asked for the lord's blessing in various points of their life, or for the community as a whole, many of the requests rousing a resounding amen from the others. I had been to church before, many times to be honest, but I had never seen such genuine worship before, or since, it was pure, humble, filling, and almost seemed to be the way it was meant to be done.

 Everyone ate together, and shortly after breakfast I was heading back to the hostel to do a little work in exchange for my stay. I must admit I felt a little strange sitting in on such an event, but I also felt very welcomed, like they had completely opened up to me without ever being asked to do so. I had let it slip that I had been a carpenter back in the world and so they had me sure up the bunk beds in the hostel, which apparently they had been meaning to do for quite some time now. This sort of work had always been enjoyable to me, and it didn't take long for me to finish, so I decided to stick around for the rest of the day to help out in the deli and learn a bit more from these fine folk. They let me wash dishes after the lunch rush for awhile, and even fed me a few times before the day was out. As I worked I just tried to take in how they managed to maintain such an honest sense of community? It was mind boggling, I didn't think people could live like this, that humans selfish nature would tear a place like this to shreds from the inside out but here was the yellow deli, running smoothly for decades and growing stronger with the years.

    We parted that evening as new friends, and I felt grateful to have met these odd, yet incredibly friendly, hippies here in the middle of Vermont. I had gained a new perspective on life, and the value of that simply can't be measured. I had experienced kindness not only given freely but offered without instigation. I had seen a collaboration of people who had managed to live in peace and harmony amongst each other, and with hopes of influencing the word to do the same. Even now when I look back on it all it's hard to make complete sense of, but I feel like my life has been deeply impacted by these people, and I hope that I can find a way to pay forward the pure kindness that they had given me.

    I had just cut a new walking stick after having the same one for well over a thousand miles. My old friend had grown dark from wear and natural oils from my hand, the base was stripped of bark and it had started to lose its youthful spring giving it a risk of breaking with too much weight. Unfortunately, my new companion was a little hesitant to begin working with me, I wasn't used to having a stick the proper height for my back and the rough bark felt strange in my hand. Nevertheless we set out together, navigating the trail heading north again with less than five hundred mile to Katahdin. I remember the first real spot where I would test my new tool, a large pile of rocks where I planted the base of my walking aid on a boulder and braced against it to make my way down another sizable stone. Then my damn walking stick slipped and I went on my ass, with quite a bit of force I might add, subsequently bouncing to the ground below in pain and frustration. A fine way to start a partnership I remember thinking, little bastard wasn't getting off that easy, I had just cut it green from a downed tree alongside the trail and I wasn't about to take from nature without using it. It would appear that I needed to make a slight adjustment to walking with my new 'friend' but I figured that would come in time, or at least I was hopeful it would.

As I went walking I started to wonder if I had been using the word subsequently correctly. It was hardly used in common conversation from my part but after falling due to my new stick and subsequently bouncing to the ground I decided to ensure that it was the proper adverb to use. By breaking it down into root words, that being sub, sequence, and the prefix ly, I was able to make a better analysis of what the word meant. Sub, meaning below, sequence, meaning a series of events, and ly, to make the word and adverb, it appeared to me that this particular word was meant to mean the next action below in the series. So I had derived the true meaning of the word subsequently and subsequently I can use it better. While it was nice to know I had been using English correctly I was suddenly struck by how strange of a topic it was to be thinking of! I had all the time in the world to think on the great mysteries of life, to solve the major problems plaguing mankind, to devise theories for existence and plan for the future yet here I was thinking of the word subsequently! Why was I wasting my time on such a thought? Admits my bewilderment over my own mind I found the greatest truth, when else would I have time to think of such things?

My time in the Green Mountains of Vermont was nearly at an end as I neared the New Hampshire border, and I'll admit I was sad to see them go. The town of West Hartford greeted me close to sun down which I found a little discouraging seeing as I would now have to hike in the dark to reach the next shelter four miles ahead of me. It seemed to be a bit more than I cared to handle that day and so when I crossed the white river on a large road bridge I decided to try and find someplace close by where I could set up camp and not disturb anyone. While snooping around the upper bank of the large, swift moving river I heard a bell begin to ring not far off, and not a church bell but more like the one a man would expect to hear from the deck of a small ship. On the front porch of a small home stood a man and a young boy just ringing away and as our eyes met the man motioned me over with a wave of his hand and calling out to offer me a drink if I cared for one. With nothing to loose I figured I may as well see what exactly all the ruckus was about, and if nothing else they could probably direct me to the nearest patch of trees where I would be able to rest for an evening. Thus I had arrived at the home of the Heart family, a meeting I would not soon forget. While standing on the front porch being offered a soda or coffee I hear a voice from inside the house ask if I'd like a Bud Light? So that's the kind of party it's going to be! Before I knew it I'm standing in the kitchen of these fine folks home sipping cheap beer, eating fully dressed hotdogs, and taking shots of Crown Royal Whiskey! After a few hard drinks and several hours of playing Call of Duty Black Opps they asked if I cared to spend the evening in the living space above their garage, and seeing as I was a little intoxicated it seemed like a proper idea.

Apparently the backstory here is that during a massive flood the White river swelled well over its banks and the Heart family's home had been severely damaged because of it. Thus they were forced to inhabit the garage while they performed renovations. Fortunately their insurance company came through for them and they not only had enough money to fix the damage done by the river, but also improve the place quite a bit. As a by product of all this they now had a proper space in the garage where people could stay, and the Hearts frequently offered it to thru hikers who passed by, trail magic at its finest! The Hearts have helped quite a few hikers over the years, and I for one am incredibly grateful for the kindness they showed me. Should anyone happen to pass by West Hartford on the AT listen for the bell, if you're lucky you'll meet some of the better folk I had ever come across.

12.5 THE ROAD TO KATAHDIN

I was never destined to be a college man. My hands are best suited to work with wood and nail as opposed to pen and paper, and my head is far happier to puzzle over measurements and fractions rather then spreadsheets and projections. I had tried college when freshly out of high school, but it just turned out to be the most expensive party that I'd ever attended and thus left before ever really starting. That being said, if ever I had the desire to be a unhappy, academically minded, normal American I certainly would have set my sights at Dartmouth College in Hanover, New Hampshire! The town is packed with the certain charm that is prevalent in the greater New England area--old buildings packed closely together and covered with ivy, a few well groomed parks, local businesses aplenty and an Ivy League school, all in one quaint little town. That and the people here are extremely aware of the AT and go well out of their way to accommodate thru hikers. Not only do many of the local eateries offer free sustenance to the revered northbound thru hikers of America's grand trail, but many of the citizens have taken it upon themselves to care for the wayward, sunbathed philosophers venturing through their fine city. There were multiple coolers of soda set out alongside the roads, some of which had telephone numbers upon them that hikers could call for a free place to stay! Truly, Hanover is a haven for hikers!

What attracts me most about the Dartmouth College however is not their prestigious curriculum or long list of 'accomplished' alumni, but rather their outdooring club known as the DOC. Further perpetuating the idea that Hanover is a perfect hiker haven, the college has designated a social club specifically for going on the trail and making sure that it is well cleared and properly blazed. They really do a fantastic job, and should I had ever had the privilege of studying along side these brainy backwoods bastards I would have undoubtedly be academically expelled within a semester simply from spending all my time in the woods and not the class room. I admire their passion for both study and nature, though I would like to argue that I had in fact learned far more during a day of quiet reflection among the trees than a day fawning over school books and school work itself. Still, the DOC is a wonderful group of individuals and I thank them greatly for all of their hard work.

While all of the AT is marked by the little white bastards I've come to know as friends, the DOC had at one point done things a bit differently. The school colors for Dartmouth College are black and orange, and in a fit of school spirit the DOC at began blazing the trail with a three stripe pattern utilizing these colors. The infamous off beat blazes became known as tiger blazes but sadly the phenomenon was short lived, as the AT Conservancy soon put the kibosh on the individualistic practice. Still, the unique blazes have become part of trail lore and some of the faded markings can still be seen by those who know to look for them. I for one am a fan of the idea of customized blazes for bits of the trail, though I know it would soon become confusing as thru hikers would have to know in advance what to look for. However, even in the most regulated environment there is room for experimentation, and the worst that can happen is the idea is short lived but is nevertheless bound to be treasured by those who partook in it.

New Hampshire was proving to be a very unique state right from the start, and in all the right ways. After passing through the town of Hanover the landscape changed dramatically, becoming very rocky, rising and falling rapidly yet still densely forested and extremely green. It had been rumored that northern folk are far too busy to bother with switchbacks, and while I thought it just to be a jab at how people in the south prefer to take it easy whenever possible, it would appear that the rumors had some sort of factual base. Those who forged the trail here seemed to be looking for any and every excuse to change elevation, darting upwards over every available peak and dropping back into the valleys in between just as quickly, showcasing countless cliffs and stunning vistas. When I say stunning I mean it in more than one way, for the trail would allow one to walk right to the edge of a descent that would undoubtedly be fatal if one were to take one step in the wrong direction, towering over boulders and fully grown trees alike! It was on one such vista that I stopped for lunch one afternoon, and being bold, decided to rest with my feet hanging over the edge, looking over a gorgeous and unobstructed wooded valley with several rocky summits in the distance. As I sat just a fart away from certain death a familiar figure approached from up the trail, along with new company: Mountain Mime and a young man named Half Rack. Half Rack had gotten his name from a deer antler that he had managed to find in Tennessee and decided to carry the rest of the way; he was the quiet type, tall and thin with dark hair and a surprisingly well groomed appearance for someone having been in the woods for nearly half a year. It would seem that I would be keeping pace with the pair of them for the time being, and I must admit I was beyond grateful for the companionship.

Indeed it was so--Mime, Half Rack and I would meet up and pass by each other time and time again, divulging little adventures of the day when we could. One such meeting came on the front porch of a man named Bill Ackley, whom I find to be the spitting image of a crazy old backwoods kook, though certainly a kind and generous one. Bill had set up a little sign on the trail advertising free ice cream and water, which had recently become two of my favorite things, and as rumor has it the man is a damn fine coquette player. Whether or not the latter is true remains to be seen, though I have no cause to doubt it, though the former I managed to confirm. On a warm New Hampshire day I can think of nothing better than a cool ice cream sandwich with good friends.

As the four of us sat about enjoying the day, I brought up the fact that Emerald was in the area and that I was conflicted on my next course of action. I didn't want to lose pace with these lads but I figured she would be no more then a half day behind at this point, and I wondered if it would be better to put in less miles to see if she would catch up. As luck would have it this was a question that answered itself, for as we sat about enjoying the simple life Emerald came strolling up the side trail to meet us at Mr. Ackley's home for wayward soul searchers. Furthermore, it would appear that she was no longer hiking alone, for alongside of her strode a thin, young man with curly blonde hair and clad in the apparel of our people, namely dirty shorts and shoes, and while he was indeed out for a good trek I had not had the pleasure of meeting him before hand. As Emerald greeted our small gathering with hugs all around, I got to meet this fellow who, after an unfortunate endeavor involving a lost eating utensil, had decided to call himself Sporkless.

Truly the greatest part of the entire hike was meeting new people, like minded individuals with an emphasis on action over idea, all sharing the same discovery that comes from being nearly lost in the woods. While I consider my actual hiking team to be comprised of Dozer and the like I strongly bonded with these four hikers, and I enjoyed every step of the way with them. Before we departed from Bill's home we decided to take advantage of the scale that he had hung on his front porch, each of us weighing our packs in turn to see who was hauling what. While my companions were all weighing in at roughly thirty pounds fully loaded, my pack was a staggering fifty, literally twice as much as Sporkless--but they don't call me Gizmo without reason. While nearly everyone around me was shocked at the amount of weight I was carrying this late in the game it really came as no surprise to me, I had made it this far and full well intended to carry on as such. I had carried far heavier burdens before starting the trail, after all. While nearly every other thru hiker in the history of the trail had sought to lose bits of their burdens over the course of the journey, I, for the most part, had maintained mine. I felt it a sort of personification of life, that I would always choose to shoulder more then I should to be more useful, reliable, and prepared, not just for myself but for others around me. Every step with this great weight upon my back made me that much stronger, and while in life there are a great many things that I will never fully be able to let go, I can bare them without hesitation. Hard lives breed hard men, and while I do not consider myself to be born greater than others I do know that I have already done and will continue to do what many will not. And so the five of us took off down the trail again, thanking our host and each of us carrying our burdens, but I for one had never felt so free.

Hiker-ism: Tree Line

(Noun) Ever been drinking heavily one evening and feeling just fine until your drunken buddy thinks it's a grand idea to buy a round of tequila at one AM, which is always the one that takes people from standing steady to pass-out drunk. Trees do the same thing but with atmosphere--at a very specific line the air is too thin and the trees can no longer grow above it.

Of all the paths that I had wandered, there has been no more magnificent and challenging route than that which winds through the rough and rugged White Mountains of New England. I can never tell if they were the most beautiful or if their beauty was exaggerated beyond measure because of the amount of effort required to traverse them, but either way, the feelings of awe were greater here then anywhere else and my footsteps have hardly since felt so profound. Thru hikers had been talking about the White Mountains since the Blue Mountains in Georgia, and I remember the strange sort of vibe that was present amongst my company leading up to this formidable mountain range. It was almost as if we were warriors on the verge of a battle that would secure our names in legend for all time. Like Achilles and his horse we approached the great stone walls, not sure what to expect but thirsty for the taste of battle against our strong and ever-ready foe, preparing for what seemed like ages and finally arriving on the blessed ground that would seal our fate. This is really the last place where a NOBO thru hiker can fail, the final challenge before the great Katahdin itself, and I for one was ready.

While the first peak in this majestic mountain range has long been disputed among hikers I, along with many others, feel it is Mount Moosilauke (Moo-sa-lock) near the city of Glencliff, New Hampshire. This particular peak is the first one to present one of the strangest phenomenon that is to be observed in the mountains of the east coast: a natural low elevation treeline. While I had known these things to exist in the Rocky Mountains, thousands of feet higher than anything on the AT, I could not wrap my mind around how this was happening on the east coast. Still, as I climbed the rocky path up the side of Mt Moosilauke thee trees grew shorter and thinner until they suddenly broke, leaving nothing but a rocky and barren summit overlooking forests and mountains as far as the eye could see, completely unobstructed thanks to this natural wonder. As I continued upwards the trees fell behind, looking like an ancient phalanx lining up in preparation to rage against the summit, growing roots as they waited for the battle call to sound. No such call had ever come over the barren fortress, though the wind did pick up, causing the temperature to drop noticeably and chilling my skin in turn.

Perhaps I had made a bit of an error on this particular day, for it had been an incredibly cold winter and spring had hardly taken hold, despite this being the first day of summer. The first day of summer holds a special place in the heart of thru hikers, for not only does it signify the arrival of the finest days of the year to hike in the north east, but it is also well known to be Hike Naked Day and is to be celebrated by all. I'll admit, I had decided to forgo the full monty as the Whites were rumored to be populated with a fair number of families out for a day hike, which proved to be true, however I did strike out in naught but my boots, hat, ever present belt, and underwear to fully take in the season. As I had mentioned before this may have been a little more then I bargained for, as the winds of Mt Moosilauke became quite fierce, and even my legs which had become hearty and well warmed felt chilly on this the first day of summer, but all was manageable provided I kept moving. Completely exposed, in more than one way, above the treeline I smiled as I passed a few hikers hunkering down between the rocks atop the mountain, acting as though all was normal and feeling very confident seeing as I can't recall any other time which my legs had been so damn fit. That, and I was riding a massive wave of endorphins brought about from months of stress-free strolling through America. It's a grand thing to be so comfortable nearly naked in front of strangers, to know that one is literally being judged and not care in the slightest what others may think. It was a freeing experience; I had not only become solidified in myself while being absent from society, but managed to maintain it in the presence of others. I was free from social stigma, from cultural norms. I am who I am, and not even a situation that many would have nightmares about could shake me from such comfort.

The Whites were far from a nightmare however, in fact quite the opposite. If the amazing summit of Mt Moosilauke isn't enough to make ones day, the descent along Beaver Brook certainly is. Starting off as a small, high elevation spring, the brook is hardly more then a few trickling threads of water carving through half frozen grass as it leads the way down the mountainside. Personally I think this particular descent may be the steepest one on the entire trail, dropping over twenty two hundred feet in less then a mile and a half! There were points where rebar had been hammered into a massive, and rather slick, rock face, holding thick boards in place to make a stair that proved to be far more difficult to navigate than any other man made feature I had encountered. Without the stair system however the path would have been impossible to traverse, and potentially deadly, seeing as one slip would send a hiker cascading downhill with nothing to slow or stop his tumble until the bottom of this super-slick stone the size of several small homes stacked atop one another. That all being said, the brook began to become simply marvelous, as with every inch it seemed to grow in size and speed, leaping over cliffs and stone to form majestic waterfalls, each one greater and more awe-inspiring than the last. I found myself stopping frequently, not just to plan out my next few potentially hazardous steps, but also to observe this grand water feature. While the best of the Whites was yet to come unbeknownst to me at the time, I remember this welcome to the most challenging section of the AT perfectly, and even in years past I think back on it frequently and fondly.

I'm fairly certain there is no spot of flat ground in the entire White Mountain range! Not only is the trail ever blitzing to the top of every rock and peak in the entire National Park, but it does so over rock scrambles that some would consider to be full out climbing walls. I had thought that I had seen some of the worst around the Dragons Tooth in Virginia, but that was a cake walk compared to the unnamed accents I was now crawling over. I remember looking at some of these exposed stones baring blazes and thinking that my eyes must be deceiving me, they were incredibly challenging even for me after over a half a year on my feet, and would undoubtedly be enough to break all but the most mentally sound hikers.

At one point while bouldering up one of these rock faces that even young and nimble mountain goats would choose to avoid, I grabbed a small tree at the top in an effort to hoist myself over the unkind obstacle. This happened to be a fine and yet somehow foolish idea, as indeed I was now over the bulk of the rocks but now stuck clinging to this over-sized sapling well over twenty feet in the air with nowhere to switch my handholds. Thinking quickly I swayed against the tree, letting my pack weight shift freely with each increasing swing, until finally building enough momentum to propel me the few remaining feet over the rock face and face plant safely onto the plateau. Not the smoothest of landings, but it worked, and though a little scratched I was over this obstruction and moving forward on to the next one less then twenty yards ahead. So it was traveling in the Whites, a thrilling mix of challenge and danger, with some of the most amazing sights I had ever seen.

What sights they were indeed! From the splendid panoramas of the Kinsmen to the powerful springs and rivers ripping through the valley floors, it seemed like every turn provided another chance to be taken aback by the raw, unfiltered, regal beauty of the north east. Perhaps the grandest of all, in my experience at least, would be Franconian Ridge in the very heart of the range, though this came after a night of equally beautiful company.

I could nearly devote a chapter to this night alone, yet I'll try to be brief. I had been keeping pace with Mime, Half Rack, Emerald, and Sporkless fairly well over last few days, though per usual they had managed to keep their daily pace well above my own, making for long days on my part. Still, by chance I needed to stop into Lincoln, New Hampshire to resupply and thus hitched in independently to serendipitously find these fine folk had done the same. The five of us had commandeered a large section of a local fast food joint to store our gear as we all took turns venturing forth to procure provisions for the coming days. Though I was simply here to stock, up the four of them had a slightly different idea and decided to use one of Sporkless' local connections to secure a proper night's rest. Thru hikers tend to stick together if possible and so they offered me the same opportunity should I wish to join them, and I must say I was far too intrigued to let the offer slide by. It would appear that Sporkless was a member of a local hiking/climbing club, or something like that, who had several huts, or *lodjs* as they called them, one of which was rather close to town. So after a quick B-double-E-double-R-U-N (beer run!) we were loaded into a local shuttle and heading towards the hut for what would hopefully be a good nights rest.

Turns out that this place was the Ritz! Multiple rooms, hot shower, full kitchen, electricity, full kitchen, couches in a lounge area, proper toilets, full bloody kitchen, what more could a man ask for?! As we sat about, sipping a few local brews and rearranging our packs for the day ahead, we spent some time simply enjoying the company of others and resting under a proper roof for the night. I couldn't help but be fascinated with Mime this evening, he was still so young, being hardly a legal adult, and yet had obviously grown so much in the last few months. He still possessed a boy-like fascination over knowledge and fiction, yet I could tell that he had finally gotten a taste of the real world and was becoming a fine young man in his own right. Emerald had always been cheerful, pleasant, ever wearing a smile, though ready to let you have it should you look at her wrong, but that night I got to hear of her life before. She had been in the armed services, completed her four years, and now felt a little lost in life with no particularly clear path ahead after the blazes stopped. While walking we are all so caught up in the day that real life seems like memory, or like a movie that had been watched once or twice and promptly forgotten about. Fortunately, out here we had much time to think of what it was that we actually wanted to do with our lives once we returned to them, and while Emerald had no real clear path ahead she at least had some damn good ideas on the subject, which puts her far ahead of most people in my generation.

Half Rack and Sporkess remained a bit of a mystery, though I feel I got to know a bit about them as well. Half Rack remained rather quiet, but when he did interject it was frequently a quick witted jest that would arouse a quick laugh, or an insightful phrase that could start an entire conversation. Truly he was one of the more intelligent and introspective people I had encountered out here, and such wit is hard to find, and harder yet to witness. Sporkless is without a doubt a good man, having taken us all under his roof.

We ended up playing card games, which he proved to be exceptionally good at, undoubtedly a fine strategist he is and one that I would greatly appreciate the companionship of in a sticky situation, and while he did occasionally joke around he was more of the serious type and truly a born leader. I count these four as family, and while I had just recently begun reconnected with my blood relatives there's something about these individuals that had caused me to bond just as deeply and in only a fraction of the time.

This night would be common back in the world, the sort of thing I had experienced often though never really dwelled upon, however now I realized just how important this sort of interaction was to me. I had gone to find myself and now more then ever was drawn to those whom I had left behind, and it would appear that they all had become just as much apart of me as my own heart. I decided to never again let anyone in my life go without knowing just how important their friendship is to me, how sharing my life with them had brought me the greatest joy, and how irreplaceable they all are to me. I had drank away much of my time with them, though now I wished I hadn't, and what I would give to be better able to recall all of the moments I had experienced with them as clearly as the glorious mountains that I had traversed. I had made myself a new man out here in the woods, though I would have never taken the first step without my friends, and even though I plan to try for the rest of my days I don't think I'll ever be able to fully express just how grateful I am for each and everyone of them.

In the morning Half Rack made pancakes, which is always an amazing way to start a day I must say, and not long after we were shuttling back to the trail. Little did I know of the glorious day that lay ahead. It was the sort of day hikers have wet dreams about: perfect weather, low seventies with no wind and the best visibility imaginable, the perfect conditions for hiking across what is by far my favorite ridge line on the AT. As usual, I had no idea what I was about to come across but could not have been more pleasantly surprised. As I made my way up a twenty five hundred foot accent I began to wonder what was so special that they would take the trail up this hellish incline? The hemlocks grew thick most of the way, blocking any view that would be had, until I passed the treeline and my mind was absolutely blown! Miles of unobstructed, rocky ridge line, so pronounced and profound it was to be wondered if they had become enchanted or possessed some sort of mystic powers. Looking over what seemed to be the entire planet, I could see mountains in the distance that appeared smaller then ant hills. I felt as though I may be able to actually see Springer to the south if I managed to focus hard enough. I became intoxicated from the power of such beauty, my breath taken from me and my knees left shaking, my heart pounding not from exertion but from pure and absolute awe at the most regal of sights my eyes had ever seen.

As I walked the miles of Franconian ridge I could hardly go ten yards without stopping to take it all in, and if I were to smile any larger my jaw would have split clean in two. I rested a good long while atop the highest peak after winding my way through rock formations and scrambles, unable to ponder any way this sight could have been made more beautiful. As I rested I knew for certain that I had procured my first real view of Mt. Washington just beyond the ridge, one of the trails most famous peaks, and it stood still slightly covered in frost, shimmering in the noon day light like a weary giant that had stopped for a brief rest. It waited my arrival, watching my every move, looming in the distance. Filled with inspiration, joy, and determination I shouted forth a challenge to the monstrous beast before my eyes, roaring with determination and the will to conquer my waiting foe! The mountain remained silent, jesting at my frailty, not even acknowledging my challenge, but the colossus would feel me soon enough.

Hiker-ism: AMC Hut

(noun) The Appalachian Mountain Club is responsible for maintaining White Mountain National Park, and procure their funding in a rather bazaar manner. Rather then strictly seeking donations they have built several well constructed huts in the Whites, and charge people ONE HUNDRED AND FIFTY FUCKING DOLLARS PER FUCKING PERSON to stay overnight. I don't know who in their right mind would pay such an amount to sleep in a bunk room, use a privy and have a bed time, but people do it bless their hearts.

I ran out of water while traveling over the ridge, and regrettably the next available source was three miles ahead. Normally three miles would be no big deal, but my average rate of travel had literally been cut in half due to the difficult terrain. It took me over two hours to reach the source, and I felt every step of it, but the water pouring from the side of Mt. Garfield was some of cleanest and most refreshing that I had ever drank. Even though my body ached for want of water I had to drink slowly, for it was so cool that it would freeze my brain with any more then a small mouthful. The pursuit of water had left me rather tired, and so instead of pressing on to perhaps find a backwoods campsite at a lower elevation I decided to try my luck at an AMC Hut. While I had zero intent to pay the exorbitant fee to stay overnight, I had heard that they will allow thru hikers to work for a night's stay if one arrives at the right time. Being so far ahead of the bulk of hikers due to my early arrival at Springer, I liked my odds. Sprokless and Emerald had arrived there before me and had been able to persuade the crew to take them on for a night as well, which made it less likely that I would be able to; still I was here and was going to try. Gale Head Hut was indeed a fine structure, multiple rooms, a kitchen, running water, electricity, a virtual palace to a thru hiker, and the large log cabin was truly a sight to behold.

After a little banter I too was able to exchange a little work for a night's stay, which was nice seeing as the sun was beginning to set and I was getting rather tired. The crew served dinner to the guests of the hut, and there were many--enough to fill the entire dining room, which must have generated a massive amount of revenue seeing as there were well over thirty people present. After all the guests had eaten the three of us were permitted to feast upon what had not been consumed, and I must admit it was rather good food, but immediately after we set to cleaning up the place. Because I was last man through the door I was stuck cleaning the stove, which proved to be a bit more work than any of us expected, still it saved me an astounding amount of money so I didn't mind at all. While the guests were provided bunks and mats the three of us were to sleep in the dining room on the tables with our own gear, but none of us cared in the slightest; after all this had become the standard for the last several months, no need to deviate from the plan now. Not a bad deal all things considered, and I don't think I'd ever been so grateful for a midnight drink of water from a running tap in my entire life.

The waterfalls in the Whites are unmatched by any others I had seen on the AT, they were absolutely stunning! The rocky run of Zealand Falls was a grand sight, but my personal favorite lay on a side trail just a few miles from there. Therou Falls is a must for any thru hiker in my opinion, especially since it lay only a tenth of a mile off the actual trail. The river here cascades down a wide channel cut into the sandy red rock, weaving around a massive bend below and further plummeting out of view--it's a wonder to behold! I must have spent a good hour on the shore of the river, bounding about and examining the flow, playing cheerfully along the lively, powerful current. As it became time to leave I wondered if I would ever see these magnificent falls again, and it was indeed a sad thought to have. Still, I concluded that it was far better to have seen them today than never at all, and while this may be the only meeting I share with these stunning falls I will have had at least met them once more than most. I had left my foot prints on the shore of this mighty river, and while they will soon be physically washed away there will now and forever be a moment when they had once been fresh, and forever in that moment I will have stood proudly alongside Therou Falls.

What many consider to be the crown jewel of the Whites is the Presidential Ridge, containing such peaks as Mt. Jackson, Mt. Eisenhower, and of course Mt. Washington itself. It's worth warning people though that this is possibly the most dangerous place on the entire AT as well, with the trail of Webster Cliffs nearly always one slip to the left away from death and the grand summit itself boasting the worst weather in America, no joke. Still, when I climbed to Mt. Jackson, the first of the greater summits, the view was well worth it. The sky was becoming covered in dark clouds, it was apparent that a storm was approaching, and while the peak of Mt. Washington was hidden by menacing thunderheads Jackson stood underneath them and was bathed in a golden light where the sun had managed to pierce through, falling onto the mountain. It was an angelic sight, several beams of light jutting through the dark and troubling clouds, almost like spotlights in a dark theater, illuminating the air as they made their way to earth. It was peaceful and powerful, a calm before all hell attempted to break loose, and I stood in the midst of it all, unnoticed by either side. Indeed the storm did eventually set in, starting slowly overnight as I camped, but it was held at bay until after I awakened and packed up thankfully; still, it was about to be a rough day no doubt.

It's the price one pays as a hiker sometimes, several nearly perfect days must be compensated for and mother nature is quick to collect. The wind had picked up, and with every step across the Presidentials it seamed to intensify. Visibility had dropped to roughly twenty feet due to a strange sort of precipitation--it wasn't really fog, or rain for that mater, but more like I was stuck in the middle of a rampaging storm cloud! In hindsight, that very well may have been the case. With no choice other than to keep going I strode through the storm, the winds now howling past my ears, and even though my leather hat had been completely soaked through a heavy a hearty gust would still rip it from my person in an instant. I had attached a bit of twine to my head covering thankfully, and it's a good thing for I may have lost my long term friend here without it; truly that would have been a shame after traveling over twenty seven hundred miles with it. I leaned forward into the wind, trying like all hell to stay upright, battling to gain even the slightest bit of ground with the fury of nature ever trying to hold me back. My rain fly rattled on my pack, my jacket was nearly soaked through despite being designed for these conditions, my feet were getting cold, I had to squint to keep the rain from stinging my eyes, and I began to smile. This was my journey and even this mighty gale could not stop me, the mountain had accepted my challenge and with every stride I defied it. Filled with adrenaline my courage spiked, and if death itself had appeared on the trail before me I would have slapped the bastard across the face and dared him to try and take me.

Atop a wayward boulder on the edge of a mighty cliff I stood, defiant against my aggressor, and roared forth my battle cry 'HAIL TEMPEST!!' Driven mad with vigor and valor I laid forth my taunt, my challenge: bring forth thy worst oh spiteful mountain, batter my bones and see them purists, tear at my flesh and find me immortal, do thy worst for you now suffer the best, know me and fear me oh great and powerful fury for I am man and I will prevail! Bring forth it's worst the storm did, battering me with endless fury as I stood firm, head thrown back in ludicrous laughter, unmoved by my foe. For a few hours this continued as I weathered the storm until I reached an AMC hut at which I desired to stay, called simply the Lake of the Clouds, which was rumored to be the grandest hut in all the Whites.

The Lake of the Clouds was indeed a grand place; the dining room had many windows that I imagine would have provided a spectacular view on a calm day, but needless to say that was not this day. What had attracted me to this place is the rumor of a shelter option for thru hikers called The Dungeon, which serves as an emergency shelter for any poor sap who gets stuck on Mt. Washington when the huts are closed for the season. The main selling point of this less than desirable hovel is that one is only charged ten dollars to stay the night, and so I did indeed stay, invigorated from the storm but grateful for the chance to be sheltered from it and to dry out.

While the hut was nearly a resort, The Dungeon was quite a different story, and in fact I can think of no better word for the shelter other than dungeon. The heavy, metal door to this little forbidden room is on the outside of the hut, about twenty yards from the side door, and to open it one has to lift a massive lever and apply a good amount of force to render the entry point ajar. Inside is a tiny cement room, no more then ten feet by ten feet, with two decrepit bunks built inside which could hold up to three people apiece and a battered old bench pressed against one of the bunks. It was sheltered from the storm but far from dry, and I had a sneaking suspicion that even in the kindest of weather this room was still damp and dreary. Still, it smelled far better then the restroom I had used to hunker down during the ice storm in Georgia, so I didn't complain, I even got leftovers from dinner included with my stay.

As luck would have it I didn't spend the night here alone, as an old friend also happened across the hut in this mighty gale. Cola, whom I had not seen since leaving North Carolina, had decided to share The Dungeon with me this night, and I must say he looked very different from before. His mustache had grown at an alarming rate and now curled over the majority of his cheeks in one gigantic swoop, and it seemed that his smile had grown just the same for he was light heated and cheerful. The Stink-o de Mayo crew had lost two of its members, Red Beard and Apple Jacks, but Milk n' Beer was still somewhere about as well as Wingnut, which was encouraging. Truly I was grateful for the company this evening for at no point did the weather let up, and throughout the entire night the winds pummeled the hut in an attempt to tear it from the mountain side but thankfully to no avail. The nasty weather added to the effect of this tiny room being a dungeon, and while it would have been enough to detour most hikers I look back on the experience fondly; it was just one of those crazy thing that thru hikers do.

In the morning the storm seamed to have tired itself out, but that was to be short lived. I found out from the crew at The Lake of the Clouds that the day before had presented seventy mile per hour winds and that this day wasn't to be much better. Still, there was a moment early in the morning where things let up and it provided an incredible view for a matter of moments. I could see nothing in the valley below, but the clouds had broken enough where every bit of precipitation above my current elevation dissipated, letting me look over an endless sea of fluffy white cumulus clouds blanketing everything below the hut. The ridge line looked like that of a rocky cliff on side of an ocean, almost as if the mountain had been turned into an island and I stood looking out to sea, bathed in a cool mist. I had only ever seen anything like it while traveling by airplane, and to have my feet on solid ground while gazing over such a sight was astounding. Even in the worst of things there can be moments of brilliance, and just the minute or so where I was blessed with this sight made weathering the storm worth every bit of effort.

The brief reprieve from the storm was short lived, and within a matter of minutes all hell broke loose once more. I had thought about staying another day at the hut to see if I could get a better view going over Mt. Washington, but that seemed pretentious. To have come so far and weather so much, why should I wait on account of weather? So again, in the storm, I set out to meet my waiting foe, ready and able after a good nights rest; the final showdown with the greatest peak in the Whites had begun.

While Mt. Washington may not be the highest peak in the continental United States, it is known to be the most temperamental and, quite honestly, the most lethal, having claimed over one hundred and fifty lives. At the base of the foot path leading from the hut to the summit is a highly visible sign warning hikers that they should turn back in poor weather, and due to how quickly things can change on this barren rock face, that any fool who should set out even on the kindest of days should be prepared for the worst. With little more then a confident smile I passed by; I knew the dangers, and I was ready. The trail was saturated with water and my feet were already wet, a dense fog hung in the air being whipped around by high winds as nature continued to pour out her wrath upon me. I could see no farther than thirty yards before me, but thanks to many large cairns that had been built along the trail the way was easy to find. It was an eerie sight, theses large piles of stone emerging from the mist one by one as I made my way, like solemn stone guardians silently pointing the way to my fate. Saying not a word, they neither greeted nor shunned another fool trying to take on the mountain. The rocky path was uneven and unforgiving, it took quite a bit of effort to travel over and progress was slow, but even in these poor conditions I soon came in sight of what I sought. Atop Washington is an observatory where the highest wind speed on earth had been recorded at over two hundred and thirty miles per hour, and while this day was far from record breaking the winds did howl with such fury at times that I had to hold my hat and lean forward on my walking stick to make headway against them. Amongst a few cement buildings on top of the highest stone is a little brass marker hammered into the rock, the symbol of the summit, that my foe had fallen! I raised my arms aloft and cried my victory call, the day was won, and after hundreds upon hundreds of miles the final barrier between me and the Great Northern Terminus had been conquered! I felt as if I had just breached the walls of some ancient city, and while the streets were still well guarded her bounty was mine for the taking, I was invincible! I braced against the wind and laughed in triumph, what a journey it had been to get this far, and after I felt my fallen enemy had suffered me long enough I made my decent, knowing full well that I was going to make it to Katahdin.

It's worth noting that even a dieing animal still has teeth, that the final fury of a beast may slay its taker, and thus I proceeded with caution. The weather was still horrid, the way was not easy, but I climbed with far greater pleasure knowing that this mighty summit had fallen in my wake.

14 THE FINAL FRONTIER

Hiker-ism: Slack Packing

(Verb) A favorite among rich kids living off of an hearty inheritance, this method of 'backpacking' involves booking two nights at a hostel, storing the bulk of one's gear at said hostel during the day, and hiking with just enough supplies to make it a day in the woods before spending a second night at said hostel to retrieve the stored gear. Pussies...

    While I had passed the most prominent peaks of the Whites, I still had a little ways to go before I was free and clear of them. I had managed to budget far better than I had anticipated thankfully, and so I decided to take advantage of an opportunity to fast track my way out of the state of New Hampshire. In the town of Ghoam there are several hostels that one can stay at for little money, and so I decided to slack pack over the last great ridges of the state. The Barn Hostel in town is exactly what it sounds like, a barn, but with a full kitchen, washing machine, and hot shower, which I'll admit sounded amazing after being saturated in cold, high velocity precipitation for several days. When I reached the base of the Presidentials I managed to catch my second golden thumb into Gohram, and after briefly talking with the owner of the hostel, arranged to stay for two nights so as to slack pack over what's known as the Wildcats. I had high hopes for the day ahead, planning over twenty miles in the harsh and unforgiving Whites, but a proper night's rest prepared me for the day ahead and I was at it bright and early.

    I didn't like leaving so much of my gear behind--sure I didn't use most of it day to day, but I had gotten used to not worrying if I was going to need something. Thus, the process to downgrading my pack to Slack Pack status was a bit more tedious than I had anticipated, leaving behind my sleep system and many of the repair items that had been strapped to my back over the last half a year. Still, I managed to detach myself from these treasured items for the day's hike, taking only some trail mix, a few bars, and my water reservoir, promising the rest of my friends that I would be back shortly to collect them. After catching a quick hitch back to the trail where I had left it the day before, I set out, light as a feather, to reach the second road to Ghoram twenty miles down the trail.

    I can't say that I really noticed a difference being so unburdened this late in the game. The trail was still challenging, and rather than taking solace in the fact that I had nothing more than I needed for the day I felt uneasy about not being able to fix the situation if things went awry. Fortunately the weather had finally broke, bright blue skies and hardly a breath of wind with excellent visibility; I like to jest that I had no views FROM the Presidentials but I had found very good views OF the Presidentials. Indeed, looking back on Mt. Washington from the Wildcats provided a monumental sight, and it would appear the mighty mountain lay ashamed that it had been bested and thus relinquished whatever fury it had unleashed, sulking in shame at my passing.

While I feel the vistas in the earlier parts of the National Forest were a bit better than the latter, these were still astounding, especially on such a fine day. The trail showed no sign of letting up; in fact I believe that I traversed some of the more formidable inclines on the entire AT in the last of New Hampshire, though I began to feel as though I was going to miss them when there were no more to climb. I remember a particularly perilous valley surrounding the Carter Notch Hut, the last one in the Whites, that was both awe inspiring and incredibly difficult to travel. It's a quick thousand foot drop into the valley and a fourteen hundred foot climb out of it, but the views from either side are well worth the effort. There's a small lake in the center of the valley, and it's surrounded by massive, rocky mountains with spots so rugged that nothing can grow upon them, leaving huge boulder fields exposed. Being unburdened I was able to power up the ascent on the other side of this angelic valley with little difficulty, though I almost wish I had been forced to stop a little bit more so as to take in the sights. I was drawing near the final mountain, but by now knew full well that the AT wasn't about getting to Katahdin, it was about enjoying every step of the way there.

I made it back to Gorham without incident, though I got to the trailhead later than expected. Even though twilight was beginning to set in, I was able to catch a ride back to the hostel to rest and collect my gear. The Barn, being a barn, was very open with a lot of air flow through the structure, which I think helped me to rest seeing as I was so used to the outdoors; it felt homey. I was glad to be reunited with my old friends whom I had left while I blazed through the last of the Whites, and I began to reminisce about the times we shared together as I carefully, and cheerfully, returned them to their proper place in my pack. I'm glad I had tried slack packing, though I don't think it's for me, and as I slapped the full weight on my back and strapped in I felt far more like myself as I struck out for the trail again.

While I may not have noticed the difference from going from a heavy pack to a light pack, going from a light pack to a heavy pack was quite a different story! I felt the strain on my shoulders, and had far less energy than before. Summer had finally taken hold and it was starting to get hot, to the point where I was sweating for the majority of the day no matter how I was clad--shorts, no shirt, rolled down socks, it didn't matter. While I was grateful not to be cold for once it became far more tedious, for where my body heat used to help me survive the cool weather it was now a hindrance, a undesired byproduct that required extra effort for my body to remove. My shoulder had not felt exactly right since Rohn Mountain in Tennessee but had not been much of a bother until lately, and now it was increasingly becoming more and more irritating as the day progressed. I would have to stop several times in a day to stretch, removing my pack at times to exercise the full range of motion in the joint, which seemed to help but was only a temporary fix to what was obviously a bigger problem. Furthermore, I was becoming increasingly homesick, and thought back often on those whom I had left at home to go adventuring. I would sing the songs that I had come to know after hours and hours of sitting in bar rooms, hardly able to speak the words from the smiles and the surge of memories would bring. The world was my home, but my grand halls felt terribly lonely, and I longed to return to the little, dimly light room where my friends dwelt, and to show them the man that I had become.

    I recall traversing a series of rocks that I could hardly believe were blazed. The gaps between them were massive, they stood twice as tall as a man, and yet there were the little white bastards smiling upon the rocks, insisting I follow. I'm not exactly sure how, but I managed to channel my inner Spiderman and slide down the rocks backwards, keeping just enough traction with the toe of my boots to place my body where I desired to to go and land safely, and softly, on the ledges as I went. It was just another day at the office, and I would have thought nothing of it if it weren't for a little white sign near the base of this formation. I had just arrived at the New Hampshire/Maine state line, the final border crossing on the AT! For a good long time I stared at this small, wooden plank bolted to a post in the middle of nowhere, this final imaginary line that signified the last leg of my adventure, and I began to feel overwhelmed with emotion. How far had I come to view this insignificant chunk of painted lumber? How many nights had I dreamed of this moment? How the hell did I make it this far?! I felt tears welling up in my eyes, but now was not the time for that. While I had already come so far I wasn't done yet--it was time to show the world what I was made of, that Jordan Gizmo Bearss was a man of his word, and that this mighty task would be completed! With a brief outburst of pure joy and satisfaction I lept forward over the border and down the trail, moving with strength and conviction, immersed in a feeling of great satisfaction at having accomplished this mighty feat.

    Maine is by far the most remote and rugged state on the entire trail, its natural majesty is nearly untouched by man, and its few settlements are spread few and far between in this great state. New Hampshire had been the master of the Alpine ecosystem, that being one above the tree line where nothing grows except for a hearty, slow growing type of moss and a few scraggly shrubs, but Maine introduced a type of environment that I had not seen before. Many of the summits in Maine are covered by bogs, and the soft, muddy buildup of centuries' worth of decomposing moss growing over itself would be entirely impassible if not for a few boards placed across the surface, providing a platform to hike on. The mud in these high elevation bogs was so deep that one could not find a bottom to them even when submerging a walking stick in them up to one's grip . I had known many hikers to slip from the boards and bury a leg well past their knee in this rotten mass, and while I can not confirm it I'm sure the bogs have claimed a shoe or two, never to be seen again. While a bog naturally conjures repulsive images in the minds of many I found them quite beautiful here in the summer, where small wild flowers bloomed on the surface and a lush blanket of green covered the whole of the mountain.

While the bogs were a fine welcome to this the final state on the AT, the trail itself provided a far more memorable how-do-ya-do. By some sort of grievous oversight I had managed to miss the fine print in my guide book and planned to put in a solid twenty miles when I encountered what is known to be the most challenging mile on the entire trail, one that takes some hikers an entire day to travel through: the infamous Mahoosuc Notch. While I had no warning as to what I was approaching, but I certainly noticed once I entered this forbidding landscape, for the temperature dropped by a solid ten degrees nearly instantly and even in the dead of summer the snow never fully melts from the notch.

The notch is located between two massive, rocky cliffs, sheltered from sun and wind, and the narrow mountain pass had become filled with centuries' worth of enormous boulders which had split from the sides of these mighty rock faces in harsh New England winters. Some of these boulders were the size of mini vans, others the size of a small home, all piled upon each other creating an absolutely mind bending trail to travel. The way was reminiscent of the works of Salvador Dali, where one's eye could follow various paths in an attempt to pass through the rock field and somehow end up closer to where one started. The blazes are hard to follow at times, and I'll admit I took a wrong turn more than once, but if ever there was an entertaining place to get lost it was the Mahoosuc Notch. One would have to climb, squat, crawl, brace, and squeeze by boulder after boulder, rock after rock, ledge after ledge with progress hard to make and impossible to track. Deep cracks lay between many of the formations, many wide enough to swallow a hiker whole with one misstep, and with no good way to emerge from such a blunder. I personally took great care in my effort to traverse the notch, minding every step as I wound my way forward. At times one has to remove their pack and push it before them through a small cave made under impassible rocks resting upon each other; other times one has to brace three limbs on different stones to try and maneuver safely to the next spot of flat ground. I remember taking a wrong turn once and after passing no more than thirty feet over a deep chasm by hugging the side of a small mountain I instantly realized my misfortune, as I stood well over fifty feet above the next solid place to stand, perched atop a massive stone. "Well, that didn't work," I said aloud as I began to backtrack to the last blaze I had seen. Truly the Notch was a boggling place to wander.

It took me the better part of the day to get through the Notch, but I managed, and with enough time to keep moving before the night set in, or so I thought. There's a campsite on the opposite side of the Notch that most people choose, but feeling invigorated from such a wonderful experience I just had to keep going up the Mahoosuc Arm, a sixteen hundred foot ascent that rises sharply from the Notch. Some have decided to call this particular climb the Mahoo-SUCK Arm, and after attempting the climb immediately after the Notch I count myself among them. The majority of the incline is rocky and barren, making for good traction but leaving hikers exposed to the elements, and the heat had certainly returned after exiting the ever chilled mountain pass. I was sore, having used muscles that I had long forgotten about to get past the boulder field, I was low on water and was forced to conserve as I made my way, and even though the sun was setting it blazed harshly upon my shoulders. It took me a good hour to climb this beast, though I must admit, after a day of extreme exertion, seeing the sunset over the Notch was simply gorgeous. The yellow light shimmered off the foreboding rocky cliffs and washed the low lying hemlock forests in a soft forgiving glow that brought peace to my weary limbs, tickled by a gentle breeze atop the mighty Mahoosuc Arm.

I had planned to make it another seven miles further than I did, but that just wasn't going to happen, and so I settled on staying at Speck Pond, which happens to be the highest elevation body of water in the whole of Maine. While I am normally opposed to paying for camping I found it worth the seven dollars to have to go no further on this day. Limbs worn and weary, shoulder sore and bothered, feet battered and bruised I set up camp on one of the tent platforms as opposed to using the public shelter, knowing full well that I needed to lay naked atop my bag in an effort to recover my broken body in the cool night air.

First on the agenda was to gather water however, and I went in search of the spring. As I did so I passed by the caretaker's tent, which was occupied by a young woman with braided brown hair, reading a book in the last of the day's light. I waved a hello as I passed, and she did so in return, and I must say that she was far more lovely than expected. After a quick wash in the icy spring my weary body found enough strength to finish setting up and prepare for bed. As I went to remove my boots I couldn't help but notice just how much abuse they had taken in the day's scramble--they were nearly blown apart! The soles were cracked in multiple places and separating from the leather in the arch, the laces were splitting, and the inserts were starting to disintegrate; these boots had served me well. The Notch had taken its toll on me and seemingly everything I owned, but the wild and crazy crossing of this astounding feature is well committed to memory, and is not one to soon be forgotten.

My body was beginning to wear thin. While my legs were by far in the best shape of my life, my upper body was scraggly and weak, and I had never seen so many of my ribs so clearly before. The slight injury I had taken on Rohn Mountain in Tennessee was increasingly becoming more of a problem as my shoulder required more and more rest or stretching in a day, also my feet were completely numb in most spots. Worst of all was that after living for so long on such a strict budget, my energy levels were suffering seeing as I was never able to carry, or consume, enough calories in a day. While I had still managed to make good progress most days, the day after the Mahoosucs was an exception to the rule. For the first time in months, my body was sore and my joints refused to work properly for a good hour after waking. It would appear that twenty eight hundred miles had taken a rather hefty toll, and so I was forced to take it easy for a day, hardly making fifteen miles in all.

I ended up just shy of the road to Andover at a place called Dunn Notch before stopping for what was supposed to be a brief break, but quickly turned into a night's stay. The falls here were just plain impressive and they begged to be examined, which subsequently became the downfall of my daily labor. After crossing a broad river a good twenty foot waterfall is instantly visible, but that's nothing compared to what's in the area. There's a rocky point, hardly wide enough for a man to easily, yet boldly, walk upon, just out in front of the falls, and if one is brave enough to venture out, the far more majestic Grand Falls become apparent. I was completely surrounded by surging water while standing on the end of this natural jetty, the smaller twenty foot falls plunging into the rock behind me on the right and the Grand Falls violently fell to my left dropping farther down than I care to think about. What a sight! What power this water possessed, and how strong the rock that dared to stand before it! The Grand Falls cut the rock sharply as it fell, forming a cliff alongside the trail that could easily be missed by those who stay too well on course, but what a shame if they did.

I sat on the edge of this cliff as I ate my meager dinner that night, and decided it to be a perfect place to enjoy a pipe. It had been awhile since I took the time to enjoy a smoke. With my back resting against a well rooted tree, I watched the sun set over the valley as the water churned restlessly nearby in a most soothing manner. I watched the clouds change from white to yellow to blue to red quietly and peacefully before my eyes. I watched the first stars appear in the western sky as they outshone the sun, and as the world prepared to slumber, in turn so did I. Though before setting up camp I breathed deeply of the fresh air made cool by the smallest amount of mist reaching upwards from the falls. It was the sort of place that a man could hurry right by and miss entirely, but wonder why anyone would should he manage to stop. The sort of place one hopes of when stuck in the daily grind and can't believe exists when actually there. The subtleties of nature stride boldly into the profound for those who care to look, from the youthful spring of a seedling birthing from the earth to the gentle rumble of a grand waterfall charging headlong into serene majesty. All parts of this world are to be enjoyed by man, and I for one shall take the time to do so.

Hiker-ism: Lean-to

(Noun) Mention a Lean-to to a hardcore, military trained, survivalist and they will go on for hours as to how one can use a mess of sticks and leaves to keep the elements at bay by leaning them against something, hence the name. However, in the world of thru hiking this is another name for a shelter.

I had met many wonderful people in my travels, and from the stories I've heard from them this seems to be a constant in the lives of travelers. I considered myself to be well versed in the traveling arts, nearly a master in my own mind, and yet I managed to meet people who made me feel as if I had only just begun.

I was able to stay in Dunn Notch thanks to a habit I had of always carrying a day's more food than I thought I needed, but this set me up for a couple of big days to try and make it into Rangely, Maine. I passed over Moody Mountain, which boasts a thousand foot ascent in four tenths of a mile, and over Old Blue Mountain, nicknamed Ol' Bitch, but was able to stay on pace for the first day. Alas, the wilderness of Maine was able to captivate me again on the second as I came across Sabbath Day Pond Lean-to, but thankfully my captor proved to be a kind one. What made this particular lean-to too hard to pass up was a large, sandy bottomed lake out front, which was rumored to be the perfect swimming hole. It had been rather warm the last few days, and while I could no longer smell myself my odor must have been stifling, for several hundred houseflies seemed to consider me their best friend. While deer flies had long been a problem due to their blood sucking bite, houseflies only feast upon dead and rotting matter, thus this was obviously a sign that I was in great need of a bath. Indeed the lake was a fine one for swimming, and the rock-less bottom felt wonderful on my numb, yet somehow very tender, feet. The water was shallow and well warmed by the sun, though was still cool and refreshing, and while I can't recall how long I spent lounging about in the lake I do know that when I emerged I no longer reeked of rotten deer ass, much to the dismay of my new 'friends.'

I had already used my spare meal at Dunn Notch and thus committed myself to going hungry for the evening, but that was of little importance seeing as I had greatly enjoyed the day. I had crossed the paths of several SOBO hikers recently, and while they are far fewer in number then NOBO hikers it was nice to chat with those who I encountered. One such hiker was at the lean-to when I decided to settle in for the day, a thin, peaceful young man with shaggy blond hair and the essence of a traveler. People who have wandered for long periods of time are easy to spot, and it all in the eyes. Their gaze is straight forward but never looking at anything in particular, focused and yet relaxed; their eyes seem resonant with the beauty they had witnessed, glowing softly against stern, yet slightly smiling, faces. This particular young man had such a stare, and while I was eager to hear his story I was in no haste to start, as it would appear that we were to spend the evening together giving us plenty of time to talk.

His name was Padre, we started there, and I soon found out that this was his third thru hike on the AT, and that he had completed several other long distance hikes as well. His type was not unheard of but uncommon, for he worked hard at a seasonal job, saving money the whole time, and would then go traveling once the season let out. Padre was a fitting name for this fellow, for in the hiking world he may as well have been a bit of a holy man, and if nothing else was able to provide wonderful counsel to those who cared to talk with him. I mentioned that I hadn't enough supplies for the evening and asked if he would care to sell anything, but as luck would have it he had apparently oversupplied at the last town and was entirely willing to donate a meal. I felt guilty at first, taking generosity from another hiker who had carried this meal on their back for God only knows how many miles, but as luck would have it the fine folk in Rutland had given me a bit of tea to carry along, and so Padre and I were able to make a fair trade.

Before the day was over another pair of hikers had decided to stay at the shelter, or rather camp out front of it. While I didn't know one of the two the other was Goat Gurrl, who I hadn't seen in far too long, and I was overjoyed to be in the company of another northbound thru hiker! It would appear that her hiking partner Paco had decided to leave the trail at the last town, but she had picked up a new one, Lazy Boi. This young man would prove to be a fine companion indeed, being only sixteen years old with long thin limbs, boundless energy, and a never-satisfied sweet tooth, getting his name from a small collapsible chair that compacted to about the size of a pair of socks that he used at every available opportunity. I soon found out that the pair were siblings, Goat Gurrl being the older of the two, and that Paco was their father. They liked to use the geographical pun that Paco had reached DUNN Notch then exclaimed AND-OVER which was the name of the town a few miles away. I didn't realize how big of a role these two would play in my hike, seeing as I considered it to be nearly over by now, but there's a special place in my heart for these two because of the miles we did manage to travel together.

After a rainy night together I parted ways with the sage Padre as Goat Gurrl, Lazy Boi, and myself headed north to Rangely to resupply. Rangely quickly became one of my favorite stays on the trail for one simple reason: the Hiker Hut. Located not even a half mile from the trailhead, the Hiker Hut is an off-the-grid hostel that offers little more than a sound building to sleep in, a shuttle into town, and a hot meal--no electricity, no running water, simplicity at it's finest! As I walked down the unfinished drive to this little haven in the woods I felt as if this place was something special, for the trees gave way to a small cleared glen with a few flower beds and shanty buildings constructed on site. The bunk room was obvious to spot, with a small covered porch on the front of it, there was a small kitchen area next to it and the owners' personal hut slightly beyond that, a small A-frame building which must have been hardly big enough to stand in with a large sunflower painted upon the side of the metal roof.

While the place may have been small the idea behind it all was massive, stemming from mind the Steve Lynch, who is one of the most inspirational people I believe I had ever met. Behind every inspirational person is a story of a man who was once merely an inspired person, and Steve's story is one of a man who saw a great need in the world that he felt could be made better by his own actions. Every dollar the Hiker Hut earned in the thru hiking season goes to cover the miniscule cost of food required to run the place, and for the owner to spend the rest of the year in India building houses for mothers in need of a home. Rather than donate to a cause or organization, he has taken it upon himself to craft the change he desired to see in the world, which truly should be the aim of every man whether it be to live next to kind neighbors or remedy a grave injustice. I could have spent an entire week here, and in fact a southbound hiker had decided to do just that, but one night would have to be enough, for Katahdin awaited.

One of my personal favorite things about this little haven in the woods is the swimming hole located in the river that not only serves Steve and all who stay with him as a fine water source, but as a place to cool off on a hot summer day as well. During the resupply run into town, Goat Gurrl and I had each picked up a six pack to enjoy during our stay, and seeing as there was no refrigerator to keep them cool we had opted to store the full bottles in the river. This led to sipping several brews while we sat in the swimming hole together, skipping stones until the sun began to set, swapping stories of the trail and the world away from it. She still had many miles to travel after reaching the Great Northern Mountain, seeing as she had started in the DWG, but I was quickly running out of them; it was nice to see someone at this point who was starting to get the idea of the trail, but had ages to go upon it. I was able to give her a few ideas of where to stay along the way, and I joyfully began to reminisce about all the wonderful things I had seen along the way.

When the sun was getting low we rejoined the rest of those who had decided to stay at the hut, a few southbounders and a section hiker named Spock, who honestly looked like Leonard Nimoy and snored like a freight train. Steve had a small cooking fire going, and in one of the greatest acts of thrive-al I'd ever witnessed managed to make a massive pot of popcorn in a cast iron dutch oven for us all to enjoy. Sitting under the stars with my new friends, eating this salty snack out of my hat, which somehow tasted better this way, and sipping a beer felt like the way I wanted to live every day when I was off the trail. It was amazing to see someone who had actually managed to make it a reality.

Hiker-ism: Ford

(Verb) The act of crossing a wide stream by foot without a bridge or series of stepping stones, which is sure to ruin your pedicure.

As stated before, Maine is truly the wildest of the states I had traveled, and when the weather decides to get rough it can be flat out dangerous. The people who inhabit this untamed country are known as Maine-iacs, because one really does have to be a little crazy to try and settle here. If the fall, winter, and spring relentlessly bombarding you with snow doesn't choke a man out, the summer of merciless rain storms and mosquitoes is sure to stretch one's survival abilities; that and one always has to be prepared to deal with a pissed off rutting bull moose. As a hiker, a thunderstorm can be disastrous with even a momentary lapse in caution, mostly due to the environment present in the high elevation bogs. While the nasty mire that makes up the low spots of these bog is an absolute muddy mess, during a good rain the danger comes from the barren peaks around them, where large patches of exposed rock become slick as a snake oil salesman. The only other place where I had seen more exposed granite during my trip was on Stone Mountain in Georgia, and even there a bad fall wouldn't have meant potentially busting teeth on a boulder one was trying to hop to, or skidding down a steep slope until one's skin managed to gain enough traction to stop the slide. While I normally preferred to hike alone I chose to stick close to Goat Gurrl and Lazy Boi as a nasty bit of weather rolled in over the mountains of Maine, just in case I met with some misfortune.

While I was able to avoid major injury, I'll not forget crossing a mountain known as The Horn, a barren waste of stone and shrub in the middle on Maine. I'm sure the view from this monster is amazing on a clear day, but today was not that day. I'm fairly certain the winds were higher during my trek across the Presidentials, but the rain was undoubtedly worse, for instead of a heavy mist being whipped around at high speed, it felt as if someone was throwing buckets of water sideways at me! I would crouch, scramble, brace and use my hat in an attempt to shield myself from this torrent with the siblings close at hand, ever moving forward against the fury. Even while taking every possible precaution I did slip once, dragging my knee along the stone for a fair distance, leaving a large bloody sore on top of my patella. It was useless to bandage it in this weather; tape wouldn't stick to my dripping wet skin and any gauze I carried would have been instantly saturated. So I left it to bleed in the elements, hoping the rain would clean it well enough as I pressed forward in the storm.

The three of us made it to an old logging road after making it sixteen miles in these conditions when the weather broke a little, and we had to decide what our best course of action would be. There was a shelter about three miles ahead, but it would be hard to reach before dark, and the clouds seemed to indicate that this was only a brief reprieve from the storm, not its end. The perils of hiking after dark over these rugged mountains seemed to be a bit more than we cared to experience, and the road here was sheltered by a thick forest of hemlocks on either side and the large flat area would be a fine place to dig into for the evening, and so we did. The importance of tent stakes had become apparent in recent poor weather, for they not only kept the tent in one place during the night but also kept the rain fly taught, which greatly increased its ability to keep the elements at bay. We dug in as best we could, hammering stakes into the old road bed with the aid of the back end of my hatchet, and prepared for the night ahead.

I was right in making the assumption that we were far from out of this predicament, and not long after we set up the storm set back in. This was unlike anything I had seen out here in the woods; my tent shook violently in the strong winds, the rain hammered the sides of my shelter, and while it didn't leak or break it wasn't able to keep everything completely dry. I would have been sleeping in a hearty pool of water if it had not been for my sleeping mat, and as the night went on I started to wonder just how much abuse my tent could take having already served nearly a half year of continuous use,

Needless to say sleep was hard to come by that night, but I did manage to find some, emerging from my home early next morning, far from dry, but safe, and with the worst now behind me. Goat Gurrl was nowhere to be seen, but Lazy Boi, who had weathered the storm in a hammock I might add, was still about, and he seemed to be in far better shape than I was. I swear if I attempt another long distance hike I'm bringing along a bloody hammock! It was the worst weather I had seen in the wild and this kid was faring far better while carrying less weight, using less space, with shorter setup time, and he got to sleep in a fucking hammock every night! I asked what became of his sister, and apparently she had suffered the worst out of all of us, for one of her tent poles had broken in the night and while she had made it till the sun came up, she opted to make for the shelter at first light to try and find a little sleep there. It was a relief to know she had made it alright, but I felt bad that it came with such discomfort.

The repercussions of last night's weather were far from over, as I couldn't tell if the trail had been blazed in a river or if the trail had simply become a river due to heavy rain--both options seemed likely. Fortunately visibility had been restored and I was able to see for ages as I made my way, the mountain sides seemingly alive with muddy rivers charging down it, almost as if the rock was attempting to shake off the night as well. Something I failed to recognize when I began the day's hike was that all this water had to go somewhere, and thanks to physics that would have to be the lowest available area. The lakes rose, the bogs swelled, and most notably the rivers cutting through the valleys became raging, deadly, concentrated beams of nature's fury, charging recklessly along their course, capable of easily pulling trees from their roots, shrubs from their banks, and hikers from their feet. When I came to the banks of the Carrabassett river I rejoined the company of Goat Gurrl as well as a pair of other hikers, and the reason why these fine folks had gathered here was simple--the river was simply uncrossable. The water had risen well over a foot, completely covering the tall grasses that grew on its banks, and while there was normally a board laid over half the river to help hikers across, the thing was being bashed against the rocks, tethered in place by a cable that held it close to its origin. It was a sight to behold, and it was obvious that the best course of action was to wait a day and attempt a crossing in the morning.

While the best option was to wait, it wasn't the only option. I had walked across the whole country, my final destination was nearly at hand, and this ticked off body of water dared to stand in my way! I was not having it; I had overcome too much to stop unless I willed to do so and this river was not about to slow my progress. While the other hikers tried to find a good place to set up for the night I studied the river, walking up and down its bank looking for some place that wasn't a churning mess of death and may allow me to cross. About a hundred yards upstream I found such a place, and while the water was still moving quickly it didn't look like instant suicide to attempt. It was here that I would make my stand.

Stripping down to my boots and undershorts I left my gear upon the bank in case I suffered the worst, believing it better to be swept away unburdened should the river truly prove to be uncrossable. I would return for my belonging if I was able to succeed, but for now it was better to keep things safe and make three trips instead of loosing bits in one failed go of things. Taking only my walking stick I drew a few deep breaths and took my first step into the river, submerging my battered boot well beneath the surface. It didn't take long to realize what I was getting myself into; my walking stick would quiver as the water rushed around it and my socks began to pull against my leg as the current grabbed hold. The water was cold and unyielding, chilling my legs as I strode into waist deep water, the stones slick beneath my feet. As I reached the center of the raging rapids my legs shook as I lifted them, taking all my strength and a great deal of focus to attempt to plant them against the rocky bottom as the water surged around my stomach. Every step was laborious, every second seemed like an eternity as I imposed my will forward, trying not to think of the peril that would befall me should I slip, until finally I began to stride through shallow water once again, emerging unscathed upon the other side.

In a fit of victory I planted my walking stick firmly upon the shore, letting it be known that I would achieve this crossing, even though I knew it was only the first time I had succeeded. After a moment's rest to collect myself I ventured across again in much the same way, leaving my stick to see if I could cross without it, as this is how it would have to be done on my final attempt. Again victorious I retrieved my gear for what would undoubtedly be the worst of the endeavor, strapping my clothes atop my bag and securing the little odds and ends as best as I could before braving the river one last time. I did not place the straps over my shoulders, but rather planted my palms underneath them where my shoulders would normally rest and pinning my elbows close to my sides to keep the strongest grip I could before stepping forth once more. It had been hard to maintain my balance unburdened, being able to lean and move as I needed in order to remain upright, but now I had to suffer the worst of the river to keep my gear safe. Hoisting my pack at full arm's length to keep the base of it from being caught in the mighty flow of my greatest obstacle, progress was slower than ever before, and every fiber of my being strained to remain upright. My mind was racing, my legs quivered, my heart was pounding yet still I remained steadfast to my goal, too far to turn back as the river made a full effort to remove my footing stuck firmly in the middle of its fury.

One small, strenuous step after the other the river challenged my efforts, and with every step I proved my worth, I persisted until finally emerging upon the other bank, champion of this focused rage! With a glorious call I declared my victory; I would not be stopped, not now, not ever! My companions, safe and dry upon the bank where I had left them, cheered my triumph, though it was obvious that they, being of far sounder mind than myself, would not attempt to share it. Honestly, this was the most foolish thing I had done in my travels, and yet I felt I needed to do it. I had mended my broken spirit out here in the woods, and I needed to know that no matter what may come in the future I would not again be ripped from such a sound state of mind. To me this was not just a dangerous river crossing, this was a profound symbol of my life, a message to the entire world that I would not back away from what I desired. This was a personal test, not just of my physical strength, but of my will, and I now knew that that anything that may come to pass in my life I can overcome! As I dressed myself again to travel down the trail I felt a profound sense of serenity, the like of which I had not known ever before, and while I do not believe I shall ever attempt something so risky again I will always remember just how strong my will can be.

There were a few south bound hikers on this side of the river, all of which were planning to do the same as my companions on the other side, that being to wait it out, and they marveled at my my success. A young couple remarked that it was rather brave of me to try such a thing, and perhaps it was, but on the other hand perhaps it was entirely foolish. I guess the reality of it all depends slightly on the outcome, a little on who's telling the story, and mostly on whoever is listening. I later found out that the day and night before my perilous river crossing my companions and I had weathered the category one Hurricane Arthur, and that it was uncommon for one to stretch so far north. It was an odd series of events that had come to pass during this stage of my hike, and I am not only glad to have survived them, but also proud to have championed my will to them.

Along the way I had seen some amazing mountain peaks. From the wind swept bald of Bluff Mountain in North Carolina to the barren rocky mound of Saddleback, Maine, each one offered its own unique beauty. Whether it be astounding vistas, odd rock formations, still dense forests, or some other odd personality trait, every one was a pleasure to traverse. That being said, some defiantly stick out in my mind more than others, one such summit being Bigelow Mountain in Maine. I've heard tell that there are sixty seven summits that break four thousand feet in the whole of New England and Bigelow just so happens to be one of them, but it's not the difficulty of the climb that makes this particular mountain so stunning. Rather, it's the very summit itself that grabs my memories, or at least the last hundred feet of elevation, for even after everything I had been through I had not seen anything like it. The trail was barren, void of plant life, narrow, rugged--it looked like some place where a great, wise, yet dangerous sage would make his home. It was almost as if the place had been engulfed in flame just prior to my arrival, and as the footpath swayed left and right yet ever upwards, also it somehow managed to get narrower with every step. In the last bit of the ascent one is reduced to climbing over large rocks in an oversized natural stair in order to reach the highest point where one may stand on a rocky plateau, hardly large enough for one person, and look over a massive lake below, with sharp drops on all sides.

  When I arrived here it was after a twenty five mile day, the wind blew rather vigorously over the unprotected ridge, and the sun had set so low that everything resonated with a fiery red hue, further adding to the effect of recently scorched earth. It's rumored that one can see the final mountain from here on a clear day, and while I felt I had phenomenal visibility I didn't know where to look, so I didn't bother and simply braced against the wind for a moment and listened to its gentle song across my ears. I felt as though a wave had broken over me, refreshing my soul and revitalizing my spirit atop this astounding summit and I let loose my victory call, boastful and triumphant. I had come to thoroughly enjoy my daily victories and the smaller things in life. I didn't need a grand meal to be made happy by food, just a Little Debbie's snack cake. I didn't need a million dollar home, for I assure you I found my little green tent just as satisfying. From the gentle caress of an overhanging sapling to the passing of an ancient tree, the smallest river stone to the grandest vista, I derived immense and all-encompassing fulfillment from the little things. If ever there was a lesson to be learned from the many months I had spent wandering it was certainly to never take even the smallest thing for granted, and to breathe in satisfaction from even the smallest of victories.

  The end seemed to be drawing more and more near, for the next morning atop Avery Peak is the two thousand mile marker. The trail changes a little every year and thus I had crossed the actual two thousand mile mark while climbing Bigelow, but still the presence of an actual marker was entirely fulfilling. It had been a solid twenty eight hundred miles of foot travel to get here, and I had made two thousand of them in uninterrupted wilderness along this great trail. While I did take a moment to revel in this achievement I didn't take all that long; there were still miles to be done, and I planned to see every last one of them.

The adventure was far from over, even though the idea of climbing the Great Northern Mountain was starting to become a tangible reality. The final state was still rugged and wonderful, presenting at least one good challenge a day. Sometimes it would be a steep incline, others a hearty rock scramble, and more and more frequently it would be a swift and wide river to ford, for which I started to take my boots off, seeing as their integrity was coming into question. I remember one such crossing, where I had arrived at on the same day as a family of day hikers who may have been swept away while crossing here if it had not been for a secure rope stretched from bank to bank. The youngest of these hikers seemed to spend more time holding fast to the line with her feet blown sideways in the current then she did with them underneath her, which made for quite a humorous sight.

While the trail wound through the woods strategically in order to encounter the rivers where one should be able to wade through on foot, the Kennebec was one that could not be so easily crossed. I do not believe that even the strongest of swimmers would have been able to pass this mighty body of water while laden with a full pack, and after having witnessed its power in person I'm not sure if one could cross even if completely unburdened! With no suitable bridge close by, those who maintain the trail had come up with a rather unique solution to the Kennebec river crossing, and that was to employ a man to ferry hikers across, two by two, in a little canoe. The guidebook came in handy again as I drew near to this point, making it very clear that this service ran only at certain times during the day and to be sure to arrive as soon as possible in order to ensure your crossing. In light of this, my two companions and I decided to stay at a shelter that lay less than four miles from the Kennebec, where I had the pleasure of meeting back up with Cola, who had much of the same idea. This was a welcome reunion, especially since we would be crossing in pairs, and having an even number of thru hikers just seemed to be more efficient.

The four of us left bright and early in hopes of being the first across--it was rumored that the wait could become rather long if there were a multitude of people attempting to cross, and so we made to jump to the front of the line. It's a gentle slope down to the bank of the Kennebec and I would highly recommend the hike, for it's a lovely stroll through tall pines, alongside a pleasant tributary winding its way to meet the might river. For a while during the day I thought the tributary WAS the Kennebec, for it certainly was too strong to ford, but what a surprise I was in for once I actually arrived on the southern bank! I can with no real certainty say just how broad the river is but I wager it's well over two hundred yards of swift black water, and while I may not be the brightest of chaps, when it comes to mighty river crossing even I knew that attempting to swim this river would be utter suicide. Fortunately, our plan to arrive early paid off, we were soon able to spot activity on the other bank as the ferry man made an appearance before crossing over to meet us with two southbound hikers. The ferryman was quite a character, clad in a pair of cover-alls and a broad brimmed straw hat; he was all smiles upon greeting us with a sort of simple backwoods charm that comes from years of living a simple yet fulfilling life. He was a giant of a man, standing well above me and far wider to match, complete with a hearty stomach that shook when he laughed, and it was obvious that he was no stranger to hard work.

Before crossing, all of us had to sign a waiver releasing our fine chauffeur and his employer from liability for any loss of gear or life, which was a bit unnerving when being faced with such a mighty river. Still we signed as he loaded our gear into his chariot, and after we strapped on a life vest we were loaded in ourselves, slowly making our way to the other side. As planned I rode with Cola, who sat in the middle of the craft while I took a seat near the bow and our host resumed his post in the stern, ready and able as we first aimed upstream to ensure the current wouldn't sweep us past our destination .

It was quite a chore gaining the necessary headway before heading across; the current was so strong that if we brought the craft any more then a paddle length away from the bank progress would be entirely halted by the might flow of the Kennebec. I was no stranger to paddling into a unfavorable currents, having spent years surfing, but the majority of my upper body strength had been lost in the months of hiking and I was wearing thin before we even made for the other bank. I soon realized just how strong this giant of of a man was, as he was able to persist even with little help from myself or Cola, and he was even able to jest and joke as he rowed, saying that he had done this crossing upwards of forty times a day during the busy season. While I found such a feat hard to believe I had little cause to doubt it as we finally turned north the brave the river, hoping for the best and trying hard to maintain our balance.

What a mighty river it was! I hadn't ever battled against such a current, even in the biggest of surfable waves, as the waters of the Kennebec broke upon the side of our little craft. The canoe bobbed up and down violently as we rowed forth--it was no wonder why we had to sign a waiver before attempting the crossing, but Cola and I tried hard not to think about that while stuck in the middle of thing. My shoulders ached as they strained against the mighty flow of the river, paddling headlong with the aid of my host, who honestly seemed right at home being tossed about in the furious waters of the Kennebec. After an intense effort and what seemed like an hour of labor we reached the other shore, tired, slightly wet, but safe and sound and a little upriver of where we intended to land. The ferryman brought us safely to dock in a small, sheltered cove as the nose of the canoe rested upon the shore, and Cola and I nearly tripped over each other in our haste to stand upon solid earth again. We collected our gear and thanked our mighty host again for safely bringing us across as he smiled and waved before heading back to collect other hikers, and while I was glad to have met him I think that I shall keep my boots firmly planted on dry ground if ever I seek to go wandering again.

    Something that will ever motivate a long distance hiker is the thought of food. I got the strangest cravings for things during my hike, as well as acquired a few new tastes along the way--for example, a love for a brand of soda called Moxie. I first tried it due to the fact that I had hiked with a lovely woman who went by such a name, and continued to drink it because I had never tasted anything like it before and seeing as it's only available in the northern half of New England. While I tried to pick up a bottle of this strange elixir at every opportunity, my original desire for it was sparked by the crossing of a mountain near the town of Monson that bore the name Moxie Bald. While the large granite summit was quite lovely, shortly after arriving I felt the need to depart for town in hopes of procuring a draft of the elusive tonic, and thus put in a hearty day of hiking to reach the little mountain haven.

    Monson is so small that I doubt anyone would have bothered to place it on a map had it not been such an important stop on the AT. There is literally nothing north of this little town as far as the trail is concerned; no supply points, no well-traveled roads, nothing but a hundred miles of remote wilderness until the base of Katahdin and Baxter State Park. Monson is the last chance for northbound hikers to have a hot shower and collect basic supplies before braving what is known as the Hundred Mile Wilderness, and both of the opportunities come at a hostel known as Shaw's. It's a simple hostel, with a few multi-floor bunk rooms set up on sight, the most prominent of which has a full kitchen on the ground floor that sadly isn't for hiker use. Nevertheless, Shaw's offers reasonably priced, proper beds, a hot breakfast in the morning, and cans of soda for fifty cents, with a good supply of Moxie always on hand. Goat Gurrl, Lazy Boi and I all took the opportunity to rest one last time in a proper bed on the AT, and I must admit that being full well aware of this fact made it a rather strange stay.

The only other things in the entire town worth mentioning are a gas station and a small bakery which both carry a few hiking essentials, the bakery having a good stock of Pop-Tarts and the gas station having beer. Goar Gurrl and I decided to take this final trail town opportunity to pick up a twelve pack of ale and enjoy each other's company. We stayed up past actual midnight chatting, her about the miles south she still had to go and me about getting back home. I had become rather homesick recently and was full well ready to get back to it, though I knew that I would soon miss life out here in turn. It was a complex surge of emotions that night at Shaw's, both good and bad, and while I didn't exactly know how to handle all that I was feeling I did know that in the morning I would still be on the trail, and that I needed to be sure to enjoy it while I could.

Indeed the morning came, and a bit too soon as far as I'm concerned, due to the copious amounts of booze I had consumed and the lack of time I had to sleep it off. Still I managed to rise in time for breakfast, and thank God for it because I'm not sure how I would have managed to get along without something to boost my energy levels. I hadn't awoken with bloodshot eyes, a minor headache, and a hangover since I had a stable job, seeing as drinking had long been my method of coping with things I didn't wish to be doing. I'm not sure if it's more common for thru hikers to drink or to rest here in Monson; while our bodies had well conditioned us to rest whenever possible, our minds all seem to be racing with thoughts of the final stretch of trail. Either way, this hangover was enough to make me realize that heavy drinking is definitely not the way I want to be dealing with stress in the future--it just seems to hold me back more then get me through, as became apparent this fine morning. Still, after three eggs and sausage I was ready enough to get underway, finally allowing myself to be full well Katahdin bound.

The Hundred Mile Wilderness is a grand undertaking, a true test of how trail-savvy a hiker is, pitted against the wild with nothing but what can be carried and no help available should things go wrong. While it is possible to get a ride out of the Hundred Mile, it's a difficult endeavor seeing as the roads are far apart and hardly traveled, forcing hikers to call in a rather costly shuttle if they truly need to be extracted. That, and cell service is profoundly unreliable; anyone who wanders these woods needs to be full well ready to depend only on one's self, and I undoubtedly was.

I hate to admit it but I did feel a bit nervous as I took my first steps into the wilderness, there were a lot of things that could go wrong here and I hadn't the money for a shuttle out. I had been made ready for this, I was prepared, and it didn't take long at all to get settled back into my rhythm, hiking forward through the final test laid before me. The hardest part is undoubtedly the first half of the hundred mile stretch, boasting the last real mountains before Katahdin and full of rugged river crossings.

During one such crossing I could see no good way across without submerging myself waist deep in water and having to literally climb out on the other side. There were no bridges built here, no ropes to help cross, just pure unkempt nature sporadically marked with the familiar white blazes of the AT. Fortunately, at this particular crossing a large tree had fallen across the banks not far upstream which made for an ideal place to cross. The trunk had been stripped of bark and was strangely limbless for the majority of the crossing, and so I decided to shuffle across on my hind end, ensuring that I didn't meet with another nasty fall. In one of the strangest encounters I had with the insect kingdom, and trust me I've had many, a very stubborn dragonfly decided to block my passing and refused to be stirred from its rest, even by the possibility of certain death. After failing to convince him to flee I lifted him onto my finger, where he sat the entire time I slid across what used to be his personal log, looking rather inconvenienced for an insect. This of course made the entire undertaking far more difficult, as I could now not use one of my hands for fear of squashing the proper owner of this natural bridge. Still, after a fair effort I made it across and was able to convince my new acquaintance that he should remain where I had found him by pushing him softly back onto the log from behind. Truly it was a strange start to a day.

The miles fell with ease here in the Hundred Mile Wilderness; I was a full fledged thru hiker by this point and was ready for anything. While the woods were incredibly familiar to me by now there were still moments that I would stop to take in, the peaceful lakes and pleasant vistas of Maine. I can recall with ease the most astounding place of all, for it is ever ingrained in my memory as one of the grandest moments of my entire life. White Cap Mountain is the last peak to break thirty five hundred feet before the great Katahdin, and in fact nothing beyond White Cap breaks two thousand as it stands a solid seventy miles away from the northern terminus. The trail here is not really all that difficult, it's well beaten and while it does get a little rocky here and there it's rather clear, and I passed over it with ease. Still, at the top of this mountain one can gaze over the trail south for ages, easily spotting Avery and Bigelow in the distance, especially on the incredibly clear day that I stood there.

While the view south is indeed a grand one, the thing I'll never forget about White Cap is a little side trail indicated by a painted white arrow upon a few small rocks in the direction of a small grouping of trees. Intrigued, I decided to see what could possibly be lying beyond the few scraggly shrubs that blocked my view and followed the loosely marked side trail until I came to a small vista where the shrubs gave way and I could clearly see due north. There was a little white arrow painted upon a rock no bigger than my pack, pointing towards a distant mountain range, and next to the arrow was the letter K. In awe I gazed upon the great Katahdin. Not just an idea, not just a picture, not a wooden sign indicating how many miles were left to travel, but the actual bloody mountain itself! After over seven months of hiking I could finally see it! Clear as day, standing strong against a brilliant blue sky, the final mountain, Katahdin, was at hand, and I was ecstatic! I cheered, I danced, I rejoiced, my final destination was before me and I could hardly believe it, it was almost as if I had witnessed the very face of God. After I regained my senses I took off back to the AT, light hearted and steadfast while feeling like a school child on the first day of summer vacation. I could see it, I could do it, and I was on my way towards my greatest of accomplishments.

I began to encounter a massive influx of southbound hikers. While I had been running into one or two for months, I was now sharing shelters with well over twenty at a time, and they were adorable! They were easy to spot, every one of them in bright clothes freshly washed and free of wear, keeping to themselves at shelters and not yet trusting those around them, bright eyed and bushy tailed, ready to take on the trail ahead. I hadn't the heart to tell them of the hardships that lay ahead; they would know soon enough.

After consuming my evening meal I set about to enjoy the rest of the evening alongside the brook. With feet out-of-boots and dipped into the cool water I enjoyed a pipe, listening to the falls and relaxing after a fine day's hike. As I sat there a group of three northbound hikers showed up at the shelter, and trust me they were easy to set apart from the rest. Without hesitation they made themselves at home, tossing down their gear and making casual conversation and smelling to high heaven. I hadn't seen these chaps before, but soon found out that I had heard of them as I introduced myself. They went by the names Grease, Spaghetti, and Papa Squats; I had read their names in the shelter logs and many of those whom I had hiked with had shared time on the trail with these fellows, good lads every one of them. Grease was soon bathing in the brook, getting looks of sheer amazement from many of the southbound hikers who could hardly fathom drinking from this body of water, let alone using it for other purposes. The others went to scout out a proper place to set up, shuffling around loose earth and venturing where others hadn't even looked, masters of their rustic environment. I myself had claimed a bit of uneven ground close to the shelter and opted to set up my tent instead of sleeping in the lean-to for the bugs were bound to be bad once the sun set, and indeed when the sun sank low the mosquitoes let me know it was time for bed. I slept well, and I imagine the other northbound chaps did as well, though I don't think the same could be said for many of the others because in the morning not a one of them looked well rested. Bless their hearts.

The Hundred Mile Wilderness seemed to be absolutely packed with incredible camping locations! There were great little flats next to raging rivers, impressive falls with tranquil surroundings, and even though the second half of this challenging section was next to completely flat, there was an abundance of clear, cool lakes that begged a night's stay. It's a shame that I didn't have two weeks worth of food or I just may have just taken the opportunity to rest at more of these other worldly places, but sadly rationing is one of the biggest challenges in this vast stretch of unoccupied wonder and I had to keep on track. That not saying that the idea of resting wasn't incredibly appealing, sometimes so much so that it was impossible to ignore. Goat Gurrl and Lazy Boi had heard of this place known as Antlers Campground that was supposed to be too amazing to pass up, so when the three of us came across it early one day they decided to rest here till tomorrow. I didn't quite feel like cutting the day short, though it seemed to be a perfect place to enjoy lunch, and so I settled in for a moment with the siblings to check out the sight.

Antlers Campground is a pretty typical backwoods camping location: no charge, no set places to set up, a privy, and a water source, which in this case was a massive freshwater lake so clear that it was hard to tell just how deep it was. The site was on a small peninsula jutting out into the lake, surrounded on all sides by water and thus the air was cool and refreshing. What I remember most about here was that for some odd reason there were no bugs, contrary to almost every other lake I had come across in Maine. I sat on the lakeshore with my boots off, munching a little something in the sunlight and just enjoying the day; it was a shame that I would have to be on my way soon. I waded in the water a little bit and washed off by splashing the water over my bearded, trail worn face, smiling as the cold water washed away a week's worth of sweat and grime. I took a nap on the shore in this blissful, warm, bug free haven, but was up before long so I could start hiking. I helped Goat Gurrl gather firewood and eventually start a small blaze so she could prepare something to eat, prompting a desire for myself to make tea, which I did. As I made to move out, the sun was starting to retire, not quite setting but low in the sky and exhausted from its daily labor. If the sun gets to rest then so should a man, and so what was supposed to be a hour or two rest alongside a pleasant lake turned into a night's stay. Sometimes the pleasant little simplicities of life can catch up with you, and while one can't afford to always live this way it's nice to just relax and find peace in the simple pleasures of living.

Despite always being surrounded by the wonders of nature I was incredibly homesick at this point, and if my mind wasn't heavy enough, my body had had nearly all that I could handle. I had never been so thin before, my limbs were worn and weary, and while I had gotten used to being tired I honestly needed to rest for a few moments several times in a day just to pick up the strength to keep going. There was one time here in the last of Maine where I was walking on completely flat ground, no roots, no rocks, nothing but level, packed earth and I somehow was able to snag my toe and twist my ankle, falling to my knees completely exhausted. The fall that I had taken crossing The Horn had still not completely healed and this pathetic little fall caused my knee to rip open again and bleed profusely. This happens to be the only time that I had to make a proper bandage during the entire trip, and it was a little embarrassing to have made it so far without injury and even more so that it came from such a stupid sequence of events, or rather the lack thereof. It was obvious, I was tired, malnourished, worn thin, and ready to go home, but there were still miles to be done and so I continued on.

In this worn and weary state I came across a small glen alongside the trail somewhere deep in the wilderness. I don't think I can point out exactly where it was for it wasn't marked in my guidebook, or on any map for that matter, simply because there was no reason for it to be. It was just a simple wooded glen with several small boulders scattered about and stacked atop of each other; moss grew upon everything here and incredibly thick turning it all a deep lush evergreen color with patches of brown where pine needles had collected. There was a tiny spring pushing out from under one of the rocks, tricking softly along its way between tall pines and their roots, and while there was nothing incredibly uncommon about this place it seemed to be somehow set apart, somehow different from the rest of the woods. Perhaps it was that it was a far deeper green then the surrounding area, or that the trees grew thick enough to block most of the natural light except for in a few areas where it poured through in soft yet vibrant golden beams. Whatever it was, I felt the need to stop here. I wasn't terribly tired, for I had just rested, nor was I hungry, but I felt connected here, and so I stood in the middle of this simple, yet majestic glen and I started to weep. It just hit me here, that I was going to make it, that I had accomplished so much over the last seven months, and as the tears started to stream down my face I fell to my knees, pack and all, and simply could not contain myself. Frankly, I did not wish to contain myself, for even after suffering immense heartache for the last three years I had never been able to outwardly express it in even the slightest of ways. I believe that this was because I had managed to cope and exist with my emotional burdens, but I had not felt like things were ever going to be ok again, that I would have to continue feeling the weight of my scars even though I was mended and moving forward. Here in the shadow of the Great Northern Mountain I finally felt like things were ok, that they were more than ok, that they were good, and getting better, that I not only had to endure life but that I could honestly enjoy life. This journey had restored me to sanity. It reminded me that I was in control of my own life, that I do more than just survive the worst, but also thrive and grow in the middle of it. So overwhelmed by this total sense of relief I continued to weep, whispering the words 'Thank you' again and again for only the trail to hear, leaving the pain and hurt there on the forest floor. I grew into myself at that moment, rising to my feet again feeling not just empowered or invincible, but also very much at peace. Like the ocean after a storm that had just breathed forth great destructive power but now sat calm and sarnie, supporting life and prosperity with vast, tranquil waters. Struck by a sudden, complete, all encompassing realization of my travels I reached for my journal and inside the front cover I wrote in reference to the trail: 'In this place the proud may be turned humble, the weak can become strong, and the broken be made whole.'

After six days and nights I made it to Abol Bridge Campground, which meant that I had arrived at Baxter State Park and that the Hundred Mile Wilderness was now behind me. All that was left was to go up the great Katahdin itself, and while it's known to be a formidable hike I don't think that anything short of death would have stopped me from reaching the top of that rock. All that was left in my wallet was a five dollar bill, which I used to buy a few things to eat that evening and a can of beer for the summit tomorrow--it was going to be a day to celebrate. From the small, self contained store on the bridge it was an easy five mile hike into Baxter State Park, to reach the base of Katahdin where I decided to spend my final night in the woods.

At the base of the final mountain is a small campground, decent stream, gravel road, and a ranger station which one has to visit if they wish to stay the night here. Anyone can camp at the base of Katahdin, but thru hikers are offered a chance to stay at the Birches, which is well removed from the other sites so as they wouldn't have to deal with our stink or the noise. The shelters are run down, the privy isn't as nice, it's on a strange side trail, and the only real benefit to staying at the Birches is that it's a lot cheaper! So as I entered the ranger station I was met by a well built, enthusiastic fellow dressed entirely in well pressed tan garments that indicated he was undoubtedly employed by the National Park Service. Indeed he was the ranger in command and after a brief exchange I informed him that I was a northbound thru hiker who wished to camp, and he informed me that it going to rain tomorrow so it was best to make my attempt early. After I thanked the fellow we came to the point where I had to pay for my stay, seven dollars in all, which after a good ten minutes of digging about in my pockets and pack I managed to come up with in silver change, leaving me with nothing left but a fistful of pennies and a few nickels, what a ride. All northbound thru hikers who stop at the station are given what's known as a Katahdin number, which signifies what number hiker your were to arrive this year. It would appear that in Two Thousand Fourteen I was to be the forty sixth northbound thru hiker to complete the Appalachian Trail. I refused to think about it really, I hadn't gone up the mountain yet, there were still five point two miles to go, I hadn't earned it yet. Instead I decided to head to the campsite to set up one last time, though it didn't feel any different than before, just another night in the woods at that point.

As the sun set I lay in the shelter with Goat Gurrl and Lazy Boi, preparing for the day ahead. I had made a habit of looking over the guidebook at night to try and plan out what was to come, though this time it seemed fairly simple, go up the bloody mountain bright and early and be back down before noon, it was incredibly surreal. I savored every moment of that evening, from positioning my gear to caring for my aching feet, while I had been dreaming of this moment for so long it didn't register that it was actually here, and so I slept easy and woke before dawn to begin the final day. Goat Gurrl had bought way too much oatmeal in Monson and so she decided to prepare a hot breakfast for the three of us, and after filling my stomach and strapping on my boots it was time to be off.

The weather was indeed a bit rough and I was grateful for the early start. A heavy fog hung in the air, limiting visibility, and it was obvious that a good storm was on its way in. While the trail was far from dry nothing could dampen my spirits as I made my attempt; I was finally here, and I was going to complete this mighty task once and for all! I studied everything intensely, it was like my first day on the trail all over again, I just couldn't get over the beauty of my surroundings. The trees seemed greener, the water was clearer, even the trail itself which I had trampled over for nearly twenty two hundred miles seemed more profound as I knew I would soon be at its end. I stood next to Katahdin Falls for a good long time, like the falls I had seen near Springer in Georgia they captivated me, and I was made happy by them. I was a little depressed that the great mountain was shrouded in such a thick mist, I had been dreaming of this for so long and would have preferred better conditions, but I had not the time nor the desire to wait and so I continued on, hoping to catch at least one good view from the rocky side of Katahdin.

About halfway up the trail breaks from the familiar wooded path into a series of boulders called the Gateway, which is strangely reminiscent of the Mahoosuc Notch, only going vertical. It was while passing through this treacherous terrain on the side of great Katahdin that I decided to take a rest and reflect before continuing to the summit. On a small rock in a flat section of the trail I sat looking over the trail I had just traveled, attempting to grasp the weight of what I had accomplished. I thought of the people I had met, from my hitch out of Fort Lauderdale to the Hiker Hut in Rangely and all the help they had provided. Of the great flat cattle lands of Florida, the frosted cotton fields of south Georgia, of Stone and Springer Mountains. I recalled the Smokies and Gatlinburg, the snow at Overmountain Shelter, the dry grass of Greyson and her wild ponies. Shenandoah and Harpers Ferry, Annapolis Rocks, the Mason-Dixon line, Duncannon, The DWG, and the green sea of Highpoint. I recalled the views of NYC, and the day passing through Sages Ravine into Massachusetts. The blissful Green Mountain range and the challenges of the Whites, the rivers, the peaks, the scrambles, and the gambles. I thought back fondly on the laughter and the hardships, the simplicity and peace I had found, the strain and anguish I had pushed past-- three thousand damn miles on foot across America had brought me to this moment, one final moment where I would seal my right to it for all time. Some have gotten to this point and said that it all felt like a dream, but not me, this was the most real thing I had ever done in my entire life, the memories of it ringing clearer than any others, what a ride it had been!

 I felt like this called for a final celebratory act of hiker trash, and I had two things that I had been wanting to do for some time now. First, I had carried a packet of MRE ice tea mix in my pack since I left Wilmington, just waiting for the right moment to use it, and seeing as there would really be no other moments past this one it seemed like the thing to do. So I shook the dark sugary crystals from their pack and into my water bottle, shaking the mixture together for a moment before sipping on what may have been the world's finest iced beverage on the side of glorious Katahdin. The clouds began to give way before my eyes and I saw several rocky peaks emerge from the mist looking like an old painting of the Great Wall of China surrounding my position. I could not see the valley floor, nor the distant mountains, but didn't much care, this simple view was far more than I had hoped for when I started the day. Thus I commenced the second of two acts planned just for today, and I stripped off my shirt, jacket, pants, everything but my boots, hat, underwear, and utility belt to finish the hike in style. Why did I feel the need to ascend the last mountain in my underwear? I don't know, I just needed to do it. Life on the trail had been so strange and unpredictable that to finish off in some simple manner just wouldn't seem proper. There are moments in life where one thinks of something unique and memorable to do, and the majority of the time we let such moments pass without a second thought, continuing forward like always, nothing ventured, and nothing gained. Why do we do such a bazaar thing? I did not just walk across the fucking country to let it be another passive moment, and I was not born to be stagnant, I was climbing this mountain in my under shorts, I was returning to life to live it, and I refuse to let my future memories not be made!

The rocks passed by with ease and in no time at all I was standing next to Thoreou Springs, named after the author of Walden and exactly one mile from the summit. I swear I could have sprinted there! The way was flat, there were no more obstacles in my way, just one more mile to glory! With my two companions in tow I continued on, venturing onward into a heavy fog dense enough to soak my skin but I was too excited to hardly pay it any mind. My heart was racing, my senses were heightened, victory was at hand! Like a mighty warrior chasing after the last of his retreating foe I strode forth towards my immortality, seizing foot after foot of earth with each step, scanning the mist for my final destination. Someone once asked me why I wanted to go to Katahdin, what was waiting for me up there? My response was that there is a sign, about two feet by three feet, stuck into the rock of this great mountain, and it is the most glorious piece of lumber that has ever existed. I was right. For in the distance I saw it emerge from my surroundings, not even a hundred yards from my person, the last mark on the last mountain of my great journey, my time was at hand! I drew ever closer, and it became ever clearer until after climbing the last rock stair I stood not but ten feet from what I had dreamed of for so long.

In one mighty action I flung the pack from my back, letting it fall to the earth not giving a second thought about it, and I sprung forward with great force to plant my hands upon this sacred marker, triumphant at last! With a roar that must have shaken the very foundation of Valhalla I trumpeted my victory with such passion and volume that it is believed to have been heard back in the halls of Cape Fear--the wandering man had beaten the mountains, he had done it! Claiming my birthright I championed my dominance over the hills and valleys of America, and bade them hear me and know thy master's voice! With a final resounding call of 'DRAGO!' which I had breathed forth over every mighty peak from Virginia to Maine I stood atop the great mountain, and after years of struggle and strife I had finally accomplished a feat worthy of recognition and once and for all considered myself a man! I jumped for joy, I raised my arms and beat my chest, I spun about like a damn fool in the mountain mist, until I exhausted myself in celebration and collapsed next to the sign that spurred my greatest moment of triumph. My companions cheered me on, they still had miles to go but now had witnessed the indescribable joy that comes from a mighty feat of personal achievement, and in turn became inspired to seize it for their own. With a smile at least ten miles wide I pulled the beverage from my pack with fits of ludacris laughter bursting from my lungs in between each exasperated gasp for air, and I ripped the can ajar pouring its contents down my throat until my lips runneth over and it ran down my person. I couldn't care less, I was overjoyed, ecstatic, driven mad with satisfaction as I enjoyed this, my moment, my summit, my glorious finale.

As I began to compose myself I climbed atop the sign as many hikers before me had done to have my picture taken by Goat Gurrl; I struck a mighty pose holding a beer in one hand with a walking stick grasped in the other and slung over my shoulder. My skin was worn but my legs stood fast and strong, my hat drooped over my ears, soaked in the mist, the tools on my belt stood atop my limited clothing, and my eyes shone bright as they gazed back over the trail. The smile shone forth underneath the scraggly, yet impressive, beard I had managed to grow, my heart was full, my soul was complete, and damn it all I was just happy. It was now that I started to feel the intense surge of emotions that I do not believe can be described in this or any language, an emotion so complex I have simply decided to call it Katahdin. It's a simultaneous mix of intense joy and sorrow, so happy to have made it and so sad it's over. I was ecstatic to return home but grief stricken to be leaving, I was overjoyed that I had no more miles to go and yet crushed that there were no more miles to go. Certainly more glad than depressed however, I stood beyond the last blaze on the last mountain on my last day in the woods and gazed at the route I had taken here and had to take again to return to the base. After standing in silence for a good, long while I uttered aloud "Time to go home." Now... just exactly how do I do that?

15 ON HOME

As my companions and I made our way down the mountain, in the same manner in which we had scaled it, the weather, again, let up once we reached the Gateway. This time however the clouds had cleared well enough to see the whole of Katahdin and a good ways beyond it. In the distance a few other mountains made themselves known to my eyes, and I wondered how long it would be before I would gaze upon distant mountains again. The steps fell under my person just as they had before, and they felt no different; in fact, they fell quite gladly for they were making their way home at last! Home, what a thought that was, I hardly knew for sure what exactly to call home at this point. I did remember however the great comfort and joy brought about by the bar in Wilmington as well as the people who dwell there, and so by my own definition it must be home to me. I passed the falls, wandered over the last rocks and stones until I arrived again at the base camp, my hiking finally complete.

Not having any more blazes to follow was a bit of a reality check, and I didn't really know how to progress from this moment. With less than a dollar to my name and nothing of value to trade I wasn't sure how to get to where I wanted to be, and so I asked the ranger back at the station what most hikers do at this point. He was just as cheery as before and congratulated me on my success before telling me that he could give me a ride as far as the gate of Baxter State Park, where he recommended I try and hitch into the town of Millinocket. This seemed like the most solid option so it became my plan, and before long I was hopping in the back of the ranger's truck to leave the woods one last time. The ranger asked that I ride in the bed of the truck, and I didn't blame him, if he gave every northbound thru hiker a lift to the gate in the cab of his vehicle, he would never be able to get the smell out of the bloody thing. Plus, the rushing air felt nice against my damp and dirty skin and it was almost like taking a shower, or at least the closest thing I'd known to one in quite sometime.

When the short trip was through I thanked the ranger, turned in a few papers to a fellow at the gate to prove I had hiked in on the Trail, and strode off down the road in hopes of someone coming along who didn't mind picking up a wayward vagabond. I got lucky, a shuttle from the hostel in the town was returning from the gate after dropping off a few southbound hikers and didn't mind giving me a lift to town, and why wouldn't he, they were the only hostel around for a hundred miles and more hikers meant more business. Little did he know that I planned to urban camp that night seeing as I had no money, but he didn't need to know that and so I graciously thanked him for the ride.

There's not much to the town of Millinocket, just a few bars, a laundromat, a couple of fast food joints, a hostel, and the AT Cafe where thru hikers can sign their name on a ceiling tile. I had hoped to make it back home by some strange series of hitching, but that didn't seem too possible and frankly, I just wanted to get home. I had one card left to play, though I somewhat hated to do it, for my folks had offered me a loan should I need it when we last talked, and if the offer still stood it was too good to pass up. After three thousand miles getting by on the kindness of strangers, a decent tax return, and scavenging dumpsters and hiker boxes I felt I had proved my point, and if I had help waiting I could now shamelessly accept it. Still, as I finally turned my phone back on I was hesitant to call and ask for a loan, but I dialed the number and waited to see if anyone would pick up on the other end. My mother became the first to know of my success, and she seemed nearly as happy about it as I was. Through the years she had seen me act aloof from afar for far too long, and even when I did live with her and my father I was never really all that reliable. But that had obviously changed now, which I believe she found a bit of solace in. Shortly thereafter my father became the second to know, and as I spoke with him I gleefully shared a few stories before getting to the business matter of the call. I had done my research before making the call thus I knew I didn't need much to get home to North Carolina--a bus ticket would cost just under eighty dollars, and so I didn't ask for more than that.

I made sure it was known that this was to be a loan, not a gift, I didn't want my trip to end on that note, but still my Father insisted he give me at least two hundred bucks; it had been a long hard journey and he felt I deserved a hot meal and a shower. Reluctant, I accepted. Sometimes it's too much work to refuse kindness, and he was right, I was absolutely starving! It was still early in the day, and my Pops was more than eager to run off the the bank and deposit cash into my bank account so I could access it immediately, and while I'm not a fan of banks in general sometimes a nation wide chain of such things comes in handy. Again I assured him that this was only a loan and that I was thankful for the help, but he nearly cut me off in saying that it was no big deal and that he was happy to do it. There had been far too few times in my life where my father and I had spoken on friendly terms, all of which being the fault of my own I'll admit, and I remember very clearly the end of this conversation. I had just expected a quick good bye like we always shared but this time he told me that he was proud of me, which are words that had not often been on his lips. It was a bit stunning, and while it was not expressed at the time I can't think of another conversation that meant so much to me. If the trail itself had not been enough for me to feel confident in my coming of age this certainly did, and I carry it with me always.

In a matter of hours I was no longer broke and staying at the hostel in town, figured I owed it to the place for the ride out of Baxter, plus the hostel offers a free shuttle to Medway every morning where I could catch a couple Greyhounds on home. Spaghetti and Papa Squats were staying here as well with much the same plan, and so we enjoyed the evening together like soldiers after a war, ready to get on home.

I parted ways with Goat Grrl and her brother Lazy Boi here in town-- they had a relation in the area that was to aid them in getting back to the DWG after a quick reprieve with their family. It was sad to see the last of my trail family go, but it had been a fine journey with the two, and we all planned to keep in touch.

The long trip home had finally begun. In the morning, just as I had planned, I hopped aboard the shuttle to Medway with Spaghetti and Papa Squats to catch a bus to Bangor, where I would hop on another heading south to North Carolina. It didn't seem real at the moment, and it all happened rather suddenly; the idea of traveling more then twenty miles in a day seemed like an alien concept and not having to hike left me restless. Nevertheless my body was still worn and welcomed the chance to rest as the wheels rolled underneath my person and the mountain countryside passed by at an alarming rate. The road to Bangor seemed like a blur, and I remember very little of it, but I do know that three AT thru hike alumni had arrived in this fair city beat to shit and hungry as hell.

Even though the three of us had only spent one night together on the trail and never hiked an inch of it in company, we had instantly become good friends and thus decided to stick together as long as possible. We figured there had to be something worth doing in a town this size--after all, we just spent the last several months in the woods, thus making every single modern convenience an absolute indulgence! And so we set about first to find a proper place to sleep for the evening; the two of them were kind enough to let me sleep on the floor if they booked a hotel room, which seemed far more favorable then finding a WalMart to sleep behind. They were taking a plane out of town in the morning and thus wanted to find a place either close to the airport or with a shuttle to it in the morning, so after scouring the Internet for a solid five minuets we somehow managed to find place that would suit their needs. It was a good five mile walk from the bus stop to the hotel we had found, but that didn't bother us in the slightest. What's another five miles on flat, paved ground?

The hotel may as well have been a mansion as far as I was concerned, for it was by far the most modern place I had stayed at since leaving for Fort Lauderdale! They had everything! Semi freshly vacuumed carpet, a TV in the room, a door that locked, an elevator, and that's not even the best stuff! Words can hardly describe just how cool a mini fridge is. It's a tiny personal box that you can put stuff in and keep it cold--I could buy milk and not have it spoil! How about temperature controlled air, what sort of magnificent devilry is that?! I recall going to the faucet in the bathroom and just laughing as I turned it on and off; fresh, clean, safe to drink water on demand is one of the single greatest things that has ever existed in this or any dimension, I can fucking assure you of that. Most people would have considered this place a bit rundown, but not us, this place was the freaking Ritz and they even offered free breakfast in the morning!

Life back in the world sure has some real positive aspects to it, and while I was simply enamored with the hotel room Spaghetti had something he had been wanting to do for a long time: go to a movie. There's very few things in life so entertaining as to go see a film in a theater, and while most would consider it such a simple thing to do, but this was an event that nearly sent the three of us into a frenzy. There just so happened to be a theater not but a block from the hotel, and so it just seemed like fate that we were to go there. Before we did however, I decided it best to pick up a few beers from a nearby gas station; if I wasn't paying for the room I could at least spare a few dollars for some fellow hikers to have a few brews. I can't recall how long it had been since I had been able to stroll into a walk-in beer cooler, but damn it all if it wasn't amazing after spending so much time in the summer heat! Eighteen pack in hand I returned to the hotel to deposit the bulk of our bounty, save for the few that we threw into our pockets to perhaps enjoy at the theater.

    This theater was my kind of place. The only thing that indicated that this old building was currently showing films was a cheaply made, large wooden sign pinned to the top of the building in an attempt to welcome people to the theater. Old dirty brown bricks made up the walls of this building, and the parking lot was cracked and uneven with tufts of grass growing where the asphalt split. The lobby had been redone as recently as nineteen ninety and behind the cracked and dented counter stood a single employee to sell us our tickets and preform every other task behind the concession stand. I can not completely confirm it, but I think this single employee was also in charge of switching on the projectors as well as every other task required to keep this wounded bird flying, and by some grace of God she managed to do it. Since it was the middle of the day our tickets only cost five dollars a piece, and in no time at all we were the only ones sitting in a large dark room in fairly comfortable seats, watching a film for the first time in ages. It was certainly not a disturbance to anyone else as we cracked open the refreshments that we had brought, and throughout the entire film no one else showed up, which is possibly because we hadn't yet been able to wash out the thru hiker scent from our clothes.

    As the film finished up it became a bit concerning to me that there had been no one else in the theater, and I couldn't help but wonder why. Here was a freaking air conditioned, publicly accessible building that not only showed films for five bucks, but even had a place that one could even drive right up to! Why were people not taking full advantage of this astounding feat of modern engineering!? Perhaps the greatest shame in recent life is the complete disregard for the wonders that we have created, that people not only don't visit the woods but don't even go to the places they had destroyed the woods to make! It's simply depressing, the lack of appreciation so many have for the abundant opportunities waiting not but a few moments from their own home, that theaters fall into disrepair, that parks go unkempt, that countless wonderful small businesses go under simply because people have no interest in visiting them. After having so little for so long I can not understand it any longer, and while I had been guilty of such things in the past I now find it impossible to carry on with such disregard. Perhaps the greatest shame in the modern age is truly not that we don't like these incredible things that we have created, but rather that we have grown tired of them.

I parted ways with Spaghetti and Papa Squats the next morning, not even really saying goodbye, for I had to wake far sooner than them to get to the bus station on time. I wanted to take a shower before breakfast, but Spaghetti had washed his pack in the tub the night before and it was still drying there in the morning. It's incredible just how much filth a pair of hikers can leave in a bathroom in less than twelve hours! After a few beard trimmings and a gear wash the bathroom looked like it was set up on the trail, completely covered in dirt and grime. I had decided to keep my beard until I returned home, and thus didn't contribute to this madness, making the mess all that more monumental! I must admit it was impressive, even for us.

After a few mile walk I arrived at the Greyhound station, and shortly thereafter the bus arrived to take me back home. The dusty old dog sat parked out back, a forgotten mode of transportation by the majority of Americans, the engine rumbling out its diesel fueled melody, glistening in the Maine summer sunlight. The driver loaded my pack underneath this fine craft that had served many well over the years; dented and dirty from ages of loyal service it didn't seem to mind carrying another wandering soul on home, and so I boarded, ready for the trip. I took a moment to stand here in the fine state of Maine, knowing that there would be no new places to see along the way. It was bittersweet to be leaving New England, but I'd like to believe we parted as friends. The bus seats were nice enough, each one being far more roomy then those on an aircraft and more comfortable, and as I claimed one for my own the old dog took off down the road, SOBO at last.

I don't know why this has become a lost mode of transportation, for I found it far more pleasurable then flying and just slightly less enjoyable then traveling by train. The world flew by the large glass windows, changing from woods to towns to pastures and back again. A few times I saw mountains, other times wide open spaces doted by patchwork farms as the wheels rolled on beneath me, and with nothing much to do I just watched and smiled, always thinking of those whom I was returning to. While it was a nice ride for awhile, thirty six hours is a long time to be doing anything and so it got a bit dull at times, but I'd sleep when I could and just relax when I couldn't, though if I had no place special to be I suppose I would have enjoyed it a bit more. Nevertheless, after a change of coaches in New York City and Richmond, Virginia, I crossed back home into good old North Carolina, nearly home at last. One last change of buses in Raleigh meant I was only two hours from Wilmington, and with every passing moment my smile grew wider and my heart grew lighter. It's hard to tell if I wanted to savor these last few moments of travel or just get them over with, but since I was stuck aboard this mighty carriage I tried to do the former by looking over the land that was somewhat familiar to my eyes. The pines grew tall, full of long green needles, and underneath them a mix of wasteland weeds and vines that I had known well. The farmland seemed endless, full of crops nearly ready for harvest, rolling by in a sea of wheat, corn, and tobacco that rose and fell with the gentle slope of the land with the occasional river cutting through it. The moment that the Greyhound passed into New Hanover County is one I'll not forget; there's a mighty river there and a good sized bridge, which meant I was nearly there. Even more memorable was the sighting of second greatest sign I had ever seen in my life, a large metal sculpture along the side of the road with the word Wilmington spanning across its center. I was home. As the bus finally came to a stop in a small paved lot at the end of I-40 I rose to exit and stepped forth on familiar earth once more, tired, worn thin, dirty, dressed in rags, bright eyed, dingy, and flat out stinky but relieved and glad to be back.

    As I took my first step off that bus I raised my arms above my head as if to embrace the land I had so long ago left, laughing as I went to collect my pack for a final time. I was dirty, smelled like absolute shit, my scraggly, patchy beard touched my chest and my mustache curled upwards at the ends, held in place by a layer of sweat and dust. I had left seven months ago weighing about two hundred pounds and returned hardly a buck sixty, my legs had never looked better and my arms had never been thinner. The pack that had served me without fail was scratched up and faded, my clothes faired much the same and barely clung to my person, having being reduced to threads. Boots blown to bits, shoulder sore as shit, this battered bag of bones was finally back home with a heart full of cheer and a head full of memories my smiling lips couldn't wait to talk about. All the more I had left to do was strap on the pack and walk on to where I knew my friends would be, good old Cape Fear Wine and Beer.

    There was roughly five miles between me and my house, but my feet laughed as they strode over them, falling quickly enough as I wandered down the streets I knew so well. I walked past the fountains and statues at the edge of downtown Wilmington, turning on Second Street to avoid the hustle and bustle of Front, plus this gave me the chance to walk down a familiar alley as I had envisioned many nights while out on the trail.

Between the post office and an old brick building I turned to stroll down this last block that stood between me and my friends. The jasmine vines grew thick here but it seemed I had sadly missed their flowering season this year, still my smile couldn't be contained and stretched with every step until giving way in joyful laughter. I'm no longer walking, I'm dancing my way down the alley, memories of what feels like another life begin to stir inside my mind, and my weary shining eyes lay at last upon the great drinking hall I call home. The last steps fall, I am home, I have done it!

My arms stretch forth to grasp the wrenches aesthetically welded onto the double doors as handles, and with one mighty action I pull them towards me as I stride once more into the place I had missed so much. I raise my arms and give a quick shout to those about--guess who's back in town kids!? Faces that were not just familiar but family look up from their pints and pool, from the coolers and taps and across the bar to see this wayward son returned home, and all at once they realize what I had done. Eyes stared in disbelief and jaws dropped open, I think a few of these fine folk didn't even recognize me at first, but they did soon enough and my hero's welcome commenced. I had never received such a welcome as this! People rushed to greet me with smiles as wide as my own, we laughed and embraced, it didn't matter that I smelled like the back side of a brown bears ass, I held my brothers and sisters close bursting at the seams with pure and unfiltered joy. My friend Josh came first, followed by Seth and Kris, them being the fine staff of this great hall, Chad and Shane close behind, Megan fell to the floor in disbelief and I in turn dropped to embrace her, the call had sounded and others were on the way, their boy was finally home and the celebration commenced. Before a proper sentence could be formed by any of us they brought me a slice of pizza and a full pitcher of high gravity IPA; with pats on the back and cheers I stood among my family again after my great adventure, all of us sharing in my victory. Before long others arrived and rekindled the reunion as we greeted once again, there were tears, there were beers, not a frown to be found during the entire night. I met Lector with a heartfelt hand shake, Maaika and I cried in each others arms, Greg, Steve, Tony and Rockabilly Lawson all gathered near and I had never felt so loved as in this glorious moment. I'm sure there were others but the memory is hazy as I was presented with drink after drink until I could hardly stand, all I can be certain of is just how glad I was to be home.

I had gotten used to waking up in new and strange places, although over the last seven months I had gotten rather fond of remembering how I got there. It appears I had forgotten the cardinal rule of Wilmington; don't drink like a local until you are a local, and I had fallen out of practice. Still, when I awoke in the morning I roused myself from some strange bed and wandered into the next room to find that Maaika had been kind enough to let me stay in her guest room, and she insisted that I take a shower. Apparently during the night we had thrown my God awful clothes into the wash and they were as clean as I can ever remember them being, waiting for me once I gave myself a proper scrubbing. The folks at the bar had given me a clean shirt to wear the night before, though I was still very fond of the last one I had purchased from them for it had been on my back for the majority of my travels. However, after I had given myself a proper shower I let the new replace the old, and we all took a little joy in that event.

Over the next week or so I met again with everyone and began to share my stories. I didn't care to drink as much as I had when I left because I now valued my experiences so much more, and didn't want to lose any ever again. I nearly cried over a Chop's Deli sandwich, which had long been one of my favorite local eateries, and again when the owner Brad burst from the office to greet me, giving me the single longest hug I had ever received. Seriously, it went past the awkwardly long phase, back into joyfully acceptable and back to awkward again before he released me, but I must say I didn't mind at all. I met with Brian, Katie, John, Jenkins, Jason, Christian, and Joan, whom had brought me to the start of my great journey and I lifted her from the ground as we met, glad to be reunited with my old friend. There were toasts and cheers, not just to me but from me to my friends, I had gotten to know just how much they meant to me and I wished to let them know it. I remember meeting back with Ashley whom had encouraged me to go in the first place and I thanked her for it, I truly believe I wouldn't have gone if she hadn't said go. The barber who gave me a hair cut grabbed my lengthy locks which I was now able to pull into a pony tail and lopped it off in one go before throwing it onto my lap. Fresh clothes, new hair cut, trimmed beard, and good friends I felt like a new man. What a ride it had been.

I soon realized that I had fallen out of practice when it came to conversation. Part of my brain was still off on the trail and while I was glad to be back in the world of hot food and cool air I would find myself sitting in silence outside. It was all very new and strange to me now--I could hear light bulbs humming in a quiet room which I had never noticed before. I was nearly hit by cars a few times when I would forget to check for them as I walked across streets. My hiking gear was now placed in storage with my tools, though I had taken to carrying around a smaller backpack at all times and felt a little naked if I was ever without it. Sitting still seemed like a chore so I would go for walks often, usually taking several in a day just to wander the streets and parks I had known from long ago. I remember the moment when it finally all settled in: I was sitting in a coffee shop on Front Street and pulled my trusty trail journal from my pack to write a final entry in it.

"It would appear the adventure is over, the steps have been laid, the mountains fell conquered, and there are no blazes left to follow. As I write, my heart begins to ache as it longs once more for the back woods I had long called home. No new land lay ahead and I began to slowly settle back into the life I had set for myself. As I write however, my eyes are drawn to the pages of this journal that have yet to be filled, and I realize a profound truth. While there is no vast wilderness to wander or new peaks to discover my journey is far from over, everyday brings something new and with it nearly infinite possibilities to explore new ventures. I do not believe at this point that I will ever travel so far for so long again, but will derive much satisfaction from my friends, vacation, and life anew. Reluctantly I resume my proper name and identity, but perhaps the pack, Gizmo, and I shall set off again for a quick walk about. Until then, I am home. I am home, and it is good."

Made in the USA
Middletown, DE
01 October 2020